Collins

Perfect Maths 4

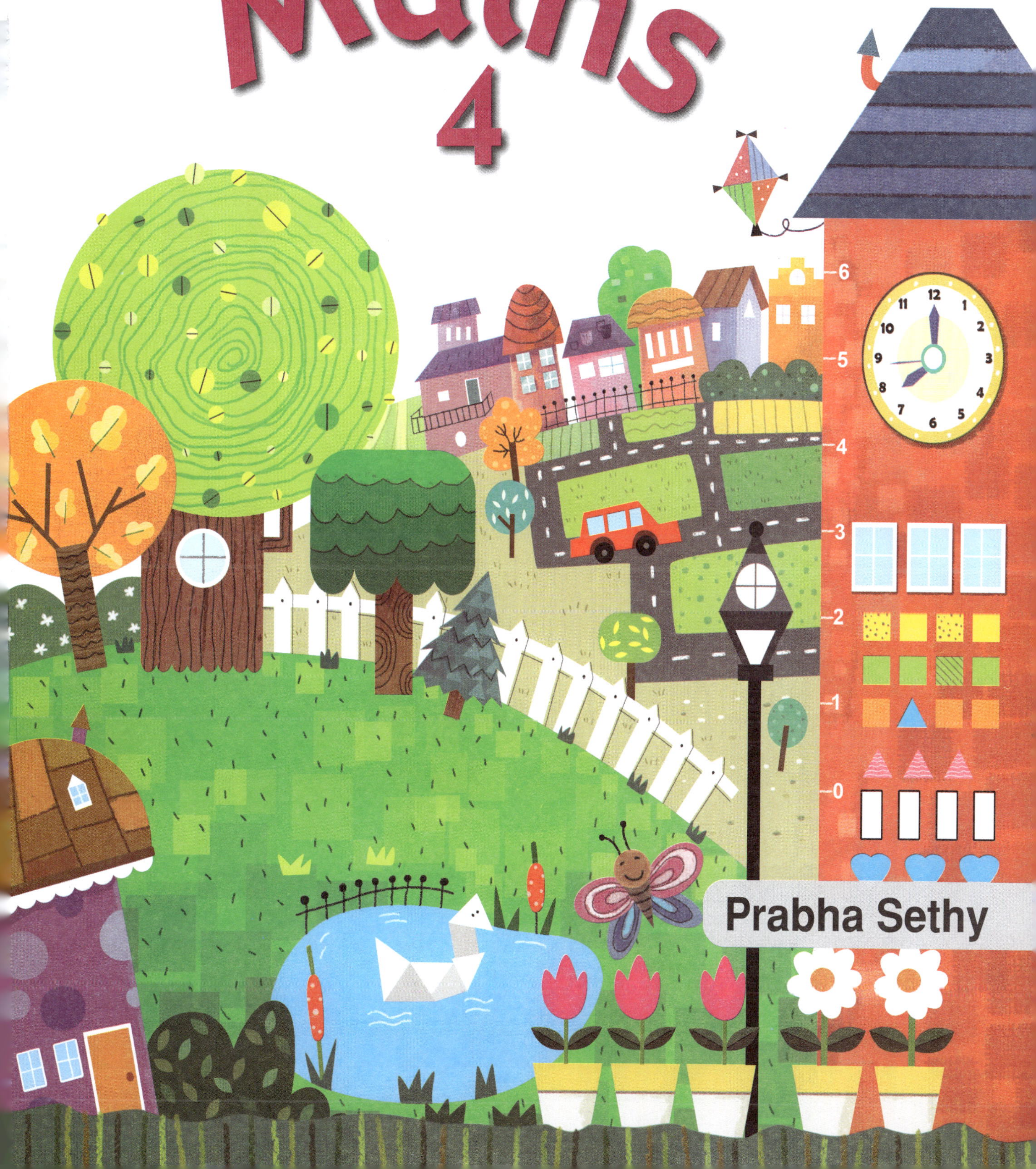

Prabha Sethy

Components of DigiSuite

Student + Teacher

- **a** animations
- **ilt** instructor-led tutorials
- **ia** activities
- **w** worksheets
- audio
- **g** games
- **v** videos

Teacher-only

- **lp** lesson plans
- **w** worksheets
- **tn** teacher's notes
- **ak** answer keys

Preface

Perfect Maths is a series of eleven books for Classes Nursery to 8. The books for the Foundational Stage, previously referred to as Grades Nursery, Lower KG and Upper KG, would be the base to make the series complete in providing a strong foundation in numeracy, starting from ECCE till the middle stage. The series adheres to the guidelines of the **National Education Policy (NEP) 2020**, aligns with the vision of the ***National Initiative for Proficiency in Reading with Understanding and Numeracy*** (NIPUN Bharat) and aims to make mathematics more relevant to students in a non-threatening way.

The books for Foundational Stage 1 to 3 (Grades Nursery to UKG) are focused on the holistic development of a child. Based on **Numeracy Skills**, **21st Century Skills** and **Multiple Intelligences**, integrated and interdisciplinary approach, experiential learning, the books aim to help a child be "**Happy to Learn**". The unique blend of direct instructions, play-based structured activities, investigations, stories and rhymes provide the children ample opportunities to develop their numeracy and literacy skills.

The books for Classes 1 to 8 follow the ***5E Learning Model***. The 5E Learning Model provides an activity-oriented approach to the series to make mathematics engaging for students through emphasizing connections between mathematics and day-to-day experiences. This series adheres to the guidelines of NEP 2020 completely, with the effective integration of its features with **21st Century Skills**, **Art Integration**, **Experiential Learning**, **Cross-curricular** and **India Focus**. The skill building questions and the varied exposure to situations provided in the pages of this series keep the learners at the centre and focus on making them future-ready. The series also aims to make students aware of the United Nations **Sustainable Development Goals** (SDGs), so that they can become SDG Pioneers, Champions or Ambassadors.

SAFAL in ***Perfect Maths:*** This series also strives to make a shift from rote-learning to competency-based learning, in accordance with **Structured Assessment For Analyzing Learning (SAFAL)**. The components of SAFAL—critical thinking, inquiry-based learning and analysis-based learning—are woven into the features such as Exercises, Mental Maths, Chapter Revision, Skill Up!, Worksheets, Reasoning Worksheets, Review/Assessment Corner and PISA Corner (Classes 6 to 8).

We would like to take this opportunity to thank all the teachers and educationist, especially Ms Rajni Kaushal, who reviewed the books and provided their feedback, which helped in improving the quality of the content.

Feedback, invaluable comments and suggestions from users are welcome.

Authors

About the Author

Prabha Sethy, formerly a teacher at Welham Boys' School, Dehradun, with more than 30 years of experience in teaching mathematics, brings in resources from everyday life into her content.

Key Features

The key features of ***Perfect Maths*** are completely aligned with the **National Education Policy (NEP) 2020** and the vision of the ***National Initiative for Proficiency in Reading with Understanding and Numeracy*** (NIPUN Bharat). These meticulously designed features, based on the ***5E Learning Model***, can be used as learning strategies to enhance the understanding of key concepts in mathematics and increase practical learning and problem-solving by bringing in real-life contexts from outside the classroom while providing some form of experiential learning. These key features also aim to help the learners shift from rote-learning to competency-based learning, in accordance with ***Structured Assessment For Analyzing Learning*** (SAFAL).

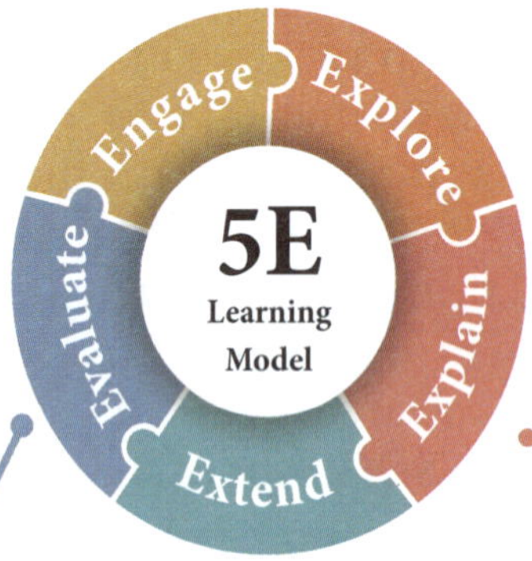

To capture the attention of students, get them mentally engaged and make connections between past and present

- Maths Around Us
- Let's Get Started
- Common Errors
- Go Easy!
- Vedic Maths (Classes 6 to 8)
- Eminent Mathematicians
- Poster

To enable the students to explore the concepts through hands-on activities, investigations, etc.

- Maths Lab Activity
- Crosswords
- Puzzles
- Mental Maths
- Worksheets
- Maths Mela

To enable the students to understand the main ideas of the topics

- Learning Objectives
- Note
- Solved Examples
- Concept Map
- Key Concepts

To enable the students to stimulate thinking and apply prior and current knowledge to real-life situations

- Do You Know?
- Word Problems
- Skill Up!
- SEE Learning

To review, assess and evaluate what students have learned

- Exercises
- Chapter Revision
- Reasoning Worksheet
- Review Corner
- PISA Corner (Classes 6 to 8)

Adherence to National Education Policy

21st Century Skills (21 CS)

- **Learning Skills**
  - Critical Thinking
  - Creativity and Innovation
  - Collaboration
  - Communication
- **Life Skills**
- **Literacy Skills**
  - Information Literacy
  - Media Literacy
  - Technology Literacy

Art Integration (AI)

Cross Curricular (CC)

India Focus (IF)

Happiness Quotient (HQ)

Experiential Learning (EL)

SUSTAINABLE DEVELOPMENT GOALS

Each feature has been tagged with colour-coded icons to easily identify the type of skills and learning being addressed!

About the Features

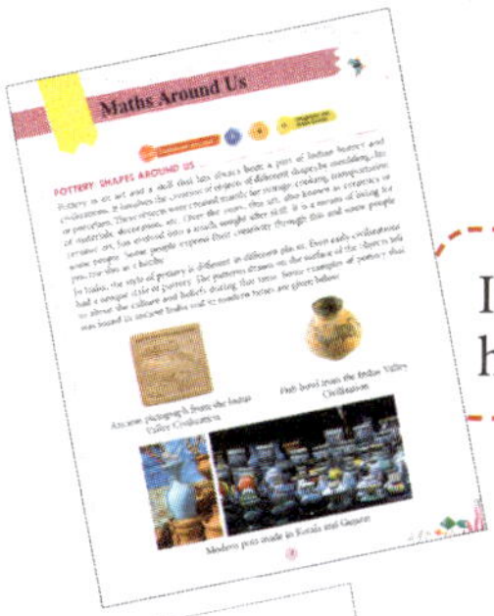

Interesting information and activities to connect maths with Indian history, art, culture, real-life situations and financial literacy

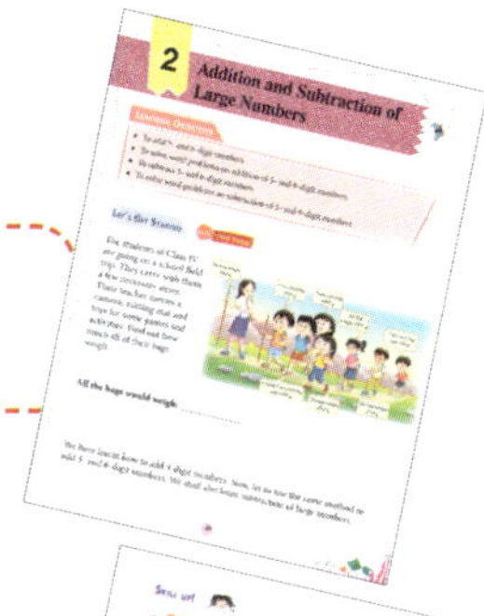

Chapter starter in the form of a picture-based exercise

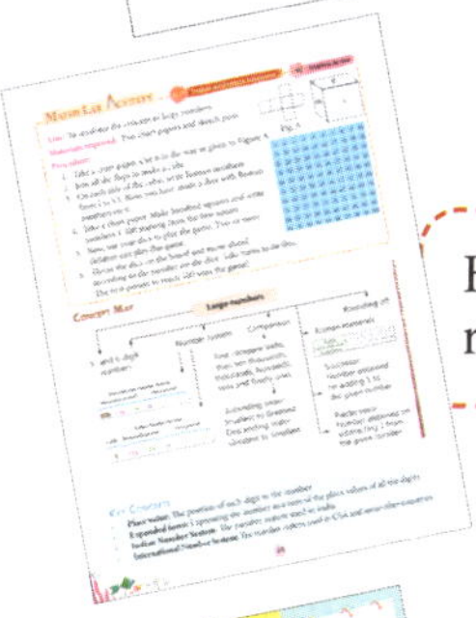

Hands-on activity to help in improving investigation, reinforcement and extension of concepts just learnt

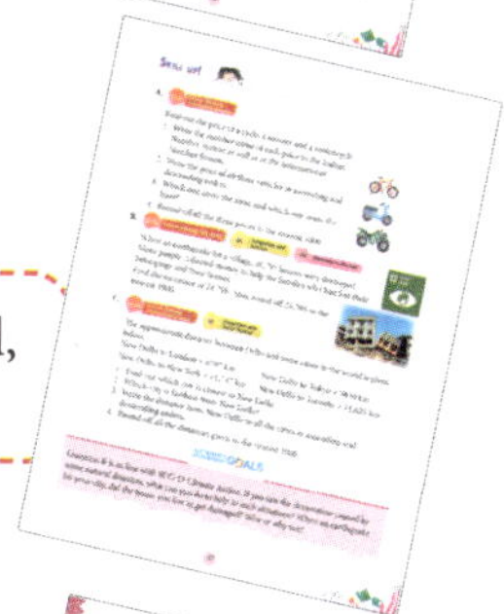

A variety of questions catering to inquiry-based, discovery-based, discussion-based and analysis-based learning

Picture-based, fun, problem-solving questions to reinforce concepts

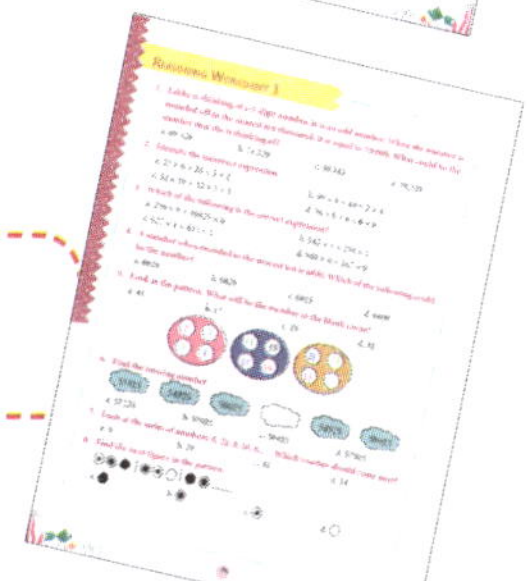

Questions to stimulate rational thinking using mathematical skills

Special stories to promote social, emotional and ethical learning

Model making or hands-on project ideas to enhance learning beyond the classroom

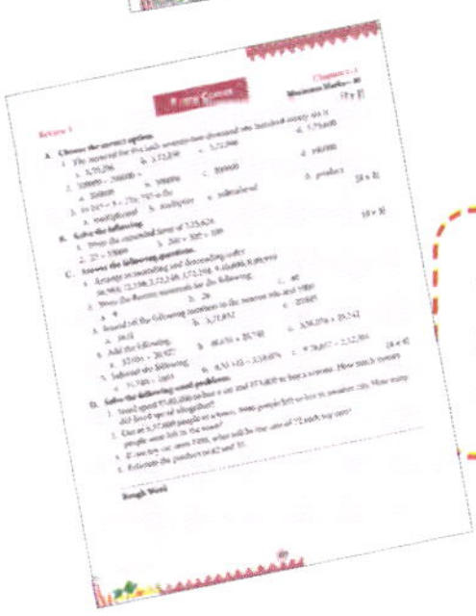

Sample test papers at the end of the book for additional practice (Classes 6 to 8 Assessment Corner based on the **New Assessment format**)

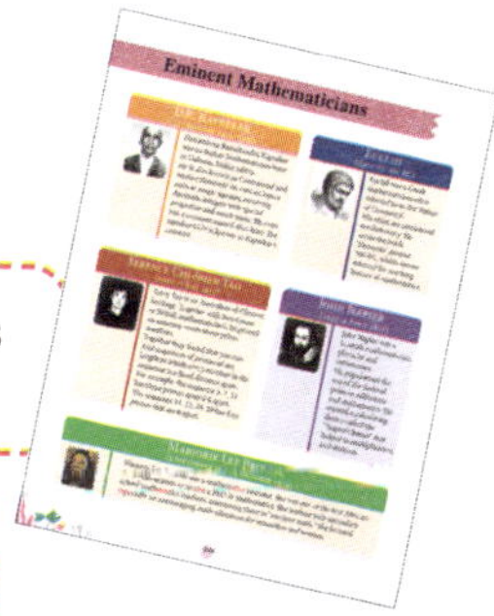

Brief write-ups on eminent mathematicians and their contributions

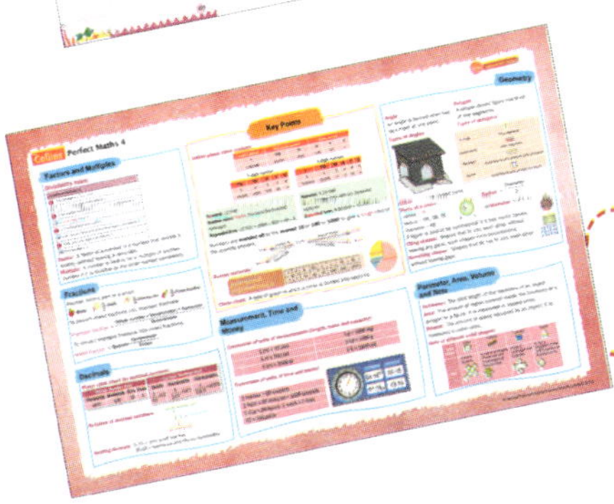

Informative colourful posters to focus on some important concepts or facts

Contents

Maths Around Us

21 CS Creativity and innovation IF AI CC Integration with Social Studies

POTTERY: SHAPES AROUND US

Pottery is an art and a skill that has always been a part of Indian history and civilizations. It involves the creation of objects of different shapes by moulding clay or porcelain. These objects were created mainly for storage, cooking, transportation of materials, decoration, etc. Over the years, this art, also known as ceramics or ceramic art, has evolved into a much sought after skill. It is a means of living for some people. Some people express their creativity through this and some people practise this as a hobby.

In India, the style of pottery is different in different places. Even early civilizations had a unique style of pottery. The patterns drawn on the surface of the objects tell us about the culture and beliefs during that time. Some examples of pottery that was found in ancient India and in modern times are given below.

Ancient pictograph from the Indus Valley Civilization

Fish bowl from the Indus Valley Civilization

Modern pots made in Kerala and Gujarat

Suppose you had to leave behind a legacy that could become a part of history in the future, what would you draw? Design and draw your own pattern on the pot given below.

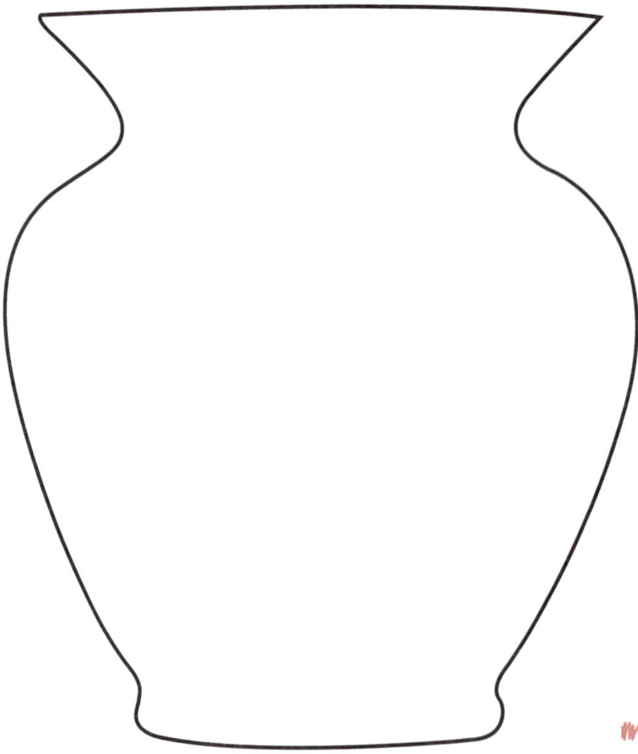

Write a few lines about what your design or your drawing means.

1 Place Value of Large Numbers

Learning Objectives

- To read, write and expand 5- and 6-digit numbers
- To find place values of the digits of a number
- To compare numbers
- To learn about Roman numerals
- To round off numbers to the nearest 10, 100, 1000 and 10,000

Let's Get Started

HQ Happiness My Goal

Bhawna and Rahul are playing a game. They need to complete a mission to move to the next stage. Help them complete the mission by solving the questions given below.

A. Read the number name given below. Write the number by putting its digits in the correct places.

Six thousand seven hundred twelve

Th	H	T	O

B. Can you make the greatest and the smallest numbers from the digits of the above answer?

1. Greatest number: ☐☐☐☐
2. Smallest number: ☐☐☐☐

You have learnt about 4-digit numbers in your previous class. Now let us learn about numbers larger than 4-digit numbers.

5-DIGIT NUMBERS

Have you ever seen a football match? How many people do you think watch a football match in a stadium? It could range from 10000 people to 99999 people or more. These numbers are 5-digit numbers.

Face Value, Place Value and Expanded Form

The face value of a digit is the digit itself. In 26185, the face value of 2 is 2, 8 is 8 and so on. The place value of a digit depends on its position in the number. Place values are categorised into different groups known as **periods**. The ones, tens and hundreds places come under the **ones** period. The thousands and ten thousands places come under the **thousands** period.

Thousands period		**Ones period**		
TTh	Th	H	T	O

> **NOTE**
>
> A comma is used to distinguish the periods in a number. To distinguish the thousands from the ones period, a comma is placed after the thousands period. So, the number 26185 can be written as 26,185.

When the place value positions are written on top of the digits of the numbers, the place values of the digits become clearer. *The place value of a digit in a number is the product of the digit and the value of that place.*

Ten thousands	Thousands	Hundreds	Tens	Ones
TTh	Th	H	T	O
2	6	1	8	5

Place values

- 5 ones = 5 × 1 = 5
- 8 tens = 8 × 10 = 80
- 1 hundred = 1 × 100 = 100
- 6 thousands = 6 × 1000 = 6000
- 2 ten thousands = 2 × 10000 = 20000

The expanded form of a number is the method of expressing the number as a sum of place values of all its digits. Once you know the place values of the digits of a number, you can write the expanded form of the number. For example, the expanded form of 26185 is 20000 + 6000 + 100 + 80 + 5.

Reading 5-Digit Numbers

Numbers can be read if you know and understand the expanded form of the numbers.

Expanded form of 26185 = 20000 + 6000 + 100 + 80 + 5

Read aloud the expanded form of the number. This will give you the name of the number.

Number name: Twenty-six thousand one hundred eighty-five

Common Errors

Number name of 58729

Fifty eight Thousands **and** Seven Hundreds **and** Twenty nine 👎

Fifty-eight thousand seven hundred twenty-nine 👍

Mental Maths

Write the place value and the face value of each digit in 75618.

Digit	Place value	Face value
7	______	______
5	______	______
6	______	______
1	______	______
8	______	______

6-DIGIT NUMBERS

The greatest 5-digit number is 99999. On adding 1 to 99999, we get the number 100000. This number has six digits and is read as **one lakh**.

Indian Number System

The figure given below shows the position of place values under the **Indian Number System**. When you start from the right and move left, the first three places are ones, tens and hundreds. In the Indian Number System, the ones, tens and hundreds come under the ones period. The thousands and ten thousands come under the thousands period. The next period after the thousands period is the lakhs period.

After the ones period, put a comma to the left of hundreds. Then, put a comma after every two digits.

Lakhs	Thousands period		Ones period		
L	TTh	Th	H	T	O

Note

The smallest 6-digit number is 1,00,000.
The greatest 6-digit number is 9,99,999.

International Number System

There is another place value system known as the **International Number System**. Here, the place values as well as the periods are different from those in the Indian Number System.

In the International Number System, the first three places from the right, ones, tens and hundreds come under the ones period. The thousands, ten thousands and hundred thousands come under the thousands period. In this number system, we put a comma after every three digits, starting from the right.

Thousands period			Ones period		
HTh	TTh	Th	H	T	O

Place Value and Expanded Form

Consider the number 9,15,274.

Number name in Indian number system: Nine lakh fifteen thousand two hundred seventy-four.

Expanded form: 9,00,000 + 10,000 + 5000 + 200 + 70 + 4

Lakhs	Thousands period		Ones period		
L	TTh	Th	H	T	O
9	1	5	2	7	4

Reading 6-Digit Numbers in the Indian Number System

To read number names correctly, write the place value positions on top of the digits. First read out the number in the lakhs period. Then read out the number in the thousands period, and then read out the number in the ones period.

For example:

L	TTh	Th	H	T	O
5	6	9	1	3	4

Five lakh sixty-nine thousand one hundred thirty-four

COMMON ERRORS

Read aloud the number name of 5,76,204.

Five lakh seventy-six two hundred four

Five lakh seventy-six thousand two hundred four

Reading 6-Digit Numbers in the International Number System

To read numbers in the International Number System, first read out the 3-digit number in the thousands period. Then read out the 3-digit number in the ones period, starting from the hundreds position.

For example:

HTh	TTh	Th	H	T	O
6	2	9	1	7	3

Six hundred twenty-nine thousand one hundred seventy-three

SOLVED EXAMPLES

Example 1: Write the number name and the expanded form of 3,42,958.

Solution:

Number: 3,42,958

Number name: Three lakh forty-two thousand nine hundred fifty-eight

Expanded form: 3,00,000 + 40,000 + 2000 + 900 + 50 + 8

Example 2: Write the number and the expanded form of four lakh thirty-two thousand eight hundred sixty-two.

Solution:

Number name: Four lakh thirty-two thousand eight hundred sixty-two

Number: 4,32,862

Expanded form: 4,00,000 + 30,000 + 2000 + 800 + 60 + 2

Example 3: Write the number and number name for one lakh three hundred forty-six in the International Number System.

Solution:

Number name in the Indian Number System: One lakh three hundred forty-six

Number: 1,00,346

Number name in the International Number System: One hundred thousand three hundred forty-six

Number in the International Number System: 100,346

EXERCISE 1A

1. **Write the place values of the underlined digits of the following numbers.**

   a. $2,4\underline{6},135$ b. $\underline{7},12,690$ c. $5,\underline{3}8,421$ d. $3,19,\underline{0}45$ e. $2,39,10\underline{0}$

2. **Write the number names of the following numbers in the Indian Number System.**

   a. 2,35,734 b. 1,26,507 c. 8,35,149 d. 3,70,815 e. 8,46,712

3. **Write the expanded form of the following numbers.**

   a. 56,198 b. 23,706 c. 217,562 d. 342,984 e. 5,29,103

4. **Write the numerals for the following number names.**

   a. Twenty-three thousand four hundred sixty-two

   b. Seven lakh fifty-two thousand one hundred five

   c. Five lakh eighty-one thousand four hundred twenty-eight

5. **Write the number names of the following numbers. Identify which system of numeration is used by observing the comma placement.**

   a. 3,29,658 b. 9,00,632 c. 284,210 d. 791,004

COMPARING NUMBERS

We compare numbers to find out whether:

- the numbers are equal,
- a number is greater than the other,
- a number is smaller than the other.

While comparing two numbers, we first check the number of digits in both the numbers.

Comparing Numbers with Different Number of Digits

If the number of digits in both the numbers is not the same, then the one with more digits is the greater number.

Consider two numbers 7,35,049 and 9987.

Here, 7,35,049 has six digits and 9987 has four digits.

Six > Four

Hence, 7,35,049 > 9987.

Comparing Numbers with Same Number of Digits

If the number of digits is same in both the numbers, then compare the first digit (from the left) of both the numbers. The number that has the greater first digit is the greater number.

56780 < 66780

If the first digit is the same in both the numbers, then compare the second digit (from the left) of both the numbers. The number that has the greater second digit is the greater number.

67780 > 66780

If the second digit is also the same in both the numbers, then compare the third digit in both the numbers. This process is continued till we find the greater digit in a number. If all the digits are the same, then the numbers are equal.

67780 < 67880

67880 = 67880

SOLVED EXAMPLES

Example 4: Compare 5,72,493 and 5,72,193.

Solution: 5,72,493 > 5,72,193 because the first three digits are the same but the fourth digit (4) in the first number is bigger than the fourth digit (1) in the second number.

ORDERING NUMBERS

A series of numbers can be arranged in increasing or decreasing order.

When the numbers are arranged in increasing order from the smallest to the greatest, it is called ascending order. When the numbers are arranged in decreasing order from the greatest to the smallest, it is called descending order.

SOLVED EXAMPLES

Example 5: Arrange 63,425; 7,21,319; 1349 and 92,710 in ascending and descending orders.

Solution: Ascending order

Step 1: First check the number of digits in each number.

1349 is the only 4-digit number and the rest are 5- or 6-digit numbers.

So, 1349 is the smallest number. Write (1) on top of 1349.

(1)

63,425; 7,21,319; 1349; 92,710

Step 2: Now find the next larger digit number. 63,425 and 92,710 are two 5-digit numbers. Out of these, 63,425 is smaller because the first digit 6 is smaller than 9. So, write (2) on top of 63,425 and (3) on top of 92,710.

Step 3: Now, the remaining number 7,21,319 is a 6-digit number. So, it is the greatest number among all. Write (4) on top of 7,21,319.

(2) (4) (1) (3)

63,425; 7,21,319; 1349; 92,710

Hence, the numbers in an ascending order would be

1349 < 63,425 < 92,710 < 7,21,319.

Descending order

Step 1: First check the number of digits in each number. 7,21,319 is the only 6-digit number and the rest are 4- or 5-digit numbers. So, 7,21,319 is the greatest number. Write (1) on top of 7,21,319.

(1)

63,425; 7,21,319; 1349; 92,710

Step 2: Now 63,425 and 92,710 are two 5-digit numbers. Out of these, 92,710 is greater because the first digit 9 is greater than 6. So, we write (2) on top of 92,710 and (3) on top of 63,425.

Step 3: The last number 1349 is a 4-digit number. So, it is the smallest number among all. Write (4) on top of 1349.

(3) (1) (4) (2)

63,425; 7,21,319; 1349; 92,710

Hence, the numbers in a descending order would be

7,21,319 > 92,710 > 63,425 > 1349.

Successor and Predecessor

Successor of a number is the number that we get after adding 1 to the given number.

Predecessor of a number is the number that we get after subtracting 1 from the given number.

Consider the number 6,45,389.

The successor of 6,45,389 is 6,45,390.

The predecessor of 6,45,389 is 6,45,388.

As we keep finding successors of numbers, we move the numbers in an ascending order and as we keep finding predecessors of numbers, we move the numbers in a descending order.

$$\begin{array}{rcccccc} & 6 & 4 & 5 & 3 & 8 & 9 \\ + & & & & & & 1 \\ \hline & 6 & 4 & 5 & 3 & 9 & 0 \\ \hline \end{array}$$

$$\begin{array}{rcccccc} & 6 & 4 & 5 & 3 & 8 & 9 \\ - & & & & & & 1 \\ \hline & 6 & 4 & 5 & 3 & 8 & 8 \\ \hline \end{array}$$

Forming the Smallest and the Greatest Numbers

To form the smallest 5- or 6-digit number from the given set of digits, arrange the digits in the increasing order.

To form the greatest 5- or 6-digit number from the given set of digits, arrange the digits in the decreasing order.

COMMON ERRORS !

Form the smallest number using the following digits once:

3, 5, 0, 8, 6

03,568 ✗ 30,568 ✓

SOLVED EXAMPLES

Example 6: Form the smallest and the greatest 5-digit numbers using the digits 5, 2, 8, 7 and 9 only once.

Solution: The smallest 5-digit number formed using the given digits is 25,789 (arranging the digits in the increasing order).

The greatest 5-digit number formed using the given digits is 98,752 (arranging the digits in the decreasing order).

PUZZLE!

Who am I?

I am a 5-digit number.

I have 5 in my ten thousands place,

7 in my thousands place,

4 in my hundreds place,

0 in my tens place,

3 in my ones place.

I am ______________!

Example 7: Form the smallest and the greatest 6-digit numbers using the digits 5, 1, 7, 3, 0 and 2 only once.

Solution:

To form the smallest 6-digit number, start by placing the digits in the increasing order. If 0 is placed at the beginning, the number will become a 5-digit number. So, place the next smallest digit at the beginning, (from the left), that is 1. Then, arrange the rest of the digits in the increasing order.

So, we get 1,02,357 as the smallest 6-digit number using the given digits.
The greatest 6-digit number formed using above digits is 7,53,210 (arranging the digits in the decreasing order).

Exercise 1B

1. **Compare the numbers and put the correct sign (>, < or =).**

   a. 7,29,185 ________ 9,12,006 b. 8,26,105 ________ 8,13,987

   c. 3,84,796 ________ 3,89,530 d. 5,36,109 ________ 5,36,420

2. **Arrange the numbers in ascending order.**

   a. 5,81,723 5,81,049 5,81,900 5,81,856

   b. 4,39,185 3,58,907 8,21,063 9,10,259

   c. 7,00,000 6,81,999 9,98,998 9,99,999

3. **Arrange the numbers in descending order.**

   a. 4,39,180 8,14,295 5,63,102 9,00,724

   b. 7,21,526 7,21,987 7,27,000 7,29,546

   c. 9999 99,999 9,99,909 9,99,999

4. **Write the successors of the following numbers.**

   a. 7,28,563 b. 2,14,868 c. 5,72,006 d. 6,89,993 e. 9,50,007

5. **Write the predecessors of the following numbers.**

   a. 8,53,764 b. 9,21,305 c. 4,68,715 d. 9,99,589 e. 5,99,061

6. **Write the smallest and the greatest 6-digit numbers (without repeating the digits).**

   a. 4, 8, 7, 9, 2, 6 b. 5, 0, 4, 7, 8, 3

   c. 7, 0, 0, 8, 6, 2 d. 7, 6, 1, 0, 5, 2

ROMAN NUMERALS

The Roman Number System or the Roman numerals was used in ancient Rome. It had some basic symbols which were combined to form numbers. The basic symbols used in Roman Number System and its corresponding value in Hindu–Arabic Number System are given below.

NOTE

The following symbols are called the **basic symbols** in Roman Number System.

I = 1 V = 5 X = 10 L = 50

Numbers from 1 to 49 are combination of these symbols.

Roman Numerals	I	V	X	XL	L	C	D	M
Hindu–Arabic Numerals	1	5	10	40	50	100	500	1000

We can still see these numbers on the face of some clocks or when we refer to classes I, II, III, IV, V, etc.

DO YOU KNOW?

Roman numbers do not have a symbol for zero.

Roman numerals from 1 to 40 are given below.

1 = I		11	=	XI	21	=	XXI	31	=	XXXI
2 = II		12	=	XII	22	=	XXII	32	=	XXXII
3 = III		13	=	XIII	23	=	XXIII	33	=	XXXIII
4 = IV		14	=	XIV	24	=	XXIV	34	=	XXXIV
5 = V		15	=	XV	25	=	XXV	35	=	XXXV
6 = VI		16	=	XVI	26	=	XXVI	36	=	XXXVI
7 = VII		17	=	XVII	27	=	XXVII	37	=	XXXVII
8 = VIII		18	=	XVIII	28	=	XXVIII	38	=	XXXVIII
9 = IX		19	=	XIX	29	=	XXIX	39	=	XXXIX
10 = X		20	=	XX	30	=	XXX	40	=	XL

Rules for Writing Roman Numerals

Listed below are a few rules for writing numbers using Roman numerals.

Rule 1: When a symbol appears on the right side of a larger symbol, it is added.

Example: XI = 10 + 1 = 11

Rule 2: When a symbol appears on the left side of a larger symbol, it is subtracted.

Example: IX = 10 – 1 = 9

Rule 3: The same symbol is not repeated more than three times.

Rule 4: When symbols are placed next to each other, we first identify the basic symbol and then add or subtract the other symbols.

Example: VIII

Here, V is the basic symbol and we add III to it.

That is, 5 + 3 = 8.

Example: IX

X is the basic symbol. Subtract I from it.

That is, 10 – 1 = 9.

Rule 5: Symbols V, L and D cannot be repeated.

Common Errors

Rule 1:

12 = IIX ✗ 12 = XII ✓

Since II is being added to X, it should be on the right of X.

XII = 10 + 1 + 1 = 12

Rule 2:

9 = XI ✗ 9 = IX ✓

Since I is being subtracted from X, it should be on the left of X.

IX = 10 – 1 = 9

Rule 3:

40 = XXXX ✗ 40 = XL ✓

L = 50 in Roman numbers. Since X is to the left of L, we will subtract 10 from 50 = 40.

XL = 50 – 10 = 40

Rule 4:

18 = IIIVX ✗ 18 = XVIII ✓

Since VIII is being added to X, it should be on the right of X.

XVIII = 10 + 5 + 1 + 1 + 1 = 18

Writing Roman Numerals using Hindu–Arabic Numbers

To form Roman Numbers from Hindu–Arabic Numbers, first take the basic symbol and then decide to write the other symbols on the left or the right of the basic symbol.

For example:

3 = 1 + 1 + 1 = III

4 = 5 – 1 = IV

8 = 5 + 1 + 1 + 1 = VIII

9 = 10 – 1 = IX

16 = 10 + 5 + 1 = XVI

40 = 50 – 10 = XL

28 = 10 + 10 + 5 + 1 + 1 + 1 = XXVIII

Writing Hindu–Arabic Numerals using Roman Numbers

To write a Hindu–Arabic numeral using Roman numbers, first look for the basic symbol. If the other symbols are to the right of the basic symbols, add them to the basic symbol.

If the other symbols are to the left of the basic symbol, subtract them from the basic symbol.

For example:

VI = 5 + 1 = 6

IX = 10 – 1 = 9

XIV = 10 + (5 – 1) = 14

XXIX = 10 + 10 + (10 – 1) = 29

XL = 50 – 10 = 40

EXERCISE 1C

1. **Write the Roman numerals for the following numbers.**

   a. 7 b. 10 c. 9 d. 13 e. 15

2. **Write the Hindu–Arabic numerals for the following Roman numerals.**

   a. X b. XXXIX c. XXVIII d. XI e. XXIV

ROUNDING OFF NUMBERS

Rounding off a number means instead of giving the exact value, we give a number closer to it, which is easier to remember and use. In other words, we give an approximate value. For example, if your mother paid ₹929 for this year's school supply, you can say that your mother paid approximately ₹930.

Rounding off Numbers to the Nearest 10, 100 and 1000

Rounding off numbers means making the numbers simpler but keeping their values close to what they were. This helps in making additions and subtractions easier.

Follow these rules while rounding off a number to the nearest 10.

- To round off a number to the nearest 10, first consider the digit at the tens place of the number. If the digit to its right is 5 or greater than 5 (5, 6, 7, 8 or 9), round the number up. For example, 48 rounded to the nearest ten is 50.

- If the digit to the right of the tens place digit is less than 5 (1, 2, 3 or 4), round the number down. For example, 43 rounded to the nearest ten is 40.

Rounding off numbers to nearest 10

Round down ← | → **Round up**

0	1	2	3	4	5	6	7	8	9	10
10	11	12	13	14	15	16	17	18	19	20
20	21	22	23	24	25	26	27	28	29	30
30	31	32	33	34	35	36	37	38	39	40
40	41	42	43	44	45	46	47	48	49	50
50	51	52	53	54	55	56	57	58	59	60
60	61	62	63	64	65	66	67	68	69	70
70	71	72	73	74	75	76	77	78	79	80
80	81	82	83	84	85	86	87	88	89	90
90	91	92	93	94	95	96	97	98	99	100

Rounding off numbers to nearest 100

Round down ← | → **Round up**

0	0–49	50–99	100
100	100–149	150–199	200
200	200–249	250–299	300
300	300–349	350–399	400
400	400–449	450–499	500
500	500–549	550–599	600
600	600–649	650–699	700
700	700–749	750–799	800
800	800–849	850–899	900
900	900–949	950–999	1000

We use the same method to round off numbers to the nearest 10, 100, 1000, etc. When numbers are greater, it becomes difficult to picture the chart and we apply another rule, which is explained in the solved examples given in the next section.

SOLVED EXAMPLES

Example 8: Round off 4,31,868 to the nearest 10 and nearest 100.

Solution:

L	TTh	Th	H	T	O
4	3	1	8	6	8

4 3 1 8 6 | 8 — 5 or more?
4 3 1 8 7 0 — Yes, then round up to the nearest 10.

4 3 1 8 | 6 8 — 50 or more?
4 3 1 9 0 0 — Yes, then round up to the nearest 100.

Example 9: Round off 9,36,725 to the nearest 1000.

Solution:

L	TTh	Th	H	T	O
9	3	6	7	2	5

Since 7 (in the hundreds place) is greater than 5 we will add 1 to 6 (in the thousands place). 7, 2 and 5 will each become 0. So, 9,36,725 rounded off to the nearest 1000 is 9,37,000.

Example 10: Round off 2,63,751 to the nearest 10,000.

Solution:

L	TTh	Th	H	T	O
2	6	3	7	5	1

Since 3 (in the thousands place) is less than 5, we do not add anything to 6 (in the ten thousands place). 3, 7, 5 and 1 will each become 0. So, 2,63,751 rounded off to the nearest 10,000 is 2,60,000.

EXERCISE 1D

1. **Round off the following numbers to the nearest 10.**

   a. 27 b. 178 c. 7351 d. 82,162 e. 9,18,255

2. **Round off the following numbers to the nearest 100.**

   a. 97 b. 526 c. 1562 d. 83,427 e. 6,43,250

3. **Round off the following numbers to the nearest 1000.**

   a. 3794 b. 5281 c. 72,835 d. 8,42,500 e. 9,36,147

4. **Round off the following numbers to the nearest 10,000.**

   a. 52,358 b. 35,825 c. 2,63,389 d. 7,28,935 e. 5,67,821

5. **Answer the following questions.**

   a. Round off the sum of 2131, 1051 and 5713 to the nearest 100.

   b. Round off the numbers 18 and 132 to the nearest 10 and find the product.

   c. Round off 7,16,853 to the nearest 1000.

   d. Round off 57,867 to the nearest 10, 100, 1000 and 10,000.

Maths Lab Activity

21 CS Creativity and innovation, Collaboration — HQ Happiness My Goal

Aim: To reinforce the concept of large numbers

Materials required: Two chart papers and sketch pens

Procedure:

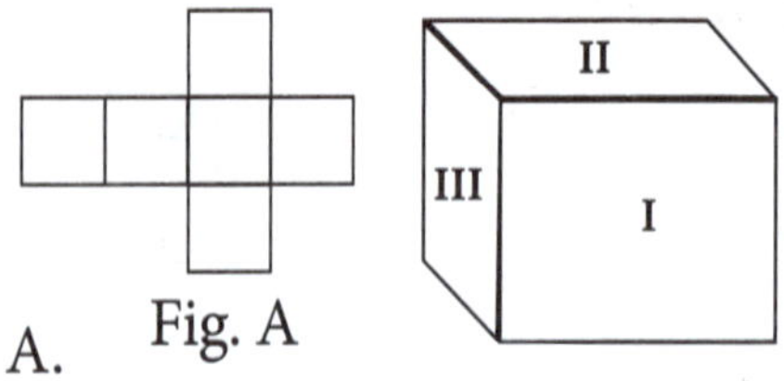

Fig. A

1. Take a chart paper. Cut it in the way as given in Figure A.
2. Join all the flaps to make a cube.
3. On each side of the cube, write Roman numbers from I to VI. Now, you have made a dice with Roman numbers on it.
4. Take a chart paper. Make hundred squares and write numbers 1–100 starting from the first square.
5. Now, use your dice to play the game. Two or more children can play this game.
6. Throw the dice on the board and move ahead according to the number on the dice. Take turns to do this. The first person to reach 100 wins the game!

1	2	3	4	5	6	7	8	9	10
11	12	13	14	15	16	17	18	19	20
21	22	23	24	25	26	27	28	29	30
31	32	33	34	35	36	37	38	39	40
41	42	43	44	45	46	47	48	49	50
51	52	53	54	55	56	57	58	59	60
61	62	63	64	65	66	67	68	69	70
71	72	73	74	75	76	77	78	79	80
81	82	83	84	85	86	87	88	89	90
91	92	93	94	95	96	97	98	99	100

Concept Map

Large numbers

- 5- and 6-digit numbers
- Number system

International Number System

Thousands period			Ones period		
HTh	TTh	Th	H	T	O

Indian Number System

Lakhs	Thousands period		Ones period		
L	TTh	Th	H	T	O

- Comparison → First compare lakhs, then ten thousands, thousands, hundreds, tens and finally ones → Ascending order: Smallest to Greatest; Descending order: Greatest to Smallest
- Rounding off
- Roman numerals

Roman Numerals	I	V	X	L	C	D	M
Hindu-Arabic Numerals	1	5	10	50	100	500	1000

- Successor: Number obtained on adding 1 to the given number
- Predecessor: Number obtained on subtracting 1 from the given number

Key Concepts

- **Place value:** The position of each digit in the number
- **Expanded form:** Expressing the number as a sum of the place values of all the digits
- **Indian Number System:** The number system used in India
- **International Number System:** The number system used in USA and some other countries

A. Choose the correct option.

1. Four lakh twenty-one thousand five hundred seven in numerals is ________.

   a. 4,21,057 b. 4,20,407 c. 4,21,507 d. 4,12,407

2. Which of the following numbers is written in the International Number System?

   a. 2,69,804 b. 9,23,184 c. 180,976 d. 9,80,15

3. Which of the following numbers is the greatest?

   a. 3,00,003 b. 3,30,000 c. 3,03,333 d. 3,00,333

4. Numbers in ascending order are written from ________.

   a. the smallest to the greatest b. the greatest to the smallest

   c. the greatest to the greatest d. the smallest to the smallest

5. The predecessor of the greatest 5-digit number is ________.

   a. 99999 b. 9998 c. 99998 d. 100000

6. Which is the smallest 6-digit number formed using the digits 3, 1, 0, 7, 9 and 5 only once?

   a. 013579 b. 975310 c. 103579 d. 135790

7. Which is the greatest 5-digit number formed using the digits 2, 7, 9, 0 and 6 only once?

   a. 02679 b. 97620 c. 90762 d. 79620

8. Which is the number corresponding to the expanded form of 4,00,000 + 7000 + 300 + 1?

   a. 4,67,321 b. 740,310 c. 4,47,331 d. 4,07,301

9. The Roman numeral for 10 + 5 is equal to ________.

   a. XX b. VV c. XV d. VX

10. 5,62,389 rounded off to the nearest 100 is equal to ________.

    a. 5,62,389 b. 5,62,400 c. 5,62,390 d. 5,62,000

B. Fill in the blanks.

1. The sum of the place value of 5 and the place value of 3 in 6,25,394 is ____________________.

2. In 5,23,974, the digit in the lakhs place is ____________________.

3. The successor of 32,548 is ____________________.

4. The difference between the successor of 999 and the predecessor of 1001 is ____________________.

C. Write T for true and F for false.

1. 7,32,590 > 7,32,590
2. 2,50,000 < 2,49,000
3. The Roman numeral for 19 is XIX.
4. The Roman numeral for 25 is VV.

D. Match the following.

1.	V	a.	30
2.	XXX	b.	22
3.	XIV	c.	5
4.	XXII	d.	38
5.	XXXVIII	e.	14

E. Complete the table.

	Number	Smallest	Greatest
1.	2-digit number		
2.	3-digit number		
3.	4-digit number		
4.	5-digit number		
5.	6-digit number		

F. Answer the following questions.

1. Write two lakh sixty-eight thousand one hundred forty-nine in numerals and words as per the International Number System.
2. Is six hundred twenty-nine thousand one hundred seventy-three different from six lakh twenty-nine thousand one hundred seventy-three? Give reasons for your answer.
3. What is the sum of the greatest 5-digit number and the smallest 6-digit number?
4. What is the smallest 6-digit number formed by using the digits 4, 0, 3, 0, 8 and 9 only once?
5. Write the expanded form of 2,43,567.
6. Write the numeral for 7,00,000 + 30,000 + 20 + 9.
7. Round off 5,49,682 to the nearest 100.
8. Write the following numbers in the descending order.
   7,00,077; 7,00,007; 7,77,777; 7,00,777; 7,70,077
9. Round off the sum of 29534, 56902 and 34059 to the nearest 1000.

A. 21 CS Critical Thinking, Information Literacy

Find out the price of a cycle, a scooter and a motorcycle.

1. Write the number name of each price in the Indian Number System as well as in the International Number System.
2. Write the price of all three vehicles in ascending and descending orders.
3. Which one costs the most and which one costs the least?
4. Round off all the three prices to the nearest 1000.

B. 21 CS Critical Thinking, Life Skills | CC Integration with Science | HQ Harmony In The Self

13 CLIMATE ACTION

When an earthquake hit a village, 24,795 houses were destroyed. Many people collected money to help the families who had lost their belongings and their homes.

Find the successor of 24,795. Also, round off 24,795 to the nearest 1000.

C. 21 CS Critical Thinking, Information Literacy | CC Integration with Social Studies

The approximate distance between Delhi and some cities in the world is given below.

New Delhi to London = 6707 km　　New Delhi to Tokyo = 5830 km

New Delhi to New York = 11,747 km　　New Delhi to Toronto = 11,625 km

1. Find out which city is closest to New Delhi.
2. Which city is farthest from New Delhi?
3. Write the distance from New Delhi to all the cities in ascending and descending orders.
4. Round off all the distances given to the nearest 1000.

SUSTAINABLE DEVELOPMENT GOALS

Question B is in line with SDG 13 Climate Action. If you saw the devastation caused by some natural disasters, what can you do to help in such situations? When an earthquake hit your city, did the house you live in get damaged? Why or why not?

WORKSHEET 1

21 CS Critical Thinking | HQ Quality Education

Fill in the crossword with the help of the hints given below.

a.					b.		
		c.					e.
d.				f.			
						g.	

Across

a. The greatest 4-digit number

b. 1 less than the greatest 3-digit number

c. Seven hundred eighty-nine thousand five hundred twenty-three in Hindu–Arabic numerals

d. The number equals to 80,000 + 7000 + 500 + 20 + 1

g. XXX in Hindu–Arabic Number System

Down

a. Nine hundred thousand fifty-eight in Hindu–Arabic numerals

b. Ninety-six thousand five hundred eighty-seven in Hindu–Arabic numerals

c. The number equals to 70,000 + 9,000 + 600 + 50 + 8

e. 34728 rounded off to the nearest 1000

f. XIX in Hindu–Arabic Number System

2 Addition and Subtraction of Large Numbers

Learning Objectives

- To add 5- and 6-digit numbers
- To solve word problems on addition of 5- and 6-digit numbers
- To subtract 5- and 6-digit numbers
- To solve word problems on subtraction of 5- and 6-digit numbers

Let's Get Started

21 CS Critical Thinking

The students of Class IV are going on a school field trip. They carry with them a few necessary items. Their teacher carries a camera, sitting mat and toys for some games and activities. Find out how much all of their bags weigh.

All the bags would weigh: ______________

We have learnt how to add 4-digit numbers. Now, let us use the same method to add 5- and 6-digit numbers. We shall also learn subtraction of large numbers.

ADDITION

Large numbers are added in the same way as smaller numbers. First add the digits in the ones place, then add the digits in the tens place, followed by those in the hundreds, the thousands, the ten thousands and the lakhs places. *The numbers that are being added are called* ***addends****. The result obtained after adding the numbers (addends) is called the* ***sum****.*

NOTE

- The symbol '+' is used when we add numbers.
- Numbers added in any order give the same answer.
- When we add 0 to a number, the answer is the number itself.
- When we add 1 to a number, the answer is the number just after it or its successor.

Addition of Two 5-Digit Numbers without Carry Forward

Let us add two 5-digit numbers, 54,435 and 12,462, without carry forward.

		TTh	Th	H	T	O
Addend →		5	4	4	3	5
Addend →	+	1	2	4	6	2
Sum →		**6**	**6**	**8**	**9**	**7**

The number obtained after the addition of these two numbers, that is, the sum is 66,897.

Addition of Two 5-Digit Numbers with Carry Forward

Here, we use the same method as above. However, in this case, we carry forward numbers to the next higher place value, wherever required.

Let us add two 5-digit numbers, 64,935 and 18,462, with carry forward.

Add the digits at each place value (O/T/H/Th/TTh) and regroup, if required. Carry forward to the next higher place value.

		TTh	Th	H	T	O
		1	1			
Addend →		6	4	9	3	5
Addend →	+	1	8	4	6	2
Sum →		**8**	**3**	**3**	**9**	**7**

The number obtained after the addition of these two numbers, that is, the sum is 83,397.

Addition of Three 5-Digit Numbers with Carry Forward

Let us add three 5-digit numbers with carry forward.

	TTh	Th	H	T	O
	1	2	1	1	
Addend	1	2	6	4	3
Addend	3	9	8	7	5
Addend +	2	4	5	2	4
Sum	**7**	**7**	**0**	**4**	**2**

The number obtained after the addition of these three numbers, that is, the sum is 77,042.

Addition of 6-Digit Numbers without Carry Forward

Let us add two 6-digit numbers without carry forward.

	L	TTh	Th	H	T	O
Addend	1	2	4	3	8	0
Addend +	8	6	3	2	0	1
Sum	**9**	**8**	**7**	**5**	**8**	**1**

The number obtained after the addition of these two numbers, that is, the sum is 9,87,581.

Addition of 6-Digit Numbers with Carry Forward

Let us add 2,95,732 and 1,38,815.

	L	TTh	Th	H	T	O
	1	1	1			
Addend	2	9	5	7	3	2
Addend +	1	3	8	8	1	5
Sum	**4**	**3**	**4**	**5**	**4**	**7**

Let us add 2,57,894, 5,31,253 and 1,64,761.

	L	TTh	Th	H	T	O
	1	1	1	2		
Addend	2	5	7	8	9	4
Addend	5	3	1	2	5	3
Addend +	1	6	4	7	6	1
Sum	**9**	**5**	**3**	**9**	**0**	**8**

MENTAL MATHS

25,760 migratory birds flew to India from Europe in December and 31,209 birds in January. How many birds flew from Europe to India in these two months?

NOTE

In addition, it does not matter which number we write on top.

But we prefer to write the greatest number on top, then the next smaller and the smallest number at the bottom.

EXERCISE 2A

1. **Add the following numbers.**

a.

	TTh	Th	H	T	O
	5	3	4	2	9
+	2	9	8	7	6

b.

	L	TTh	Th	H	T	O
	2	5	4	1	7	6
+	6	2	3	5	2	3

c.

	L	TTh	Th	H	T	O
	3	2	4	6	0	1
+	6	5	1	2	4	5

d. 532107 + 29416 + 3852 = ______________

e. 463152 + 25103 + 4318 + 294 = ______________

f. 697813 + 215347 + 37425 + 1820 = ______________

WORD PROBLEMS ON ADDITION

Certain steps need to be followed to solve a word problem. Note the following points while solving a word problem.

- **Read:** Read the word problem again and again till you understand what the problem is about.
- **Identify and underline:** Identify the important information or keywords and underline those words.
- **Choose operator:** Write short statements to understand what you need to solve. Choose the correct operator.

- **Solve:** Translate statements into mathematical operations. Then solve the problem.
- **Answer:** Cross-check to see whether you have solved the word problem correctly. The answer to the word problem must always be written as a statement.
- **Check:** Verify your answer by using inverse method of calculations.

GO EASY!

We 'add' in word problems when we know that the answer will increase by the amount given.

Look out for the word 'addition' while solving word problems:

- Total or sum
- Increased by
- More than
- Altogether
- In all
- Added to
- Together

Framing Word Problems

When an addition question is given and a word problem needs to be framed, follow the steps given here.

- Note down the quantity of the number—whether it is in hundreds, thousands or lakhs.
- Think of what these numbers could relate to, in our daily life.
- Frame the word problem accordingly.

SOLVED EXAMPLES

Example 1: In January, Sumit saved ₹5400, in February, he saved ₹2900 and in March, he saved ₹6750. What was the total amount of money he saved?

Solution:

Step 1: Read the question carefully. Note, that the total amount would be the sum of all the three numbers.

Step 2: We can summarize the problem in three short statements.

In January, Sumit saved ₹5400.

In February, he saved ₹2900.

In March, he saved ₹6750.

Step 3: Now, we can add the three numbers and write the answer in a statement form.

		2
In January, he saved	=	₹ 5 4 0 0
In February, he saved	=	₹ 2 9 0 0
In March, he saved	=	₹ 6 7 5 0
		₹ 15 0 5 0

The total amount saved by Sumit was ₹15,050.

Example 2: A factory sold 1,20,580 watches in April, 1,00,600 watches in May and 2,00,400 watches in June. What is the total number of watches that the factory sold in these three months?

Solution:

		L	TTh	Th	H	T	O
				1			
Number of watches sold in April		1	2	0	5	8	0
Number of watches sold in May		1	0	0	6	0	0
Number of watches sold in June	+	2	0	0	4	0	0
		4	**2**	**1**	**5**	**8**	**0**

The total number of watches that the factory sold in these three months is 4,21,580.

Example 3: Frame a word problem on the given addition.

	TTh	Th	H	T	O
	1	1	1	1	
	2	4	7	9	3
+	1	6	5	0	8
	4	**1**	**3**	**0**	**1**

Solution:

Step 1: Think of what these 5-digit numbers could relate to, in our daily life.

Step 2: These could be the prices of mobile phones or the number of people living in a village.

Step 3: Frame the word problem.

Given below are two different statements or word problems that have been framed based on the given addition.

1. One mobile phone costs ₹24,793 and another mobile phone costs ₹16,508. What is the total cost of both the mobile phones?
2. A total of 24,793 people live in one village and 16,508 people live in another village. How many people live in both the villages?

Exercise 2B

1. Solve the following word problems.

a. A city has 5,12,180 men, 4,00,350 women and 17,160 children. What is the total population of the city?

b. Sonam spent ₹6,25,000 to buy a shop, ₹1,32,000 to get the woodwork done and ₹50,400 on the electrical fittings. How much money did Sonam spend?

c. In the summer holidays, 43,000 people from South India went to Singapore, 24,500 people went to Dubai and 98,170 people went to London. How many people went to Singapore, Dubai and London altogether?

d. A bookseller sold 1,25,000 Maths books, 2,39,000 English books and 58,000 Science books. How many books did he sell in all?

e. A school has 58,000 tables, 58,000 chairs and 1490 cupboards. How many tables, chairs and cupboards does the school have in all?

2. Frame word problems for the following numerical questions.

a.

	TTh	Th	H	T	O
	3	2	9	4	1
+	1	8	5	9	6

b.

	TTh	Th	H	T	O
	4	6	7	2	3
+	1	8	0	9	5

c.

	L	TTh	Th	H	T	O
	7	3	5	2	9	8
+	1	6	7	4	0	3

d.

	L	TTh	Th	H	T	O
	6	1	0	5	2	7
+	2	7	8	1	4	9

SUBTRACTION

Subtraction of large numbers is done in the same way as subtraction of smaller numbers. We first subtract the digits in the ones place, then in the tens place, followed by those in the hundreds, the thousands, the ten thousands and the lakhs places.

The number that is being subtracted is called the ***subtrahend.*** *The number from which a number is being subtracted is called the* ***minuend.*** *The result obtained after the subtraction is called the* ***difference.***

10 − 2 = 8

Minuend ← 10

Subtrahend ← 2

8 → Difference

Subtraction of 5-Digit Numbers with Borrowing

Let us subtract 31,869 from 87,352. We first subtract the digits in the ones place, then the digits in the tens place, followed by those in the hundreds, the thousands and the ten thousands places.

		TTh	Th	H	T	O
			6	12	14	12
Minuend		8	~~7~~	~~3~~	~~5~~	~~2~~
Subtrahend	−	3	1	8	6	9
Difference		**5**	**5**	**4**	**8**	**3**

Wherever required, we borrow numbers from the next higher place.

The difference between the two numbers is 55,483.

Go Easy!

To check your answer

If

	TTh	Th	H	T	O
	8	7	3	5	2
−	3	1	8	6	9
	5	**5**	**4**	**8**	**3**

then

	TTh	Th	H	T	O
	8	7	3	5	2
−	5	5	4	8	3
	3	**1**	**8**	**6**	**9**

OR

	TTh	Th	H	T	O
	5	5	4	8	3
+	3	1	8	6	9
	8	**7**	**3**	**5**	**2**

Subtraction of 6-Digit Numbers Without Borrowing

Let us subtract 1,40,123 from 7,83,965.

		L	TTh	Th	H	T	O
Minuend		7	8	3	9	6	5
Subtrahend	−	1	4	0	1	2	3
Difference		**6**	**4**	**3**	**8**	**4**	**2**

Subtraction of 6-Digit Numbers with Borrowing

Let us subtract 2,86,573 from 9,53,461.

		L	TTh	Th	H	T	O
		8	14	12	13	15	11
Minuend		~~9~~	~~5~~	~~3~~	~~4~~	~~6~~	~~1~~
Subtrahend	−	2	8	6	5	7	3
Difference		**6**	**6**	**6**	**8**	**8**	**8**

Exercise 2C

Subtract the following numbers.

1. 8,32,910 – 0 = ____________
2. 7,87,878 – 2000 = ____________
3. 7,54,936 – 12,803 = ____________
4. 8,64,310 – 2,97,526 = ____________
5. 1,00,000 – 57,263 = ____________
6. 8,00,000 – 1,99,999 = ____________

WORD PROBLEMS ON SUBTRACTION

To solve word problems on subtraction, follow the same steps given under solving word problems on addition. You just need to be careful in identifying the keywords.

Go Easy!

Keywords related to subtraction:

- Change
- Decreased by
- Difference
- Fewer
- Have left
- Take away
- How many did not have
- How many more
- How much more
- Less than
- Remain
- Taller/Shorter

Mental Maths

I subtracted 30 from a number. Then I subtracted 240 from it. I was left with 253. What was my original number?

SOLVED EXAMPLES

Example 4: Sanjay wants to buy a car for ₹7,25,600. He has ₹4,89,000 with him. How much more money does he need?

Solution:

		L	TTh	Th	H	T	O
		6	11	15			
Car's cost		~~7~~	~~2~~	~~5~~	6	0	0
Sanjay has	–	4	8	9	0	0	0
		2	**3**	**6**	**6**	**0**	**0**

He needs ₹2,36,600 more to buy the car.

Example 5: Frame a word problem on the given subtraction.

	TTh	Th	H	T	O
	4	15	12		
	~~5~~	~~6~~	~~2~~	4	7
−	4	9	3	2	6
		6	9	2	1

MENTAL MATHS

	L	TTh	Th	H	T	O
	4	7	8	5	2	1
−	3	6	1	0	1	0

Solution:

Step 1: Think of what these 5-digit numbers could relate to, in our daily life.

Step 2: These could be the number of watches manufactured and sold in one month or the amount of money earned and spent by one person.

Step 3: Frame the word problem.

Given below are two different problems based on the given subtraction.

1. A factory manufactured 56,247 watches in one month. It sold 49,326 watches out of those. How many watches were left?
2. Rajat earns ₹56,247 every month. He spends ₹49,326 in a month. How much money does he save every month?

EXERCISE 2D

1. Solve the following word problems.

a. By how much is 69,107 greater than 25,658?

b. John had ₹8,47,950 in his bank account. He spent ₹5,82,160 out of it. How much money is left in his bank account?

c. A factory manufactured 7,45,000 cars in one year. Out of these, 2,79,840 cars were white in colour. How many cars were not white in colour?

d. There were 2,50,810 trees in an orchard. 1,63,490 trees were cut down. How many trees were left in the orchard?

e. A total of 9,56,930 people visited London in a year. Out of these, 6,95,710 were Indians. How many people were not Indians?

2. **Frame word problems for the following numerical questions.**

a.

	TTh	Th	H	T	O
	2	5	6	9	4
−	1	3	8	2	7

b.

	TTh	Th	H	T	O
	6	9	2	5	0
−	4	8	7	9	4

c.

	L	TTh	Th	H	T	O
	2	7	8	6	5	8
−	1	5	6	9	8	4

d.

	L	TTh	Th	H	T	O
	9	5	0	0	0	0
−	8	0	0	0	0	0

MATHS LAB ACTIVITY

21 CS Critical Thinking, Collaboration EL

1 2 3
4 5 6
7 8 9
0

Aim: To make flashcards and play number games

Materials required: Chart papers, coloured paper, glue, scissors

Procedure:

1. Cut the chart papers into small rectangles of size 4 by 3 centimetres.
2. Write numbers from 0 to 9 on the coloured paper. Make sure the size of the number is not bigger than 2 by 2 centimetres.
3. Make cut-outs of these numbers.
4. Stick each number cut-out on the rectangular chart paper. You can make 3 cards of each number.
5. Play number games as suggested below by making two teams.

   One team should take out 6 cards, for example

   3 1 7 2 6 9

Ask as many questions as you can to the other team. A few sample questions are given below.

a. Create as many 3-digit, 4-digit, 5-digit, 6-digit numbers as you can.
b. What would be the 5-digit number closest to 10,000?
c. Create as many numbers as you can between 2000 and 5000.

Concept Map

Addition and Subtraction of Large Numbers

- Addition
  - Addend + Addend = Sum
- Word problems
  - Keywords for solving addition:
    - Total
    - Sum
    - In all
    - Increased
    - Added
    - More than
    - Together
    - Altogether
  - Steps:
    1. Read the question carefully
    2. Identify keywords
    3. Choose operator
    4. Solve
    5. Cross-check the answer
    6. Write the answer in a statement form
    7. Verify the answer
  - Keywords for solving subtraction:
    - Change
    - Did not have
    - Decreased
    - How many more
    - Difference
    - How much more
    - Fewer
    - Less than
    - Have left
    - Remain
    - Take away
    - Taller/Shorter
- Subtraction
  - Minuend – Subtrahend = Difference

Key Concepts

- **Addition:** When we bring things together to increase numbers
- **Subtraction:** When we give away things to reduce numbers
- **Addends:** The numbers that are being added
- **Sum:** The result of adding addends
- **Carrying:** When the sum of digits is more than one digit, then we have to carry forward part of the sum to the next higher place value
- **Word problems:** Questions related to daily life
- **Subtrahend:** The number that is to be subtracted
- **Minuend:** The number from which the subtrahend is to be subtracted
- **Framing word problems:** Making your own word problems

A. Choose the correct option.

1. What should be added to 1,89,304 to get 9,00,583?
   a. 9,00,583 b. 1,89,304 c. 9,00,000 d. 7,11,279
2. 5,69,000 – 9000 = ________.
   a. 5,69,000 b. 9000 c. 0 d. 5,60,000
3. What should be subtracted from 9,47,385 to get 6,10,000?
   a. 6,10,000 b. 3,37,385 c. 9,47,385 d. 3,37,380
4. By how much is nine lakh twenty-three thousand one hundred three greater than two lakh seven?
   a. 7,23,096 b. 9,23,103 c. 2,00,007 d. 9,00,000
5. Rakesh spent ₹7,62,000 to buy a second hand car, ₹71,000 on its repairing and ₹31,000 on its painting. How much money did Rakesh spend in all?
   a. ₹7,62,000 b. ₹71,000 c. ₹31,000 d. ₹8,64,000
6. A factory sold 1,21,000 cycles in July, 2,59,620 cycles in August and 3,00,980 cycles in September. How many cycles did the factory sell in these three months?
   a. 6,81,600 b. 1,21,000 c. 2,59,620 d. 3,00,980

B. Fill in the blanks.

1. 2594 + 3108 = 3108 + ____________
2. 12398 + 3000 = ____________
3. 57809 + 0 = ____________
4. 5 + 3 + 100000 = ____________
5. 350000 – 4921 = ____________

C. Write T for true and F for false.

1. The result of subtracting two addends is the sum.
2. Subtrahend is the number that is to be subtracted.
3. To find the sum of two numbers, we should subtract.
4. To find the total of two numbers, we should add.
5. Minuend is the number from which the subtrahend is to be subtracted.

D. Solve the following word problems.

1. The sum of two numbers is 8,32,579. One number is 1,97,638. What is the other number?
2. Ram needs ₹9,99,500 to buy a house. He has ₹5,42,800 with him. How much more money does he need?
3. The principal of a school spent ₹5,60,400 to buy tables and chairs. If the tables cost ₹2,80,200, how much did the chairs cost?

4. Romila wants to buy a piece of land for ₹8,49,700. She has only ₹6,84,300 with her. How much more money does she need?
5. Out of 3,70,000 men in a village, 2,43,000 men work in the fields. How many men do not work in the fields?

SKILL UP!

A. 21 CS Information Literacy, Technology Literacy | CC Integration with Computer Science

Find out the price of the four most popular motorcycles in your city.
Make a report comparing the most expensive and the least expensive vehicles. You can include the difference in prices of the vehicles in your report using MS Excel or some other software.

B. 21 CS Critical Thinking, Life Skills | IF | CC Integration with Science

13 CLIMATE ACTION

When Kerala was hit by floods, many people lost their homes.
Meghna and her friends collected some money to help the people in Kerala.
The girls collected the following amount:
Meghna ₹1,27,900 Reena ₹2,51,800 Sanjana ₹63,000

1. What was the total amount collected by the girls?
2. Do you think this money would have helped the people in Kerala?
3. Can you think of another way of helping people in such situations?

C. 21 CS Critical Thinking

Rajesh starts counting from 594. Tarun starts counting from 962.
Anubhav starts counting from 287.
If all the three children count one number in one second, who will reach 1000 first?

SUSTAINABLE DEVELOPMENT GOALS

Question B is in line with SDG 13 Climate Action. If a city experiences a flood, how can you deal with it? Are there any vital ways to cope with that situation?

WORKSHEET 2

21 CS Critical Thinking, Information Literacy

Ajay, Mohnish, Shelly and Kareena want to buy an apartment.

The apartment costs ₹9,99,000. They all have saved some money. How much more money do each of them need?

I have ₹8,00,000

I have ₹5,20,000

I have ₹6,24,000

I have ₹9,10,000

AJAY — I need ______

MOHNISH — I need ______

SHELLY — I need ______

KAREENA — I need ______

3 Multiplication of Numbers

Learning Objectives

- To understand multiplication facts
- To learn multiplication by multiples of 10
- To learn multiplication by 2- and 3-digit numbers
- To solve word problems on multiplication
- To estimate products
- To identify patterns in multiplication

Let's Get Started

21 CS Critical Thinking | HQ Living In An Interconnected Society

Lekha and Irfan are going to visit a local animal shelter. They plan to carry 2 packets of food for each animal. Observe the picture given below and answer the following questions.

A. Number of animals = ______

B. Number of food packets for each animal = ______

C. Total number of food packets = A × B = ______ × ______ = ______

D. Identify the multiplicand, multiplier and the product in the question C given above. ______

MULTIPLICATION FACTS

Adding the same number to itself many times is a long process.
For example, 2 + 2 + 2 = 6. Here, 2 is added three times.

The shorter process to get the same answer is by **multiplying** the two numbers, 2 and 3.

That is, $2 \times 3 = 6$.

To solve 329 + 329 + 329, two methods can be followed.

We multiply 329 by 3 because 329 is being added to itself 3 times.

Method 1

	H	T	O
	3	2	9
	3	2	9
+	3	2	9
	9	**8**	**7**

Method 2

	H	T	O
		2	
	3	2	9
×			3
	9	**8**	**7**

329 is the multiplicand.
3 is the multiplier.
987 is the product.

329 × 3 = 987

Multiplicand ← 329; Multiplier ← 3; Product ← 987

The numbers being multiplied are also called the **factors** of the product.

329 × 3 = 987

Factor ← 329; Factor ← 3; Product ← 987

So, the multiplicand and the multiplier are the factors of the product.

Some multiplication facts are listed below.

- **Multiplication property of zero:** 0 multiplied by any number is equal to 0.

  $6 \times 0 = 0$

- **Identity property of multiplication:** When a number is multiplied by 1, the product is the number itself.

  $2 \times 1 = 2$

- **Commutative property of multiplication:** Even if we change the order of the numbers being multiplied, the value of the product remains the same.

  $2 \times 3 = \mathbf{6}$ and $3 \times 2 = \mathbf{6}$

  Thus, $2 \times 3 = 3 \times 2$.

- **Associative property of multiplication:** If we are multiplying 3 numbers, we can multiply any two numbers first and then multiply the product by the third number. The final product will be the same.

$(2 \times 3) \times 4$	and	$2 \times (3 \times 4)$
6×4		2×12
$= 24$		$= 24$

Thus, $(2 \times 3) \times 4 = 2 \times (3 \times 4)$.

- **Distributive property of multiplication:** If we multiply a number with the sum of two other numbers, the product will be the same as that number being multiplied by each of the other numbers and then the products being added.

$2 \times (3 + 4)$	and	$(2 \times 3) + (2 \times 4)$
$= 2 \times 7$		$= 6 + 8$
$= 14$		$= 14$

Thus, $2 \times (3 + 4) = (2 \times 3) + (2 \times 4)$.

EXERCISE 3A

1. **Solve the following.**

a. $3 \times 0 =$ ______	b. $0 \times 58 =$ ______	c. $72 \times 1 =$ ______
d. $479 \times 0 =$ ______	e. $0 \times 695 =$ ______	f. $289 \times 1 =$ ______
g. $3 \times 4 = 4 \times$ ______	h. $5 \times 2 = 2 \times$ ______	i. $15 \times 11 =$ ______ $\times 15$

2. **Fill in the blanks.**

   a. The numbers being multiplied are called the ____________ of the product.

   b. When we multiply two numbers, the result is known as the ____________ of two numbers.

   c. When we multiply a number with ____________, we get the same number as the product.

   d. When we multiply a number with ____________, we get zero as the product.

   e. Even if we change the order of the numbers being multiplied, the product does not change. This is the ____________ property of multiplication.

METHODS OF MULTIPLICATION

Let us discuss a few methods of multiplication.

Column Method

Column method is the standard method of multiplication. In this method, we write the numbers to be multiplied vertically one below the other. Place the bigger number above.

SOLVED EXAMPLES

Example 1: 243×2

Solution:

Write the multiplicand, that is, 243 first. As 243 has 3 digits, this number will use 3 columns namely H, T and O.

Below 243, write the multiplier, that is, 2.

Write this under the ones column.

The multiplier is written in the next row.

Now, multiply the multiplier with each digit of the multiplicand, starting from the ones position and then moving to the left.

The product is 486.

	H	T	O
	2	4	3
×			2
	4	**8**	**6**

Put the × sign in multiplier row and then multiply.

In the ones column: $2 \times 3 = 6$

In the tens column: $2 \times 4 = 8$

In the hundreds column: $2 \times 2 = 4$

Expanded Method

To multiply numbers using the expanded method, follow the steps given below.

Step 1: Write the expanded form of the multiplicand.

Step 2: Multiply each place value with thc multiplier.

Step 3: Add all the products.

SOLVED EXAMPLES

Example 2: 243×2

Solution:

Step 1: Expanded form of $243 = 200 + 40 + 3$

Step 2: $200 \times 2 = 400$

$40 \times 2 = 80$

$3 \times 2 = 6$

Step 3: Add all the products.

So, $243 \times 2 = 486$.

	H	T	O
	4	0	0
		8	0
+			6
	4	**8**	**6**

Lattice Method

In lattice method, a grid with square or diamond-shaped spaces is used for multiplication. This method involves making a lattice depending on the number of digits in the multiplicand and the multiplier.

SOLVED EXAMPLES

Example 3: 213 × 45

Solution: As 213 has 3 digits, make 3 columns. There are 2 digits in 45, so make 2 rows.

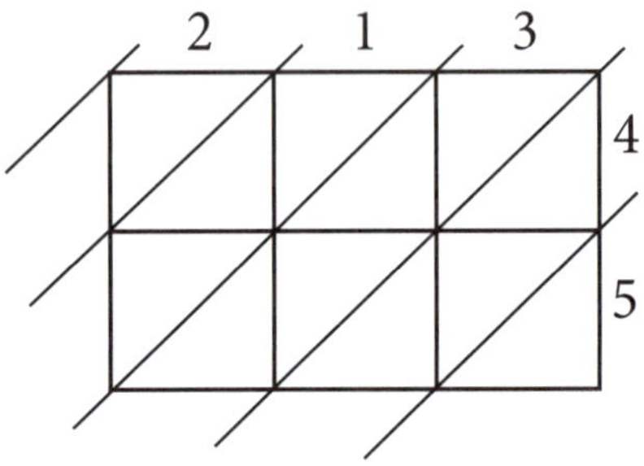

Write the numbers as shown.
Draw diagonal lines as shown.

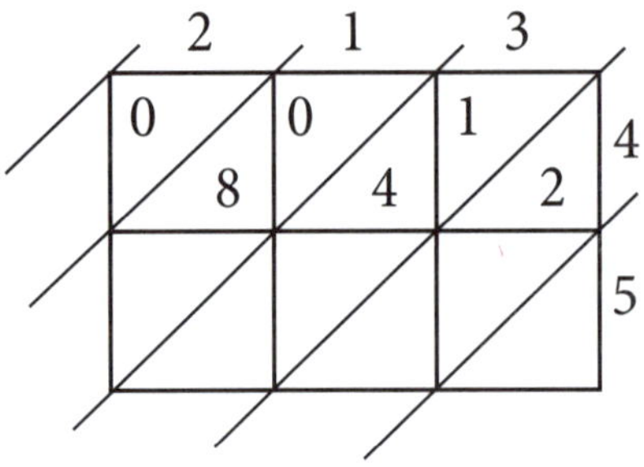

Multiply 4 with 3, then with 1, and then with 2.
4 × 3 = 12.
Write 12 as shown.
4 × 1 = 4.
Write it as 04.
4 × 2 = 8.
Write it as 08.

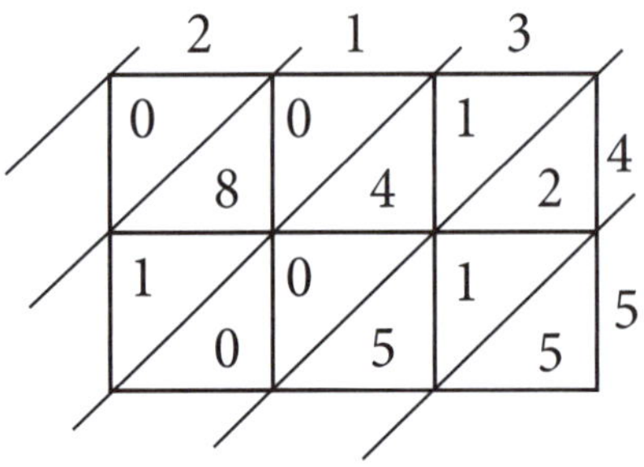

Multiply 5 with 3, then with 1, and then with 2.
5 × 3 = 15. Write 15 as shown.
5 × 1 = 5. Write it as 05.
5 × 2 = 10. Write 10 as shown.

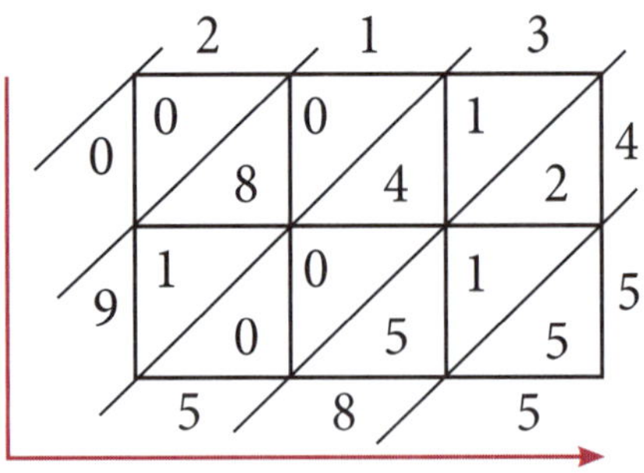

Now, add all the digits diagonally (only those numbers inside the rectangle)
For first diagonal (from the left), 0 = 0
For second diagonal, 0 + 8 + 1 = 9
For third diagonal, 1 + 4 + 0 + 0 = 5
For fourth diagonal, 2 + 1 + 5 = 8
For fifth diagonal, 5 = 5
Write down the digits from left to right.
We get, 09585 = 9585.

So, 213 × 45 = 9585.

Multiplication by 10, 100 and 1000

When a number is multiplied by 10, 100, 1000 and so on, the product is the multiplicand on the left, followed by the same number of zeros as in the multiplier.

For example,

2×10	$= 20$	19×10	$= 190$
2×100	$= 200$	19×100	$= 1900$
2×1000	$= 2000$	19×1000	$= 19,000$
$2 \times 10,000$	$= 20,000$	$19 \times 10,000$	$= 1,90,000$

Multiplication by Multiples of 10

When a number is multiplied by 10 or multiples of 10, that is, 20, 100, 600 and so on, multiply the multiplicand by the first digit of the multiplier and add as many zeros to the right of the product as in the multiplier.

SOLVED EXAMPLES

Example 4: Multiply 25 with 20.

Solution: First, find the product of 25 and 2. Then, write 0 to its right because 20 has one zero.

$25 \times 2 = 50$

Adding a zero to its right gives 500.

Thus, $25 \times 20 = 500$.

Example 5: Multiply 12 with 600.

Solution: First, find the product of 12 and 6. Then, write 00 to its right because 600 has two zeros.

$12 \times 6 = 72$

Adding two zeros to its right gives 7200.

Thus, $12 \times 600 = 7200$.

Example 6: Multiply 381 with 2000.

Solution: First, find the product of 381 and 2. Then, write 000 to its right because 2000 has three zeros.

$381 \times 2 = 762$

Adding three zeros to its right gives 7,62,000.

Thus, $381 \times 2000 = 7,62,000$.

MENTAL MATHS

1. $128 \times 10 =$ ______________
2. $128 \times 100 =$ ______________
3. $128 \times 1000 =$ ______________
4. $128 \times 10,000 =$ ______________

EXERCISE 3B

1. **Multiply the following numbers by 10, 100, 1000 and 10,000.**

   a. 5 b. 23 c. 37 d. 41 e. 75 f. 84

2. **Solve the following.**

   a. 23×20 b. 1325×4000 c. 5123×300 d. 143×20 e. 2134×50

MULTIPLICATION BY 2- AND 3-DIGIT NUMBERS

Let us now learn how large numbers can be multiplied by 2- and 3-digit numbers using different methods of multiplication.

SOLVED EXAMPLES

Example 7: Multiply 5182 by 43.

Solution:

Column Method

Step 1: First multiply 5182 by 3. Do not forget to carry forward 2 (write 2 on top of 1).

Step 2: Next, put 0 below 6 and multiply 5182 by 4. The numbers carried forward are written on top of the next higher places to avoid confusion.

Step 3: Add to get the answer.

Step 1

	TTh	Th	H	T	O
			2		
		5	1	8	2
×				4	3
	1	5	5	4	6

Step 2

	L	TTh	Th	H	T	O
				3 2		
			5	1	8	2
×					4	3
		1	5	5	4	6
+	2	0	7	2	8	0

Step 3

	L	TTh	Th	H	T	O
				3 2		
			5	1	8	2
×					4	3
		1		1		
		1	5	5	4	6
+	2	0	7	2	8	0
	2	**2**	**2**	**8**	**2**	**6**

Go Easy!

To understand better, 5182×43 is the same as $5182 \times (40 + 3)$.

$5182 \times 40 = 2,07,280$

$5182 \times 3 = 15,546$

So, $5182 \times 43 = 2,07,280 + 15,546$
$= 2,22,826$

Common Errors

2439 × 25

	TTh	Th	H	T	O
				1	
		2	1	4	
		2	4	3	9
×				2	5
		1	1	1	
	1	2	1	9	5
+		4	8	7	⑧
	1	**7**	**0**	**7**	**3**

👎

	TTh	Th	H	T	O
				1	
		2	1	4	
		2	4	3	9
×				2	5
	1		1		
	1	2	1	9	5
+	4	8	7	8	⓪
	6	**0**	**9**	**7**	**5**

👍

We put a 0 in the second row because we are multiplying with a tens digit in the multiplier.

In

T	O
2	5

2 is the tens digit.

Lattice Method

Let us multiply 5182 and 43 using the lattice method.

We will make a lattice with 4 columns and 2 rows as given below.

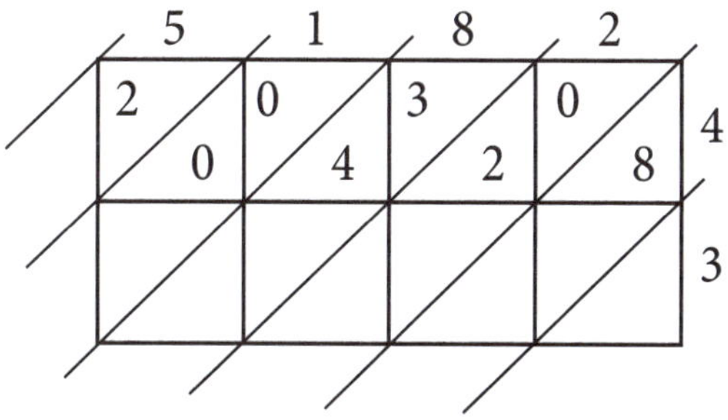

Multiply

4 × 2 = 8. Write it as 08.

4 × 8 = 32. Write 32 as shown.

4 × 1 = 4. Write it as 04.

4 × 5 = 20. Write 20 as shown.

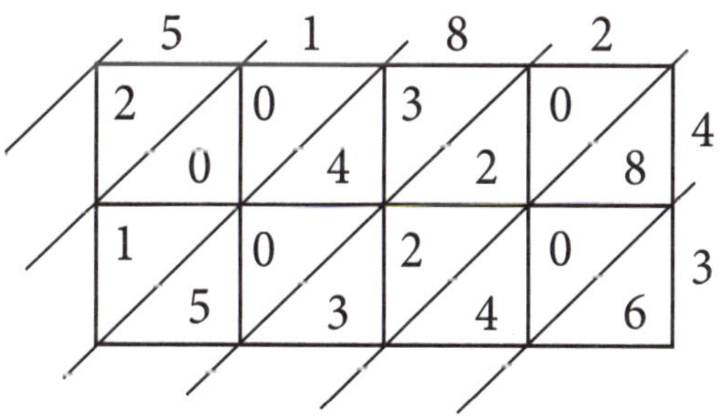

Multiply

3 × 2 = 6. Write it as 06.

3 × 8 = 24. Write 24 as shown.

3 × 1 = 3. Write it as 03.

3 × 5 = 15. Write 15 as shown.

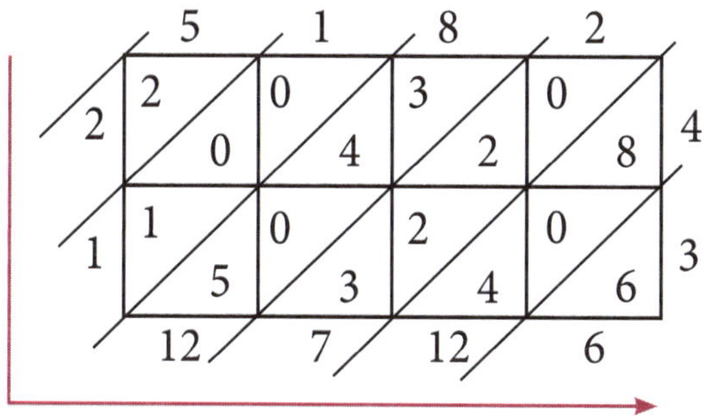

Now, add the digits diagonally (only those numbers inside the rectangle).

If the sum is a 2-digit number, keep the ones digit as it is and add the tens digit to the number on the left.

The digits we get are

2 1 (1)2 7 (1)2 6 = 222826

So, the product is **2,22,826.**

Example 8: Multiply 1532 with 467 by two different methods.

Solution:

Lattice Method

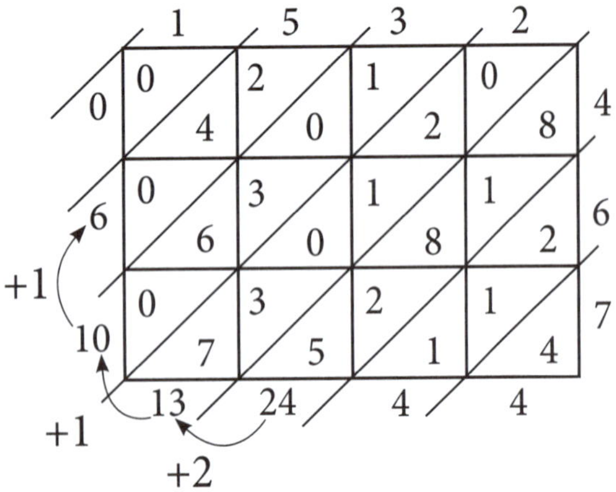

The digits we get are

0 6 10 13 24 4 4 = 715444

Column Method

	L	TTh	Th	H	T	O
			2	1		
			3	1	1	
			3	2	1	
			1	5	3	2
×				4	6	7
			2			
		1	0	7	2	4
	1	9	1	9	2	0
+	6	1	2	8	0	0
	7	**1**	**5**	**4**	**4**	**4**

So, the product is 7,15,444.

EXERCISE 3C

1. **Solve the following using column method.**
   a. 213 × 2 b. 1342 × 52 c. 12,521 × 3 d. 25 × 43 e. 323 × 231
2. **Solve the following using lattice method.**
   a. 321 × 2 b. 4326 × 79 c. 132 × 212 d. 1458 × 327 e. 926 × 541

WORD PROBLEMS ON MULTIPLICATION

When the value of 1 item is given and we have to find the value of more items, we know that the value will increase. In such cases, we multiply to find that value.

SOLVED EXAMPLES

Example 9: If the cost of a book is ₹32, what will be the cost of 30 such books?

Solution:

Cost of 1 book = ₹32

Cost of 30 books = ₹(32 × 30) = ₹960

The cost of 30 books will be ₹960.

NOTE

In this question, we have to find the cost in ₹. So, the cost should be on the right-hand side of our statements. Always remember to put the rupee symbol (₹) before the cost value.

ESTIMATION OF PRODUCTS

Estimation is an approximate calculation of a quantity or a value. Estimation of sum, differences and products of two or more given numbers help in quick calculation. Mental verification of calculations can also be done with the help of estimation.

To estimate a number, round it off to its closest 10, 100 or 1000. If the digit in the ones position is less than 5, then round it off to the multiple of 10, just less than the number to be estimated. If the digit in the ones position is 5 or greater than 5, then round off the number to the multiple of 10 just greater than the number to be estimated.

If a bus ticket costs ₹189, it can be said that it costs around ₹200. Carrying ₹200 should be enough to buy the ticket.

SOLVED EXAMPLES

Example 10: Estimate the product of the following.

a. 56×11

b. 813×87

Solution:

a. 56×11

The number 56 is rounded off to 60.

The number 11 is rounded off to 10.

$60 \times 10 = 600$

Actual product is $56 \times 11 = 616$ which is close to 600.

b. 813×87

The number 813 is rounded off to 800.

The number 87 is rounded off to 90.

$800 \times 90 = 72{,}000$

Actual product is $813 \times 87 = 70{,}731$ which is close to 72,000.

EXERCISE 3D

1. **Solve the following word problems.**
   a. One week is equal to 7 days. How many days are there in 5 weeks?
   b. 1 minute is equal to 60 seconds. How many seconds are there in 7 minutes?
   c. 1 hour is equal to 3600 seconds. How many seconds are there in 4 hours?
   d. If one shirt costs ₹450, what will be the cost of 126 such shirts?
   e. There are 476 students in a school. Each student brought ₹25. What was the total amount collected?
2. **Estimate the product of the following.**
   a. 59×21 b. 76×39 c. 520×190 d. 805×290

PATTERNS IN MULTIPLICATION

Patterns in numbers can be formed by many ways. Some patterns can be formed by using multiplication.

Remember, the product of an even multiplicand with an odd or an even multiplier will always be even.

$2 \times 2 = 4$ $2 \times 3 = 6$ $2 \times 4 = 8$ $2 \times 5 = 10$

When we multiply an odd multiplicand with an even multiplier, the product will be even and if the multiplier is an odd number, the product will be odd.

$3 \times 2 = 6$ $3 \times 3 = 9$ $3 \times 4 = 12$ $3 \times 5 = 15$

SOLVED EXAMPLES

Example 11: What will be the next number in the pattern 2, 4, 8, 16, 32?

Solution:

$$2^{\times 2},\ 4^{\times 2},\ 8^{\times 2},\ 16^{\times 2},\ 32^{\times 2},\ \_\_\_\_\_\_$$

Here, each number is being multiplied by 2 to get the next number. So, the next number will be $32 \times 2 = 64$.

Example 12: What will be the next number in the pattern 1, 3, 9, 27, 81?

Solution:

$$1^{\times 3},\ 3^{\times 3},\ 9^{\times 3},\ 27^{\times 3},\ 81^{\times 3},\ \_\_\_\_\_\_$$

Here, each number is being multiplied by 3 to get the next number. So, the next number will be $81 \times 3 = 243$.

PROBLEM SOLVING

Problem solving requires some logical thinking. Follow the steps given below to solve a problem.

1. Read the question.
2. Understand it.
3. Decide which mathematical operation to use.
4. Solve it.

SOLVED EXAMPLES

Example 13: Jasmeet pastes 4 photos on one page of her photo album. How many photos can she paste on 7 such pages?

Solution:

Read and understand

Think Start with the first information given: 4 photos on one page.

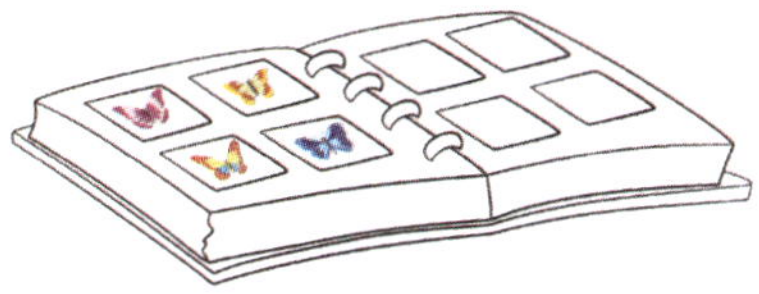

Operation: Multiplication

If on one page, Jasmeet pastes 4 photos, then on 7 pages, she will paste more than 4 photos.

Decide what to do

On 1 page	4 photos
On 7 pages	× 7
	28 photos

She can paste 28 photos.

NOTE

The answer will be more than 4, but it will not increase by 7, so we will not add. It will increase 7 **times**, so we will multiply.

EXERCISE 3E

1. Complete the patterns.

a. 1, 2, 4, 8, ________ b. 2, 6, 18, 54, ________

c. 1, 4, 16, 64, ________ d. 1, 5, 25, 125, ________

e. 2, 8, 32, 128, ________ f. 2, 10, 50, 250, ________

2. Study the pattern and fill in the blanks.

a.		b.		c.	
	$2 \times 2 = 4$		$3 \times 3 = 9$		$4 \times 4 =$ ____
	$2 \times 20 = 40$		$3 \times 30 =$ ____		$4 \times 40 =$ ____
	$2 \times 200 = 400$		$3 \times 300 =$ ____		$4 \times 400 =$ ____

3. Solve the following word problems.

a. If I put 115 books in one shelf, how many books can I put in 12 such shelves?

b. If Imo takes 13 minutes to run one round of the field, how many minutes will Imo take to run 25 rounds of the field?

c. If a movie ticket costs ₹175, how much money does the movie hall collect if 892 people watch the movie?

d. An ice cream vendor sells 132 ice creams every day. How many ice creams will he sell in 47 days?

Maths Lab Activity

21 CS Critical Thinking, Collaboration | HQ Quality Education

Aim: To revise multiplication tables

Materials required: Two dice, notepads, pencils and score sheet

Procedure:

1. Make groups of 5 children each.
2. Let each group take turns to throw both the dice on the floor or table to get a 2-digit number.
3. Everybody then starts writing the various multiplication statements for that number.

   If the 2-digit number is 12, then the various multiplication statements are

   $1 \times 12 = 12$ $\quad 2 \times 6 = 12$ $\quad 3 \times 4 = 12$

Every group then checks other group's statements. A group gets one mark for each correct statement. The score can be maintained on the score sheet. At the end of all the rounds, the group with the highest score is the winner.

Concept Map

Multiplication

Multiplication facts
1. Property of zero
2. Identity property
3. Commutative property
4. Associative property
5. Distributive property

Methods of multiplication
1. Column method
2. Expanded method
3. Lattice method

Patterns in multiplication
- The product of an even multiplicand and an even or an odd multiplier will always be even

Problem solving involving multiplication

Steps:
1. Read the question
2. Understand it
3. Decide which operation to use
4. Solve it

Key Concepts

- **Lattice:** A grid with square or diamond-shaped spaces
- **Estimation:** When the exact answer is not calculated but guessing the answer close to the exact answer
- **Problem solving:** When we logically work out the steps of a problem to find out missing values in the problem

CHAPTER REVISION

A. Choose the correct option.

1. $32 \times 1000 =$ __________.
   a. 320 b. 3200 c. 32,000 d. 32
2. $17 \times 300 =$ __________.
   a. 17 b. 5100 c. 300 d. 1700
3. $485 \times 173 =$ __________.
   a. 1,90,456 b. 1,80,456 c. 83,905 d. 1,90,455
4. $1825 \times 34 =$ __________.
   a. 60,250 b. 62,050 c. 62,005 d. 26,050
5. Raman earns ₹7980 in a month. How much does he earn in 15 months?
   a. ₹1,17,900 b. ₹1,91,700 c. ₹1,19,700 d. ₹1,71,900

B. Fill in the blanks.

1. $27 \times 0 =$ __________
2. $0 \times 567 =$ __________
3. $1 \times 2584 =$ __________
4. $45 \times 10 =$ __________
5. $13 \times 17 = 17 \times$ __________
6. $135 \times 2000 =$ __________
7. $2537 \times 40 =$ __________
8. $588 \times 70 =$ __________
9. $918 \times 547 =$ __________
10. $3479 \times 23 =$ __________

C. Solve the following word problems.

1. A total of 357 people can sit in one aeroplane. How many people can sit in 12 such aeroplanes?
2. Sandeep receives ₹450 per day as wages. How much does he receive in the following months?
   a. March 2020 b. April 2021
3. In one town, there are 1,17,300 people. Find the number of people in five such towns.
4. Afzal pays ₹5200 as rent every month. How much rent does he pay for 26 months?

5. A total of 1250 passengers can sit in one train. How many passengers can sit in 370 such trains?
6. A scooter costs ₹52,450. What is the cost of 13 such scooters?
7. One bus ticket costs ₹345. How much do 296 bus tickets cost?
8. Saif earns ₹72,000 per month. How much does he earn in one year?
9. Raghav saves ₹5300 every month. How much will he save in 4 years?

SKILL UP!

A. 21 CS Critical Thinking, Information Literacy

12 RESPONSIBLE CONSUMPTION AND PRODUCTION

Accompany your parents when they go grocery shopping next time. Estimate the total cost of all the things your parents bought. Compare with the actual bill.

B. 21 CS Critical Thinking, Information Literacy EL

Find out the monthly electricity bill of your household. Estimate what would be the yearly electricity bill. Compare the result with your classmates.

C. 21 CS Critical Thinking, Life Skills CC Integration with Science

11 SUSTAINABLE CITIES AND COMMUNITIES

Out of 2500 × 35 houses in a town, 1600 × 17 houses have rainwater harvesting. How many houses do not have rainwater harvesting? What are the benefits of rainwater harvesting system?

D. 21 CS Critical Thinking

Observe the multiplication chart given here. Find out any two numbers whose multiplication table has unique patterns.

×	1	2	3	4	5	6	7	8	9	10	11	12
1	1	2	3	4	5	6	7	8	9	10	11	12
2	2	4	6	8	10	12	14	16	18	20	22	24
3	3	6	9	12	15	18	21	24	27	30	33	36
4	4	8	12	16	20	24	28	32	36	40	44	48
5	5	10	15	20	25	30	35	40	45	50	55	60
6	6	12	18	24	30	36	42	48	54	60	66	72
7	7	14	21	28	35	42	49	56	63	70	77	84
8	8	16	24	32	40	48	56	64	72	80	88	96
9	9	18	27	36	45	54	63	72	81	90	99	108
10	10	20	30	40	50	60	70	80	90	100	110	120
11	11	22	33	44	55	66	77	88	99	110	121	132
12	12	24	36	48	60	72	84	96	108	120	132	144

SUSTAINABLE DEVELOPMENT GOALS

Question A is in line with SDG 12 Responsible Consumption and Production. What is the impact of food wastage? So, when you visit the grocery store next, always remember to buy only the quantity of food items that you can consume.

Question C is in line with SDG 11 Sustainable Cities and Communities. Why rainwater harvesting is important? Do you know any other techniques which can help maintain the quantity of our resources for future use?

WORKSHEET 3

21 CS Information Literacy, Life Skills

Make an invoice for the items sold!

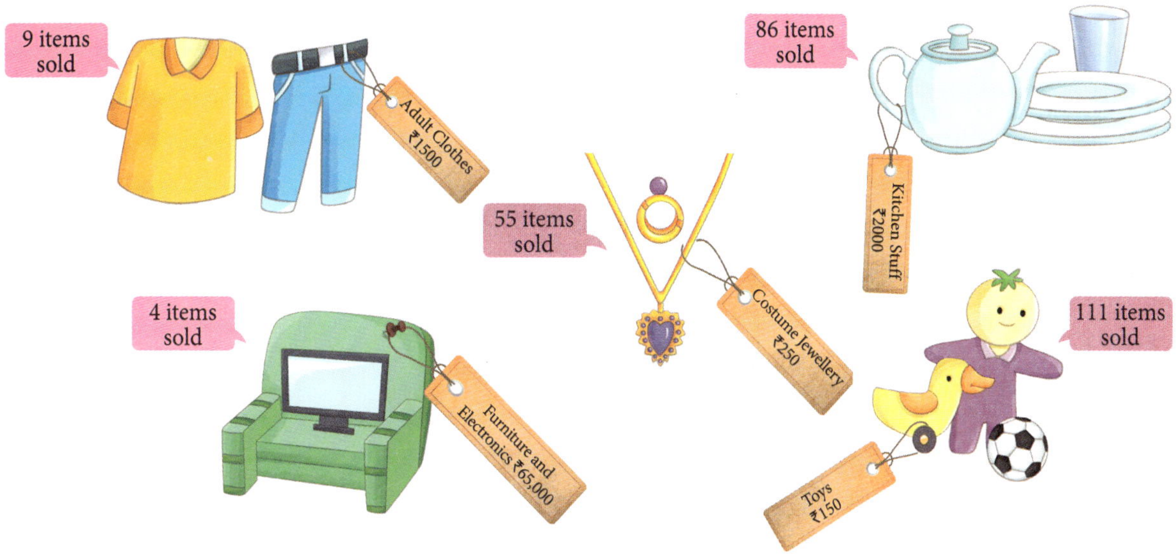

INVOICE

Invoice Number	
Date	
Order Number	
Terms	

Phone	
Email	
Contact Name	

Company	
Address	
State, Province	
Zip/Postal Code	

Item	Details	Quantity	Unit Price	Amount

Comments:	Sub-Total	
	Grand Total	

4 Division of Numbers

Learning Objectives

- To learn division facts
- To learn different methods of division
- To solve word problems on division
- To estimate quotients
- To frame word problems involving four operations

Let's Get Started

21 CS Critical Thinking

Remember, Lekha and Irfan were going to the animal shelter with animal food. If each of them needs to carry equal number of food packets, how many would each carry? Circle the correct basket. How did you find the answer? Write the steps in the space provided. Also, mark divisor, dividend, quotient and remainder in the steps.

DIVISION FACTS

Division is the process of finding how many times a number (the divisor) is contained in another number (the dividend). The number of times equals the quotient.

Some division facts are given below.

- If a number is divided by 1, we get the same number as the quotient.
- If 0 is divided by any number, we get 0 as the quotient.
- If a number is divided by itself, we get 1 as the quotient.
- Division of a number by 0 is not possible.

METHODS OF DIVISION

There are different methods of division. Let us discuss some of them.

Division by Drawing Dots

This is a very interesting method of division. Let us see how it is done with the help of examples.

Let us solve 9063 ÷ 3 by drawing dots.

9063 is a 4-digit number.

So, we make 4 boxes and mark their place values.

Th	H	T	O
9	0	6	3

Now, represent each digit of the number 9063 with dots inside the boxes. The digit in thousands position is 9. So, draw 9 dots in the thousands box.

The digit in hundreds position is 0. So, leave the hundreds box empty.

The digit in tens position is 6. So, draw 6 dots in the tens box. Similarly, draw 3 dots in the ones box.

Since we have to divide 9063 by 3, we make groups of 3 dots.

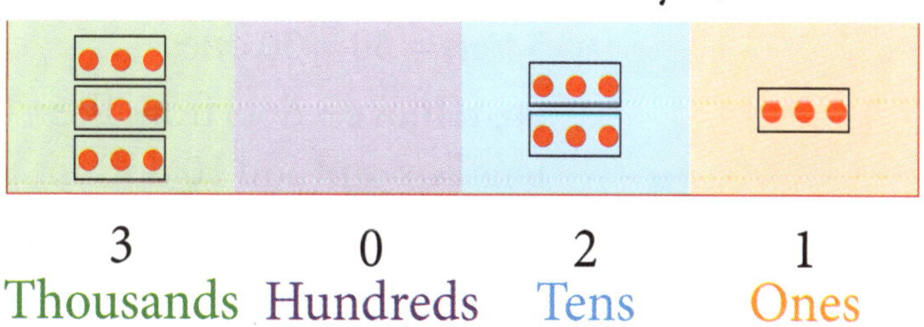

Start with the thousands box.
Thousands box = 3 groups
Hundreds box = 0 (as there are no dots)
Tens box = 2 groups
Ones box = 1 group
So, 9063 ÷ 3 = 3021.

SOLVED EXAMPLES

Example 1: 3402 ÷ 3

Solution: Represent the number 3402 with dots inside the boxes. Then, make groups of three as division is to be done by 3.

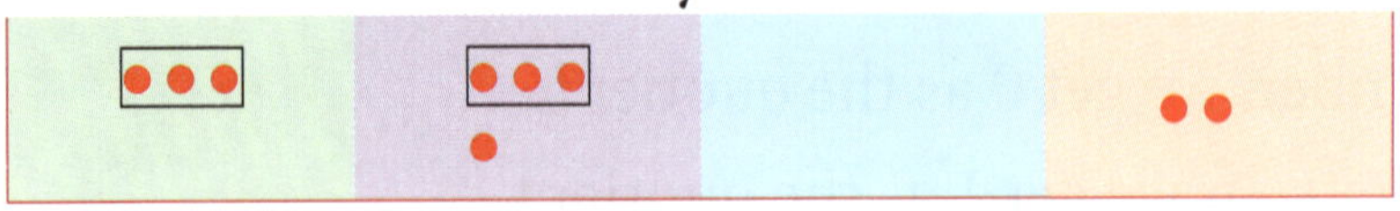

Thousands Hundreds Tens Ones

Thousands box = 1 group
Hundreds box = 1 group + 1 extra dot
What happens when we cannot make complete groups? We move the extra dot to next box (to its right).

1 hundred = 10 tens, so remove the extra dot from the hundreds box and add 10 dots in the tens box.

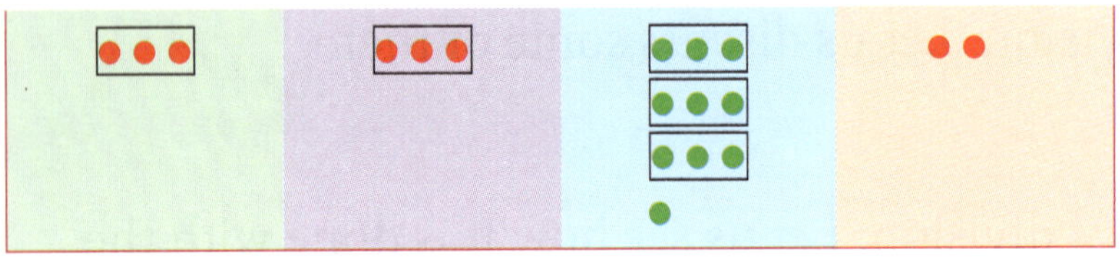

Thousands Hundreds Tens Ones

Tens box = 3 groups + 1 extra dot
Move this 1 extra dot to the ones box.
1 ten = 10 ones, so remove the extra dot from the tens box and add 10 dots in the ones box.

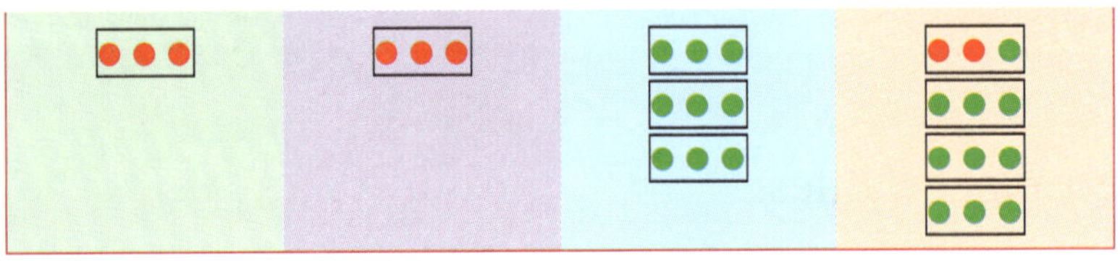

1	1	3	4
Thousands	Hundreds	Tens	Ones

Tens box = 3 groups
Ones box = 4 groups
So, 3402 ÷ 3 = 1134.

Example 2: 5738 ÷ 5

Solution: Represent the number 5738 with dots inside the boxes. Then, make groups of five as division is to be done by 5.

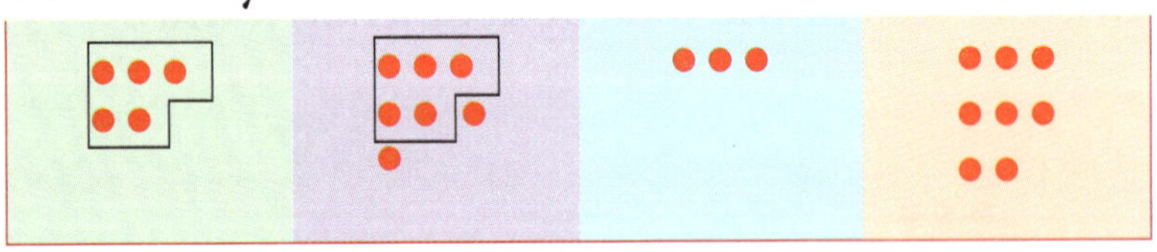

Thousands Hundreds Tens Ones

Thousands box = 1 group
Hundreds box = 1 group + 2 extra dots
2 hundreds = 200 = 20 tens
So, remove 2 dots from the hundreds box and add 20 dots in the tens box.

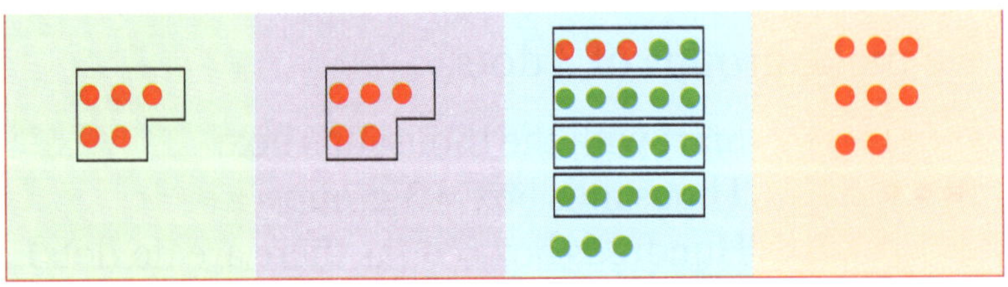

Thousands Hundreds Tens Ones

Tens box = 4 groups + 3 extra dots
3 tens = 30 = 30 ones
So, remove 3 dots from the tens box and add 30 dots in the ones box.

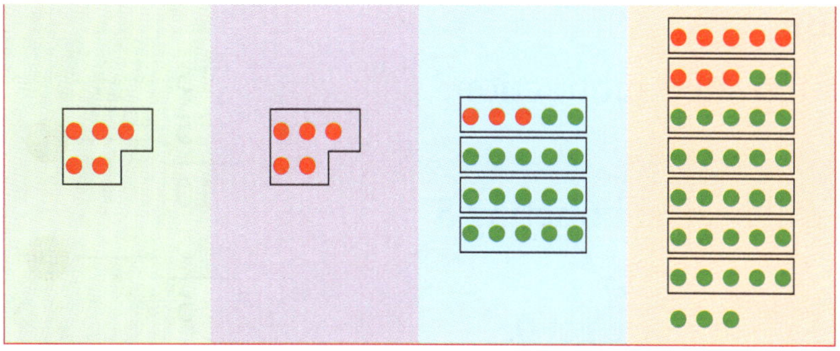

Thousands	Hundreds	Tens	Ones
1	1	4	7

Ones box = 7 groups + 3 extra dots
As there are no more boxes, the division ends here with the 3 extra dots. These 3 extra dots represent the remainder.

So, 5738 divided by 5 gives 1147 as quotient and 3 as remainder.

Division by Grouping

We can do division by grouping, that is, by distributing items into groups. The number of items per group gives us the answer to the division problem.

Let us divide 17 toffees among 5 people. To do this, first make five groups with one person in each group. Distribute the toffees one-by-one to each group.

Do you know?
The symbol, consisting of a short horizontal line with a dot above and another dot below (÷), used to represent division is called an obelus.

This shows that if we distribute 17 toffees among 5 people, each person will get 3 toffees and 2 toffees will be left.

$17 \div 5 = 3$ Remainder = 2

17 → Dividend; 5 → Divisor; 3 → Quotient

To check division
Divisor × Quotient + Remainder = Dividend
$5 \times 3 + 2 = 17$
$17 = 17$

Division by Repeated Subtraction

Division can also be done through repeated subtraction.

Let us take the example 15 ÷ 5.

Since 15 is being divided by 5, we will keep subtracting 5 from 15 till we get 0.

We subtracted 5 three times from 15 before we get 0.

Therefore, 15 ÷ 5 = 3.

$$
\begin{array}{rl}
15 & \\
-\ 5 & \text{— (1)} \\
\hline
10 & \\
-\ 5 & \text{— (2)} \\
\hline
5 & \\
-\ 5 & \text{— (3)} \\
\hline
0 &
\end{array}
$$

Division by Long Division Method

Division by 1-digit number

A teacher wants to give 4 notebooks to each student in her school. She has 6475 notebooks. How many students will get the notebooks and how many notebooks will be left?

Since the notebooks are being distributed among the students, we will divide. So, 6475 will be divided by 4 to get the answer. This division can be done by using long division method, explained in the solved example.

SOLVED EXAMPLES

Example 3: Divide 6475 by 4.

Solution:

Step 1: Start by dividing the digit in the highest place of the dividend. The digit in the highest place is 6. As the divisor is 4, find the number of times of 4 that can go into 6.

$$4 \times 1 = 4 < 6$$

$$4 \times 2 = 8 > 6$$

Only 1 four can go into 6. So, write 1 as the first digit of the quotient, on top of 6.

$$
\begin{array}{r|l}
 & 16 \\
\hline
4 & 6475 \\
 & -4\downarrow \\
\hline
 & 24 \\
 & -24 \\
\hline
 & 00
\end{array}
$$

Multiply divisor with quotient and subtract the result from the first digit of the dividend. Check if the remainder is less than the divisor.

Step 2: Bring down the digit from the next higher place, that is, 4. The new dividend is now, 24 and divisor is still 4. Now find the number of times of 4 that can go into 24.

$$4 \times 6 = 24$$

6 fours can go into 24. So, write 6 as the second digit of the quotient, on top of second digit of the dividend. Then multiply, subtract and check as done in Step 1.

Step 3: Bring down the next digit, that is 7. Repeat the procedure as shown in Steps 1 and 2.

$4 \times 1 = 4 < 7$

$4 \times 2 = 8 > 7$

Only 1 four can go into 7. So, write 1 as the 3rd digit of the quotient.

Step 4: Finally bring down the last digit 5. Now divide 35 by 4.

$4 \times 8 = 32 < 35$

$4 \times 9 = 36 > 35$

Thus, 8 is the last digit of the quotient.

Remainder = 3

```
    1618
4 ) 6475
  - 4
    24
  - 24
    007
  -   4
     35
  -  32
      3
```

When 6475 is divided by 4, the quotient is 1618 and the remainder is 3.

Example 4: 8412 ÷ 6

Solution:

```
     1402
6 ) 8412
  - 6
    24
  - 24
    0012
  -   12
       0
```

NOTE

If the remainder is smaller than the divisor, do not forget to write a zero in the quotient when you have to bring down an extra digit from the dividend.

When 8412 is divided by 6, the quotient is 1402 and remainder is 0.

Example 5: 24081 ÷ 5

Solution:

```
     04816
5 ) 24081
  - 20
     40
  -  40
     008
  -    5
       31
  -    30
        1
```

NOTE

If the first digit of the dividend is not divisible by the divisor, then consider the next digit also for division.

When 24081 is divided by 5, the quotient is 4816 and remainder is 1.

EXERCISE 4A

1. **Solve the following by drawing dots method.**

   a. 5716 ÷ 2   b. 2361 ÷ 3   c. 1552 ÷ 8   d. 2275 ÷ 7

2. **Solve the following by grouping method.**

   a. 57 ÷ 4   b. 8 ÷ 6   c. 15 ÷ 2   d. 24 ÷ 6

3. **Solve the following by long division method.**

   a. 67,893 ÷ 4   b. 92,578 ÷ 5   c. 69,247 ÷ 6   d. 73,214 ÷ 7

   e. 42,195 ÷ 2   f. 83,529 ÷ 5   g. 33,673 ÷ 8   h. 23,465 ÷ 9

Division by 2-digit number

There are 20 students in Class IV. The class needs to collect ₹640 for a picnic. How much money should each child contribute?

Since ₹640 is to be collected from 20 students, we will divide 640 by 20.

640 ÷ 20 = 32

So, each child should contribute ₹32.

SOLVED EXAMPLES

Example 6: 360 ÷ 10

Solution:

```
     36
10 ) 360
   – 30↓
      60
   –  60
      00
```

Quotient = 36, Remainder = 0

GO EASY!

10 |3 6|0

Draw a line after 1 digit from the right side, since 10 (divisor) has only 1 zero. The number on the left of the line, that is, 36 is the quotient and that on the right, that is, 0 is the remainder.

Example 7: 5386 ÷ 40

Solution:

Step 1:

```
     01
40 ) 5386
   – 40
     13
```

Since 5 is smaller than 40, divide 53 by 40. Only 1 forty can go into 53. So, the first digit in the quotient is 1.

Step 2:

```
     013
40 ) 5386
   – 40↓
     138
   – 120
      18
```

Bring down 8. Only 3 forties can go into 138, so the second digit in the quotient is 3.

Step 3:

```
     0134
40 ) 5386
   – 40↓
     138
   – 120↓
      186
   –  160
       26
```

Bring down the last digit 6. Only 4 forties can go into 186, so the third digit in the quotient is 4 and the remainder is 26.

When 5386 is divided by 40, the quotient is 134 and the remainder is 26.

Example 8: 6118 ÷ 26

Solution:

Step 1:

```
      0 2
 26 ) 6 1 1 8
    - 5 2
      0 9
```

Step 2:

```
      0 2 3
 26 ) 6 1 1 8
    - 5 2 ↓
      0 9 1
    -   7 8
        1 3
```

Step 3:

```
      0 2 3 5
 26 ) 6 1 1 8
    - 5 2 ↓ |
      0 9 1 |
    -   7 8 ↓
        1 3 8
    -   1 3 0
            8
```

Quotient = 235, Remainder = 8

Division by Short Division Method

This method is similar to long division method, but it involves more mental maths and less written calculations. In this method, the final quotient is written below the dividend in one single step.

SOLVED EXAMPLES

Example 9: a. 48 ÷ 3 b. 187 ÷ 4

Solution:

a.

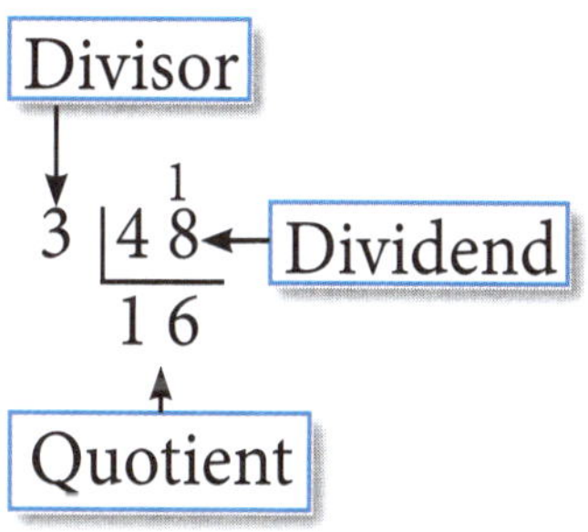

b.

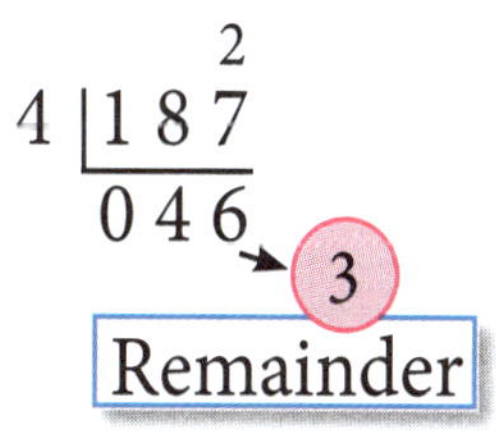

Steps	Perform the steps mentally	Write down
Step 1	a. 4 ÷ 3 = 1, Q = 1; R = 1 b. 18 ÷ 4 = 4, Q = 4; R = 2	Q below the first digit of the dividend; R above the second digit of the dividend
Step 2	a. 18 ÷ 3 = 6, Q = 6; R = 0 b. 27 ÷ 4 = 6, Q = 6; R = 3	Q below the second digit of the dividend; R is 0, so no need to write. If R is a number other than 0, write it on the right side.

EXERCISE 4B

1. **Divide the following by long division and short division methods.**

a. 70 ÷ 10 b. 240 ÷ 30 c. 8000 ÷ 20 d. 1376 ÷ 50

e. 3069 ÷ 30 f. 800 ÷ 25 g. 576 ÷ 32 h. 1755 ÷ 27

APPLICATION OF FOUR OPERATIONS IN REAL-LIFE SITUATIONS

We use more than one mathematical operations in our daily life.

NOTE

- When the value of many items is given and we have to find the value of 1 item, we divide.
- When we distribute something equally, we divide.
- The value of the item that we have to find must always be written on the right side of our statement.
- It is important to write short statements.
- The answer to word problems must always be written in the statement form.

SOLVED EXAMPLES

Example 10 Tarun's mother spent ₹285 on her grocery shopping. She bought 2 kg of apples, and 5 kg of oranges at ₹45 per kg. What was the cost of apples per kg?

Solution:

THINK

Money spent on 2 kg of apples will be = Total money – money spent on oranges

DECIDE WHAT TO DO

Money spent on oranges = 45×5 = ₹225

Money spent on 2 kg of apples = $285 - 225$ = ₹60

So, money spent on 1 kg of apples = $60 \div 2$ = ₹30

```
     3 0
   ______
2 ) 6 0
  – 6 ↓
  ______
    0 0
```

Given below is a logical working chart of this question with steps I, II and III.

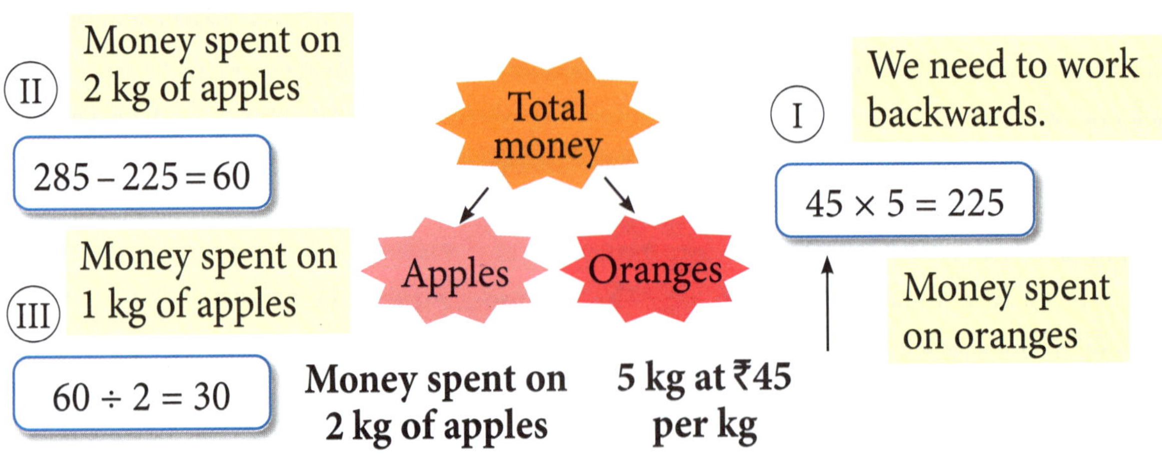

Estimation of Quotients

Estimation is done when we do not know the exact value but try to guess a value close to the actual value.

SOLVED EXAMPLES

Example 11:

There are 28 students in a class. The teacher wants to give one chocolate to each student. Chocolates come in packets, where one packet has 5 chocolates. How many packets of chocolates should the teacher buy?

Solution:

Number of packets = Number of students ÷ Number of chocolates in each packet

= 28 ÷ 5

If we have to estimate the answer, then we should change 28 to a compatible number. This means that we should check the multiples of 5 and choose the multiple which is closest to 28.

Multiples of 5 are 5, 10, 15, 20, 25, 30, 35.

28 will lie between 25 and 30 and it will be closer to 30

Therefore, 28 ÷ 5 can be written as 30 ÷ 5 = 6.

Thus, the teacher should buy 6 packets of chocolates.

Check

If we actually divide 28 by 5, we get 5 as quotient and 3 as remainder.

We need 5 full packets but since 3 students will be left, we should buy 1 more packet.

5 + 1 = 6 packets

We notice that the actual answer is equal to the estimated answer, 6.

Example 12: What is the least number of boxes required if we have to pack 183 biscuits and each box can contain 12 biscuits?

Solution:

Number of biscuits = 183

Number of biscuits in 1 box = 12

```
      0 1 5  ——→ No. of boxes
1 2 ) 1 8 3  ——→ Biscuits
    - 1 2↓
    ------
      0 6 3
    -   6 0
    ------
          3  ——→ Biscuits left
```

The above division shows that we need 15 boxes, but there are still 3 biscuits (remainder) left.

Since the question wants the **least** number of boxes required, we will add 1 more box (for the remaining 3 biscuits) to the 15 boxes.

$15 + 1 = 16$ boxes

Thus, the least number of boxes required is 16.

Framing Word Problems

How do we frame word problems if the calculations are given to us?

We can do so by following the given steps.

Step 1: Look at the numbers involved.

Step 2: Look at the mathematical operations involved.

Step 3: Think of what you can relate to with these numbers and operations.

Step 4: Frame your word problem.

SOLVED EXAMPLES

Example 13: Frame a word problem for the following calculation.

$$(32 + 8) \div 20$$

Solution:

Step 1: The numbers involved are 32, 8 and 20.

Step 2: 32 and 8 are being added. Their sum is being divided by 20.

Step 3: We can relate 32 and 8 to the number of burgers or to the number of roses.

Step 4: Anil brought 32 burgers and Tarit brought 8 burgers. These burgers were distributed among 20 students in the class. How many burgers did each student get?

OR

Priyanka has 32 red roses and 8 pink roses. She divided them equally into bunches of 20 roses each. How many bunches can she make?

Example 14: Frame a word problem for the following calculation.

$$200 - [(2 \times 60) + (1 \times 35)]$$

Solution:

Step 1: The numbers involved are 1, 2, 60, 35 and 200.

Step 2: 2 is being multiplied by 60.
1 is being multiplied by 35.
The sum of these two products is being subtracted from 200.

Step 3: We can relate 60 and 35 to the cost of tickets (in ₹) and 200 to the total amount of money (in ₹). We can also relate it to 60 storybooks and 35 textbooks in a school library and 200 to the total numbers of books.

Step 4: Sunita has ₹200. She bought 2 bus tickets for adults for ₹60 each and 1 ticket for her child for ₹35. How much money is left with her?

OR

The school library had 200 books. It had 2 shelves with 60 storybooks each, 1 shelf with 35 textbooks and the rest of the books were science books. How many science books were there?

Exercise 4C

1. **Estimate the value of the following.**
   a. $72 \div 5$ b. $49 \div 6$ c. $93 \div 4$ d. $298 \div 3$
   e. $125 \div 30$ f. $495 \div 17$ g. $4320 \div 18$
2. **Solve the following word problems.**
   a. 300 students are arranged into 12 groups. How many students will be there in one group?
   b. A total of 143 boys has to be arranged into cricket teams where each team consists of 11 boys. How many teams will be made?
   c. Rajan has ₹639. He buys notebooks at ₹35 each. How many notebooks can he buy and how much money will be left?

   d. Rohit had some marbles. He gave 30 marbles to Anil. He distributed the remaining marbles equally between Sachin and Vijay. They got 60 marbles each. What is total number of marbles that Rohit had?
3. **Frame word problems for the following calculations.**
   a. $(10 + 15) \div 20$ b. $(15 + 18 + 17) \div 25$ c. $(20 \times 25) \div 50$

Maths Lab Activity

21 CS Creativity and innovation EL

Aim: To understand division

Materials required: Chart paper, ruler, pens, 100 counters

Procedure:

1. On a chart paper, make 10 rows and 10 columns. Mark each row and column with numbers from 1 to 10 as given.
2. We can do division of numbers from 1 to 100 by numbers from 1 to 10 on this chart.
3. Let us divide 32 by 5.
4. We will start placing 32 counters from row 1 to row 5 because we are dividing by 5.
5. We complete 6 columns and are left with 2 counters.

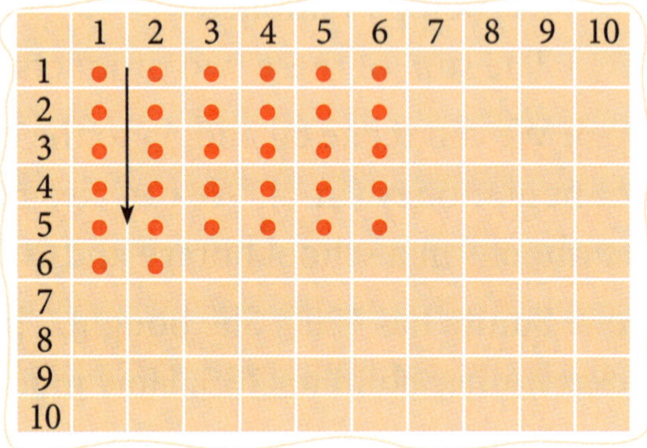

This means that the quotient is 6 and the remainder is 2.

Concept Map

Division

Division facts
1. A number ÷ 1 = Same number as quotient
2. 0 ÷ Any number = 0
3. A number ÷ Same number = 1
4. Division by 0 is not possible.

Methods of division
1. By drawing dots
2. By grouping
3. By repeated subtraction
4. By long division
5. By short division

Estimation of quotients
1. By using compatible numbers
2. By rounding off numbers

Key Concepts

- **Division facts:** Facts that apply to division
- **Estimation of quotients:** Estimating the answer of a division question
- **Framing word problems:** Making your own problems related to given calculations.
- Solving problems require more than one mathematical operations.

Chapter Revision

A. Choose the correct option.

1. 9018 ÷ 6 = ________
   a. 1503 b. 6018 c. 1805 d. 9018
2. 17,213 ÷ 7 = ________
   a. 17213 b. 7359 c. 2459 d. 2437
3. 5000 ÷ 40 = ________
   a. 125 b. 150 c. 400 d. 500
4. 4976 ÷ 35 = ________
   a. Q = 142, R = 9 b. Q = 135, R = 6
   c. Q = 142, R = 6 d. Q = 497, R = 6
5. 8445 ÷ 6 = ________
   a. Q = 1407, R = 6 b. Q = 1407, R = 0
   c. Q = 1407, R = 3 d. Q = 8445, R = 6

B. Fill in the blanks.

1. The sign for division is ____________.
2. Divisor × Quotient + Remainder = ____________.
3. 0 ÷ 18 = ____________
4. 354 ÷ 1 = ____________
5. If 12 × 15 = 180, then 180 ÷ 12 = ____________ and 180 ÷ 15 = ____________.
6. When the value of many items is given and we have to find the value of one item, we ____________.
7. Whenever we distribute something, we ____________.

C. Solve the following word problems.

1. A total of 546 mango saplings has to be planted with 13 saplings in each row. How many rows of saplings will be there?
2. A total of 360 books is distributed equally between 30 students. How many books did each student get?
3. A total of 610 apples was packed in boxes where each box contained 24 apples. How many boxes were needed and how many apples were left?
4. What is the least number of bags required to store 310 kg of wheat if each bag contains 15 kg?

D. Frame word problems for the following calculations.

1. 20 × 25
2. (20 × 25) ÷ 50
3. 20 + 25
4. (20 + 25) ÷ 3

SKILL UP!

A. 21 CS Critical Thinking

Help your mother run the house! Count the number of slices in a loaf of bread. Suppose there are 20 slices in a loaf of bread and 4 slices are eaten every day in your house. How many days will this loaf of bread last in your house? When should your mother buy the next loaf of bread?

B. Make a chart on different methods of division. You can even include creative, colourful drawings (using circles) to explain the methods of division.

C. 21 CS Critical Thinking, Life Skills HQ Harmony In The Self

Lata's mother decided to give ₹6000 towards school fees for 4 students who did very well in school. How much will each student get? Can you think of another way of helping your friends at school? What role does good education play in the development of a country?

D. 21 CS Critical Thinking, Creativity and Innovation

Observe the quotients and the remainders of numbers when divided by 10. Can you see a relationship between the digits in different places of the given number and its quotient and remainder? Find out the pattern and check if similar patterns appear when numbers are divided by 100 or 1000.

SUSTAINABLE DEVELOPMENT GOALS

Question C is in line with SDG 1 No Poverty. Education is important to eradicate poverty and illiteracy. Do you think education plays a vital role in the growth of the country's economy? Discuss with your classmates and prepare a report.

WORKSHEET 4

21 CS · Critical Thinking, Information Literacy

There are 100 students in all the sections of class II. Section D has equal number of boys and girls. What is the number of boys and girls in Section D? Count the number of students in each section. Fill in the chart given below and find the answer.

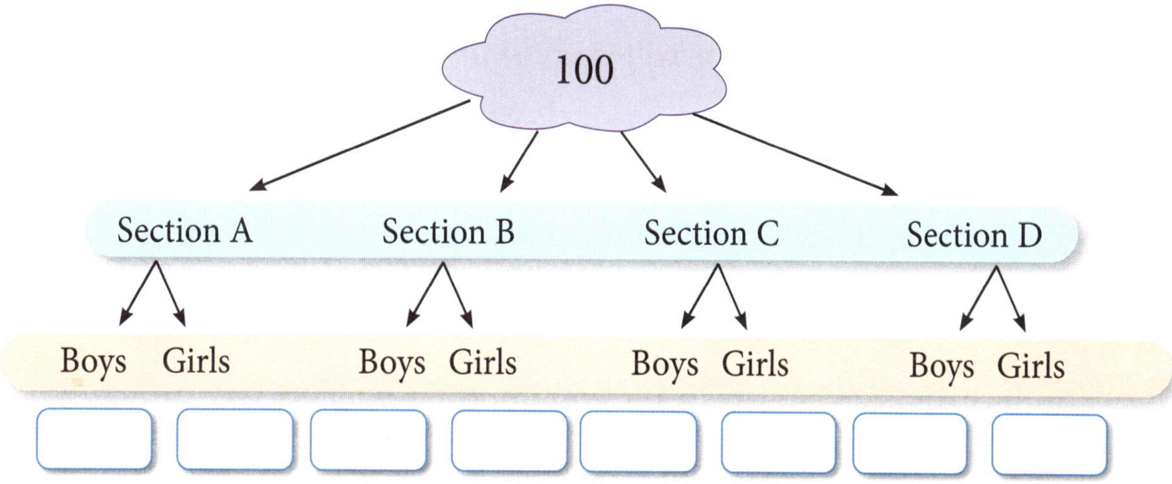

Section A

Section B

Section C

Section D

Reasoning Worksheet 1

1. Lekha is thinking of a 5-digit number. It is an odd number. When the number is rounded off to the nearest ten thousand, it is equal to 70,000. What could be the number that she is thinking of?

   a. 69,428 b. 71,529 c. 39,183 d. 79,321

2. Identify the incorrect expression.

   a. $25 \times 6 = 25 \times 3 \times 2$ b. $49 \times 8 = 49 \times 2 \times 4$

   c. $32 \times 10 = 32 \times 5 \times 1$ d. $36 \times 6 = 6 \times 6 \times 6$

3. Which of the following is the correct expression?

   a. $239 \times 0 < 16925 \times 0$ b. $542 \times 1 < 258 \times 1$

   c. $627 \times 1 = 835 \times 1$ d. $948 \times 0 = 167 \times 0$

4. A number when rounded to the nearest ten is 6820. Which of the following could be the number?

   a. 6828 b. 6825 c. 6815 d. 6809

5. Look at the pattern. What will be the number in the blank circle?

   a. 41 b. 17 c. 29 d. 31

6. Find the missing number.

   53925 54925 56025 ______ 58525 59925

   a. 57225 b. 57025 c. 56925 d. 57925

7. Look at the series of numbers: 8, 22, 8, 28, 8, . . . Which number should come next?

   a. 9 b. 29 c. 32 d. 34

8. Find the next figure in the pattern.

   a.  b.  c.  d. 

5 Factors and Multiples

Learning Objectives

- To understand divisibility rules
- To find common factors and common multiples of numbers
- To find the highest common factor (HCF)
- To find the least common multiple (LCM)
- To differentiate between prime and composite numbers
- To learn prime factorisation

Let's Get Started

21 CS Critical Thinking HQ Happiness My Goal

John and Mansi are decorating the Christmas tree with number boxes and balls. They decided to decorate the Christmas tree as a factor tree of numbers. Help them in decorating the tree by filling in the factors of the number 36.

DIVISIBILITY

When a divisor divides a dividend exactly without leaving a remainder, we say that the dividend is divisible by the divisor.

We can easily find out whether a number is divisible by another number without doing actual division. This process is called the test of divisibility. It involves certain rules.

NOTE

- To find out if a number is even or odd, we can check its divisibility by 2. An even number is a number that is completely divisible by 2. A number that is not completely divisible by 2 is an odd number.

Divisibility Rules

A number is divisible by	Divisible	Not divisible
2 if its last digit is 0, 2, 4, 6 or 8.	4,86,732	2,15,439
3 if the sum of its digits is divisible by 3.	2,85,432	2,85,433
4 if the number formed by its last two digits is divisible by 4.	9,37,168	9,37,169
5 if its last digit is 0 or 5.	8,32,745	5,86,196
6 if it is divisible by both 2 and 3.	18,342	18,346
8 if the number formed by its last three digits is divisible by 8.	6,17,168	6,17,318
9 if the sum of its digits is divisible by 9.	5,62,185	5,62,186
10 if its last digit is 0.	9,18,730	8,72,143

GO EASY!

- A number divisible by 4 will always be divisible by 2.
- A number divisible by 6 will always be divisible by both 2 and 3.
- A number divisible by 8 will always be divisible by both 2 and 4.
- A number divisible by 9 will always be divisible by 3.
- A number divisible by 10 will always be divisible by both 2 and 5.

MENTAL MATHS

Is 25,870 divisible by 2, 5 and 10?

SOLVED EXAMPLES

Example 1: Check the divisibility of 1,58,421 and 1,58,423 by 3.

Solution:

1,58,421 ⟶ $1 + 5 + 8 + 4 + 2 + 1 = 21$

As 21 is divisible by 3, the number is divisible by 3.

1,58,423 ⟶ $1 + 5 + 8 + 4 + 2 + 3 = 23$

As 23 is not divisible by 3, the number is not divisible by 3.

Example 2: Is 18,342 divisible by 6?

Solution:

Checking the divisibility by 2: it is divisible by 2 because the last digit is 2.

Checking the divisibility by 3: $1 + 8 + 3 + 4 + 2 = 18$. The number is divisible by 3 as the sum of its digits is 18, which is divisible by 3.

The number is divisible by both 2 and 3. So, 18,342 is divisible by 6.

Example 3: Are 6,17,168 and 6,17,318 divisible by 8?

$$\begin{array}{r} 0\,2\,1 \\ 8\,\overline{)\,1\,6\,8} \\ -\,1\,6\downarrow \\ \hline 0\,0\,8 \\ -\,8 \\ \hline 0 \\ \hline \end{array}$$

As the number formed by the last three digits of 6,17,168, that is, 168 is divisible by 8, the number is divisible by 8.

$$\begin{array}{r} 0\,3\,9 \\ 8\,\overline{)\,3\,1\,8} \\ -\,2\,4\downarrow \\ \hline 7\,8 \\ -\,7\,2 \\ \hline 6 \\ \hline \end{array}$$

As the number formed by the last three digits of 6,17,318, that is, 318 is not divisible by 8, the number is not divisible by 8.

Example 4: Are 5,62,185 and 5,62,186 divisible by 9?

Solution:

5,62,185 ⟶ $5 + 6 + 2 + 1 + 8 + 5 = 27$

5,62,185 is divisible by 9 because the sum of its digits is 27, which is divisible by 9.

5,62,186 ⟶ $5 + 6 + 2 + 1 + 8 + 6 = 28$

5,62,186 is not divisible by 9 because the sum of its digits is 28, which is not divisible by 9.

EXERCISE 5A

1. Circle the numbers divisible by the number given in the first column. One has been done for you.

a.	Divisible by 2	392	7,35,189	4685	5,34,176	1,73,590
b.	Divisible by 3	1,25,682	6,14,250	1,79,234	5,34,805	7,95,143
c.	Divisible by 4	5,18,612	2,13,736	1,94,635	7,38,104	9,16,532
d.	Divisible by 5	5,18,726	2,35,490	7,38,165	29,170	17,284
e.	Divisible by 6	59,387	57,432	29,796	56,981	4,36,716
f.	Divisible by 8	5,93,824	7,29,465	49,296	9,56,444	4,62,408
g.	Divisible by 9	56,183	47,916	69,831	98,714	2,13,579
h.	Divisible by 10	59,218	73,490	21,865	43,120	1,86,507

2. Circle the even numbers and tick the odd numbers.

2, 5, 7, 14, 69, 280, 1697, 5718, 6791, 9354

FACTORS

A factor of a number is a number that divides it exactly (without leaving a remainder).

When a number is divided by one of its factors, then the remainder will be zero.

For example, 2 is a factor of 18 as 2 divides 18 completely and we get 0 as remainder. 2 is not a factor of 15 as it does not divide 15 completely, leaving 1 as a remainder.

MENTAL MATHS

1. Will a number that is divisible by 10, always be divisible by 5?
2. Will a number that is divisible by 5, always be divisible by 10?

PUZZLE!

I have no other factor than myself.
Which number am I?

Finding Factors of a Number

We can find the factors of a number by recalling the multiplication facts of numbers.

Factors of 9

Step 1: Find the numbers that can be multiplied to form this number.

Step 2: Write down all the multiplication facts possible for this number.

Step 3: Stop when the factors are the same or a multiplication fact of the given number starts repeating.

$1 \times 9 = 9$ $\quad$ $3 \times 3 = 9$

As 3 is written twice at this point, we treat it as the point where the factors are repeating. Thus, the factors of 9 are 1, 3 and 9.

Factors of 24

24

$1 \times 24 = 24$

$2 \times 12 = 24$

$3 \times 8 = 24$

$4 \times 6 = 24$

$6 \times 4 = 24$

Step 1: Find the numbers that can be multiplied to form this number.

Step 2: Write down all the possible multiplication facts for this number.

Step 3: Stop when the factors start repeating.

We stop here as the factors are the same as the above statement but in reverse order.

The factors of 24 are 1, 2, 3, 4, 6, 8, 12 and 24.

NOTE

- The factor of a number is always smaller or equal to the number.
- 1 is the factor of all numbers.
- A number is a factor of itself.

MENTAL MATHS

1. Will a number that is divisible by 8, always be divisible by 4?
2. Will a number that is divisible by 4, always be divisible by 8?

Common Factors

Common factors of two or more numbers are the factors that are common to the numbers.

The **highest common factor** of two or more given numbers is the **greatest** number among the common factors. Highest common factor is known as HCF.

DO YOU KNOW?

HCF is also known as greatest common divisor (GCD).

SOLVED EXAMPLES

Example 5: Find the common factors and the highest common factor of 12 and 15.

Solution:

12

Factors of 12

$1 \times 12 = 12$

$2 \times 6 = 12$

$3 \times 4 = 12$

$4 \times 3 = 12$

15

Factors of 15

$1 \times 15 = 15$

$3 \times 5 = 15$

$5 \times 3 = 15$

To find the common factors, first find all the factors of the given numbers and then identify the factors that are common to all.

Write all the factors and then circle the common factors.

Factors of 12 = (1), 2, (3), 4, 6, 12

Factors of 15 = (1), (3), 5, 15

The common factors of 12 and 15 are 1 and 3. Here, 3 is the highest common factor.

Example 6: Find the common factors and the highest common factor of 16, 20 and 24.

Solution:

16

Factors of 16

$1 \times 16 = 16$

$2 \times 8 = 16$

$4 \times 4 = 16$

$8 \times 2 = 16$

20

Factors of 20

$1 \times 20 = 20$

$2 \times 10 = 20$

$4 \times 5 = 20$

$5 \times 4 = 20$

24

Factors of 24

$1 \times 24 = 24$

$2 \times 12 = 24$

$3 \times 8 = 24$

$4 \times 6 = 24$

$6 \times 4 = 24$

Factors of 16 = (1), (2), (4), 8, 16

Factors of 20 = (1), (2), (4), 5, 10, 20

Factors of 24 = (1), (2), 3, (4), 6, 8, 12, 24

The common factors of 16, 20 and 24 are 1, 2 and 4. Here, 4 is the highest common factor.

Exercise 5B

1. **Solve the following questions using the divisibility rules.**

   a. Is 2 a factor of 198? b. Is 3 a factor of 915?

   c. Is 4 a factor of 7349? d. Is 10 a factor of 437298?

2. **Write all the factors of the following numbers.**

   a. 10 b. 12 c. 24 d. 35 e. 40

   f. 9 g. 5 h. 11 i. 360 j. 6300

3. **Find the common factors and the highest common factor of the following numbers.**

   a. 8 and 10 b. 15 and 20 c. 18 and 24 d. 12, 18, 30 e. 15, 25, 30

MULTIPLES

Multiples of a number are the products that we get when we multiply that number by 1, 2, 3, 4 and so on.

When a multiple is divided by one of its factors, the remainder will be zero.

For example, 24 is a multiple of 6 as 6 divides 24 completely.

NOTE

- Multiples are the products in the table of every number.
- Every number is a multiple of itself.
- Every number is a multiple of 1.
- The multiple of a number is always greater or equal to the number.

The multiple of a number is always the product of factors in the multiplication fact of that number.

$2 \times 3 = 6$

2 → Factor; 3 → Factor; 6 → Multiple

$4 \times 5 = 20$

4 → Factor; 5 → Factor; 20 → Multiple

6 is a multiple of 2 and 3.

2 is a factor of 6.

3 is a factor of 6.

20 is a multiple of 4 and 5.

4 is a factor of 20.

5 is a factor of 20.

Finding Multiples of a Number

We can find the multiples of a number by simply multiplying the number with natural numbers 1, 2, 3, 4, 5 and so on.

Multiples of 2

We get the multiples of 2 by multiplying it by 1, 2, 3, 4, 5 and so on.

		×1	×2	×3	×4	×5	×6	
Hence, the multiples of 2	=	2,	4,	6,	8,	10,	12,	...

In the same way, we can find the multiples of any number.

		×1	×2	×3	×4	×5	×6	
Multiples of 3	=	3,	6,	9,	12,	15,	18,	...
Multiples of 4	=	4,	8,	12,	16,	20,	24,	...
Multiples of 5	=	5,	10,	15,	20,	25,	30,	...
Multiples of 6	=	6,	12,	18,	24,	30,	36,	...

Multiples on the Number Line

Another way of finding the multiples of numbers is to use the number line.

The multiples of 2 are shown on the number line below. Skip count by 2s on the number line to get the multiples of 2.

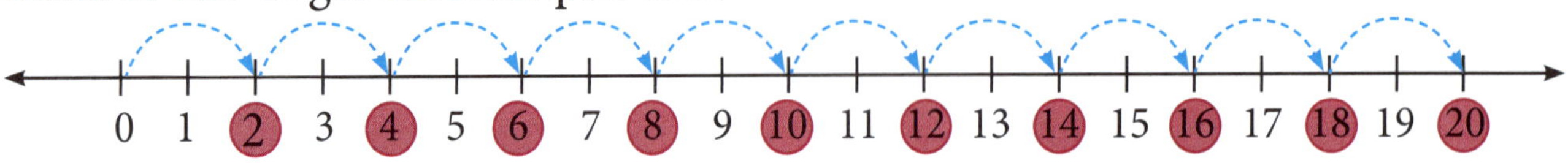

Skip count by 3s to get the multiples of 3 on the number line.

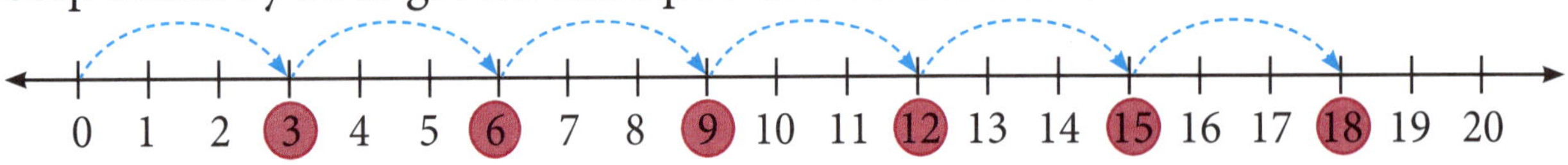

Do you know?

If on dividing a bigger number by a smaller number, the remainder is 0, then

- the bigger number is a multiple of the smaller number,
- the smaller number is a factor of the bigger number.

Common Multiples

Common multiples of two or more numbers are the multiples that are common to those numbers. The **least common multiple** of two or more given numbers is the **smallest** among their common multiples. Least common multiple is known as LCM.

SOLVED EXAMPLES

Example 7: Find the common multiples of 2 and 3 that are less than 20.

Solution:

Multiples of 2 that are less than 20

2, 4, (6), 8, 10, (12), 14, 16, (18)

Multiples of 3 that are less than 20

3, (6), 9, (12), 15, (18)

So, 6, 12 and 18 are the common multiples of 2 and 3 that are less than 20. Here, 6 is the least common multiple.

> First write all the multiples of 2 that are less than 20.
> Then, write all the multiples of 3 that are less than 20.
> After that, circle the multiples that are common to both.

The same can be shown on a number line. The numbers where the skip counts by 2s and 3s overlap are the common multiples.

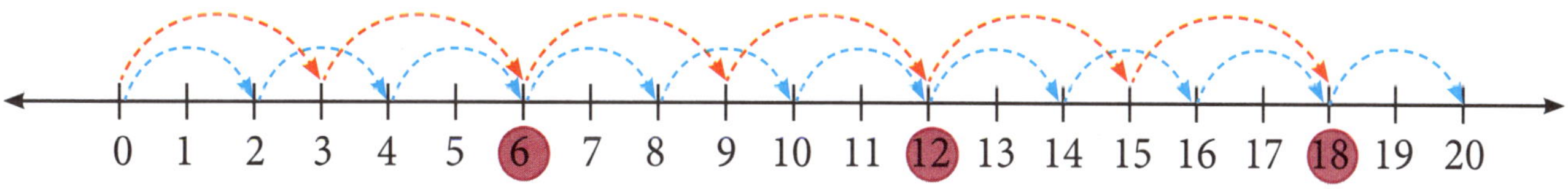

Example 8: Is 37 a multiple of 3?

Solution:

$$\begin{array}{r|l} & \;\;12 \\ \hline 3 & \;\;37 \\ & -3\downarrow \\ \hline & \;\;07 \\ & -\;\;6 \\ \hline & \;\;\;\;1 \end{array}$$

MENTAL MATHS

1. What are the first five multiples of 2?
2. What are the first three multiples of 4?
3. From the above questions, identify the common multiples of 2 and 4.

Dividing 37 by 3, the remainder is not zero. Therefore, 37 is not a multiple of 3.

EXERCISE 5C

1. Mark the multiples of 3 that are less than 20 on the number line given below.

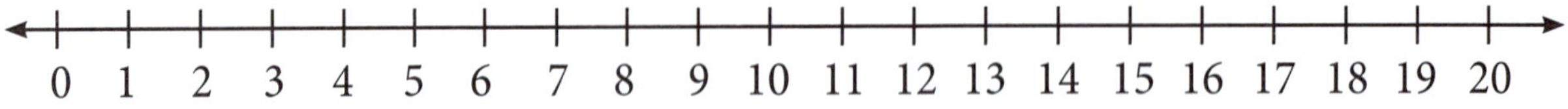

2. Mark the multiples of 6 that are less than 20 on the number line given below.

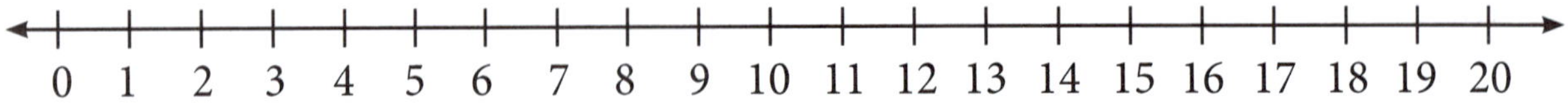

3. Solve the following.

a. Write the multiples of 6 that are less than 25.

b. Write three multiples of 5 that are greater than 9.

c. Write the multiples of 7 between 10 and 40.

d. Write the common multiples of 2 and 4 from 1 to 20.

Show the multiples on a number line.

e. Write the common multiples of 4 and 5 between 1 and 30.

Show the multiples on a number line.

f. Write the first common multiple of 2 and 5.

g. Write the first common multiple of 3 and 4.

h. Circle the multiples of 3 and tick the multiples of 5 in the numbers given below.

Find out the first common multiple of 3 and 5.

1	2	3	4	5	6	7	8	9	10
11	12	13	14	15	16	17	18	19	20
21	22	23	24	25	26	27	28	29	30

4. Find the first two common multiples of the following pairs of numbers.

a. 9 and 3 b. 15 and 10 c. 6 and 8 d. 9 and 2 e. 4 and 6

5. Find the least common multiple of the following pairs of numbers.

a. 6 and 8 b. 10 and 30 c. 9 and 11 d. 5 and 13 e. 9 and 27

PRIME AND COMPOSITE NUMBERS

There are two groups of children. One group has 7 students and the other group has 10 students. Divide each group into two groups with equal number of students.

We cannot make two groups with equal number of students!

We can make two groups with 5 students each!

$7 = 1 \times 7$ $\qquad$ $10 = 2 \times 5$

Here, 7 is a prime number and 10 is a composite number.

Prime numbers are numbers that have only two factors: 1 and the number itself. Prime numbers cannot be completely divided by numbers smaller than themselves except by 1. For example, 5, 11, 13 are prime numbers.

Composite numbers are numbers that have more than two factors. For example, 4, 6 and 9 are composite numbers.

NOTE

- 1 is neither a prime number nor a composite number. **1 is a unique number.**
- 2 is the only prime number which is even.

PRIME NUMBERS

2	7	17	29	☐
3	11	19	31	☐
5	13	23	37	☐

COMPOSITE NUMBERS

4	12	20	26	
6	14	21	27	☐
8	15	22	28	☐
9	16	24	30	☐
10	18	25	32	

Fill in the next three prime and composite numbers!

PRIME FACTORS

The factors of a number that are prime numbers are known as **prime factors**.

For example, the factors of 24 are 1, 2, 3, 4, 6, 12 and 24. Out of these 2 and 3 are prime numbers. So, 2 and 3 are prime factors of 24.

Prime Factorisation

Prime factorisation refers to the method of expressing a number as a product of its prime factors. For example,

$24 = 2 \times 2 \times 2 \times 3$

Here, all the factors are prime factors.

There are two methods to find the prime factorisation of a number: division method and factor tree method.

Division Method

Let us find the prime factorisation of 18 using division method.

Step 1: Divide 18 by the smallest prime number possible (in this case 2) by short division method.

2	18
	09

Step 2: 9 is the new dividend. Divide 9 by the smallest prime number possible (in this case 3).

2	18
3	09
	03

Step 3: 3 is the new dividend. Divide 3 by the smallest prime number possible (in this case 3).

2	18
3	09
3	03
	01

We stop when the new dividend = 1.

The **prime factors** of 18 are 2 and 3.

The **prime factorisation** of 18 is $2 \times 3 \times 3$.

COMMON ERRORS

While writing prime factors, write the factors only once. Put commas between the numbers.

While writing prime factorisation, write all the factors. Put × between the factors.

Correct	Incorrect
Prime factors of 18 = 2, 3 👍	Prime factors of 18 = 2 × 3 👎
Prime factorisation of 18 = 2 × 3 × 3 👍	Prime factorisation of 18 = 2, 3, 3 👎

Factor Tree Method

In this method, factorisation is represented pictorially.

Let us find the prime factorisation of 24 using factor tree method.

Step 1: Write 24 as a product of any two factors, say 4 × 6.

Step 2: Factorise 4 further (4 = 2 × 2).

Step 3: Now, factorise 6 (6 = 2 × 3).

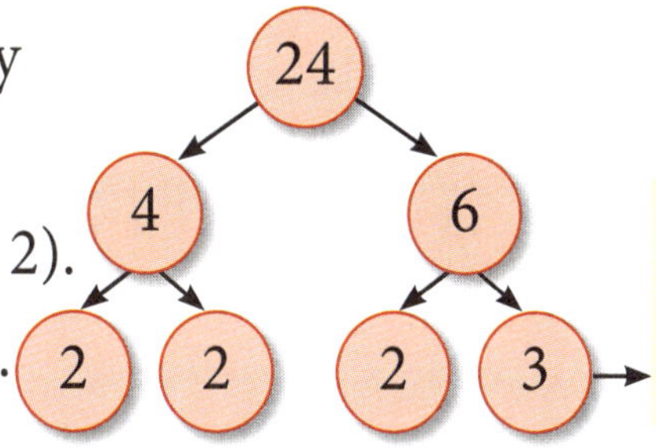

We stop at that point where all the factors are prime numbers.

Now multiply all the numbers which are at the end of the arrows.
Prime factorisation of 24 = 2 × 2 × 2 × 3
Two more factor trees using other factors of the number 24 are shown below.

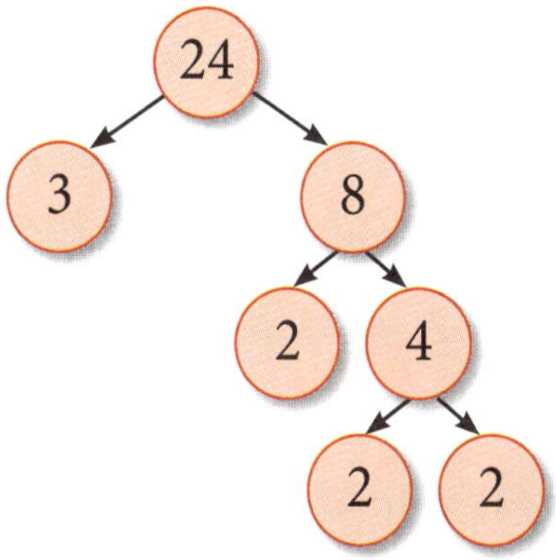

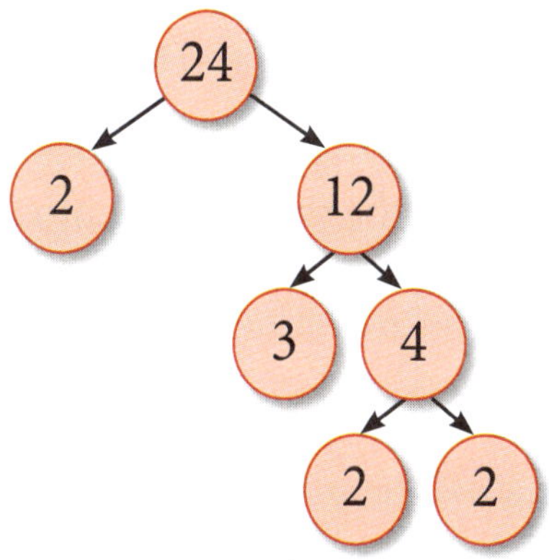

Prime factors of 24 = 2, 3
Now multiply all the numbers which are at the end of arrows.
Prime factorisation of 24 = 2 × 2 × 2 × 3

SOLVED EXAMPLES

Example 9: Find the prime factors and prime factorisation of 36.

Solution:

Division method

2	36
2	18
3	09
3	03
	01

Factor tree method

a.

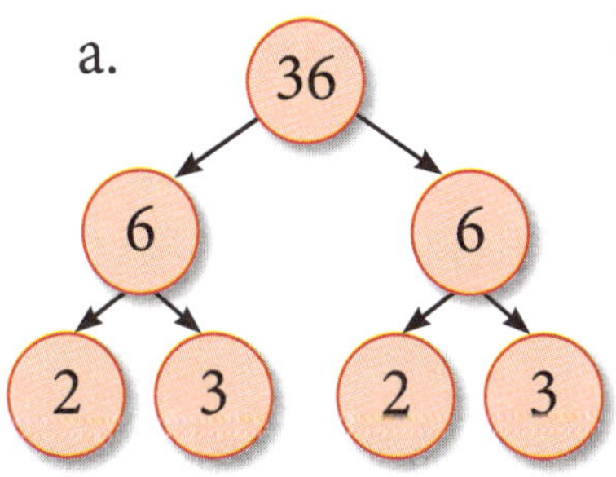

b.

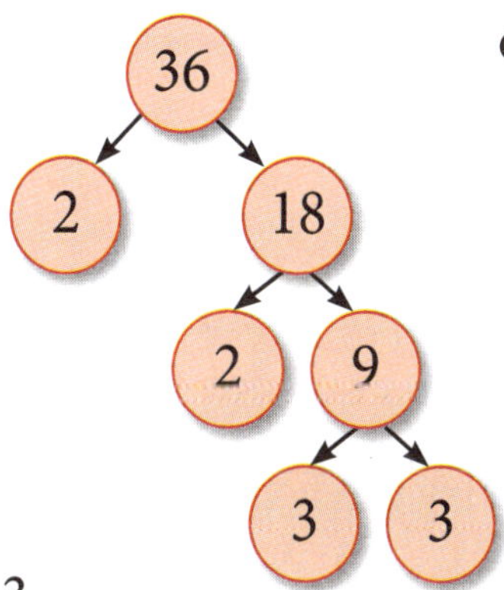

c.

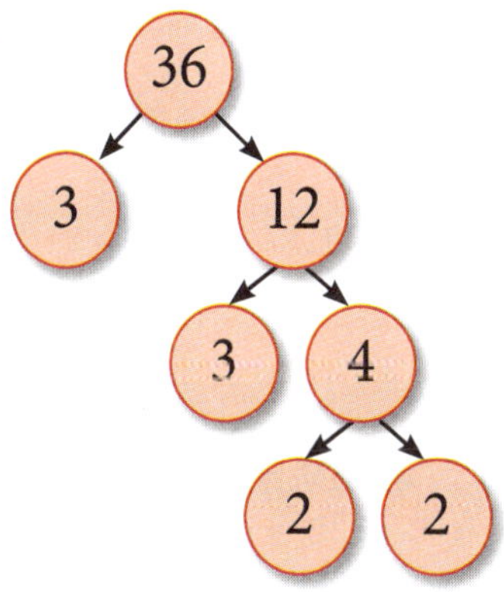

Prime factors of 36 = 2, 3
Prime factorisation of 36 = 2 × 2 × 3 × 3

EXERCISE 5D

1. **Write the prime numbers and the composite numbers between 1 and 30.**
2. **Write the prime numbers from 30 to 50.**
3. **Write the composite numbers from 30 to 50.**
4. **Find the prime factors and the prime factorisation of the following numbers.**

   a. 6 b. 8 c. 10 d. 20 e. 27 f. 30 g. 42 h. 48 i. 60

MATHS LAB ACTIVITY

21 CS Creativity and Innovation, Collaboration EL AI

Aim: To understand factors and multiples

Materials required: One chart paper, coloured sheets, glue, colour pencils or water colours

Procedure:

1. Cut the chart paper into 25 squares and paste coloured paper on top of them. You can also take some cards and paint them with different colours.

2. Start with the number 6.
3. Take 6 squares. How many kinds of different rectangles can you make with 6 squares?

(i)  $= 1 \times 6$

(ii)  $= 2 \times 3$

These rectangles tell us that the factors of 6 are 1, 2, 3 and 6.

6 is also a multiple of 1, 2 and 3.

(iii)  $= 3 \times 2$

This rectangle is the same as 2×3, it is just rotated. So, we stop here.

4. Work in pairs. Also, try this activity for the numbers: 4, 8, 10, 15, 18, 20, 24.

Concept Map

Factors and Multiples

- Rules of divisibility
- Factors of a number
- Multiple
- Prime numbers
- Composite numbers

A number is divisible by	
2	if the last digit is 0, 2, 4, 6 or 8.
3	if the sum of its digits is divisible by 3.
4	if the number formed by its last two digits is divisible by 4.
5	if its last digit is 0 or 5.
6	if it is divisible by both 2 and 3.
8	if the number formed by its last three digits is divisible by 8.
9	if the sum of its digits is divisible by 9.
10	if its last digit is 0.

Factors of a number → 2 × 3 = 6 ← Multiple

6 is a multiple of 2 and 3.
2 is a factor of 6.
3 is a factor of 6.

Prime numbers

2 7 17 29
3 11 19 31
5 13 23 37

Composite numbers

4 12 20 26
6 14 21 27
8 15 22 28
9 16 24 30
10 18 25 32

Prime numbers →

- Prime factors
  - Division method
  - Factor tree method
- Prime factorisation

Key Concepts

- **Divisibility rules:** Rules that help us to find out whether a number is divisible by the numbers 2, 3, 4, 5, 6, 8, 9, 10 without actually dividing
- **Factor:** Factor of a number is a number that divides it exactly (without leaving a remainder).
- **Common factor:** Factors that are common to two or more numbers
- **Highest common factor:** The greatest factor among the common factors of two or more numbers
- **Multiple:** A number formed when any number is multiplied with other numbers
- **Common multiples:** Multiples that are common to two or more numbers
- **Least common multiple:** The smallest multiple among the common multiples of two or more numbers
- **Prime number:** Numbers that have only two factors, 1 and the number itself
- **Composite numbers:** Numbers that have more than two factors
- **Prime factors:** Factors of a number that are also prime numbers
- **Prime factorisation:** The method of expressing numbers as a product of prime factors
- **Factor tree:** The method of finding factors of a number pictorially

Chapter Revision

A. Choose the correct option.

1. Which of the following numbers is divisible by 4?
   a. 7214 b. 4302 c. 5024 d. 9182
2. Which of the following numbers is divisible by 5 but not by 10?
   a. 5380 b. 7215 c. 4910 d. 6240
3. Which of the following options has all the factors of 18?
   a. 1, 2, 3, 6, 9, 18 b. 1, 3, 6, 18 c. 1, 2, 9, 18 d. 1, 18
4. Which of the following is a factor of all the numbers?
   a. 2 b. 5 c. 1 d. 0
5. A number that has only 2 factors is called a ____________________.
   a. composite number b. unique number
   c. prime number d. natural number

B. Write T for true and F for false.

1. 1 is a prime number.
2. 17 is a prime number.
3. 48 is a composite number.
4. 16 is a prime number.
5. 15 is a composite number.

C. Answer the following questions.

1. Use the divisibility rule to find out if 39462 is divisible by 3. Give reasons.
2. Use the divisibility rule to find out if 642888 is divisible by 8. Give reasons.
3. Which of the following numbers are odd numbers?
   294, 537, 1286, 3420, 4391, 5723
4. Circle the prime numbers and tick the composite numbers.
   2, 3, 5, 8, 11, 16, 20, 32, 39, 41, 43, 58, 63, 72
5. Find two factors of 12 whose sum is 7.
6. Write all the multiples of 6 from 1 to 50.
7. Write 2 odd multiples of 3 that are less than 10.
8. Write the prime factors and prime factorisation of 24, 27 and 36.
9. Write three even multiples of 4 and 6 less than 25. Find the least common multiple.
10. Find the common factors of 15 and 36. Also, find the highest common factor.

Skill up!

A. 21 CS Information Literacy

Make a chart of factors of numbers from 2 to 10. Then identify the prime and composite number from the factors and multiples. Given below is an example of a chart that you can make. Complete it till 20.

Number	Factors	Prime number	Composite number
2	1, 2	Yes	–

B. 21 CS Critical Thinking, Life Skills   CC Integration with Science   HQ Knowing My Needs

3 GOOD HEALTH AND WELL-BEING

If one toffee costs ₹2, how much money would you need to eat 10 toffees every day for 5 days? What would happen if you eat 10 toffees every day? Is it good for your health to eat 10 toffees every day? Do you eat a balanced diet every day? What food group would toffees fall under?

C. 21 CS Critical Thinking, Information Literacy   EL   AI

Find an interesting way to find common factors. You can use a diagram called Venn diagram. Find the common factors of 20 and 24. First list down factors of 20 and 24. Draw a Venn diagram as shown below to show common factors. In the green portion, write the factors that are common to 20 and 24.

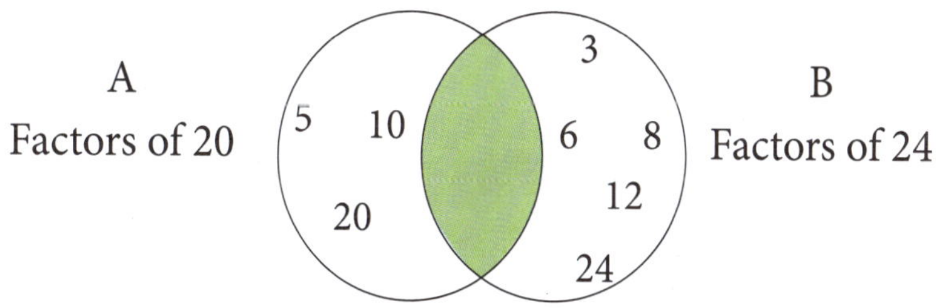

SUSTAINABLE DEVELOPMENT GOALS

Question B is in line with SDG 3 Good Health and Well-Being. Have you heard of the word 'junk food'? Is it good for your health? Find some differences between junk food and healthy food.

Worksheet 5

21 CS Critical Thinking, Information Literacy

Observe the classroom and answer the questions given below.

1. Prime groups:

2. Composite groups:

3. Prime factorisation of composite groups:

4. A and E are

6 Fractions

Learning Objectives

- To identify half, one-fourth, three-fourths and a whole
- To understand the concept of equivalent fractions
- To define different types of fractions: unit, proper, improper and mixed
- To convert fractions of one type to another
- To compare fractions
- To add and subtract fractions

Let's Get Started

21 CS Critical Thinking EL

You have learnt that a fraction represents a part of a whole. Observe the picture. How many fractions can you identify in the picture?
Circle those places in the picture where you can find a fraction. Then, write the fraction in the space provided. One has been done for you.

A. One egg used out of six eggs = $\frac{1}{6}$

B. ____________________ C. ____________________

D. ____________________ E. ____________________

FRACTION AS A PART OF A WHOLE

A fraction is a number that expresses a part of a whole object or a set of objects.

$$\text{Fraction} = \frac{\text{Part}}{\text{Whole object}} \text{ or } \frac{\text{Part}}{\text{Set of objects}}$$

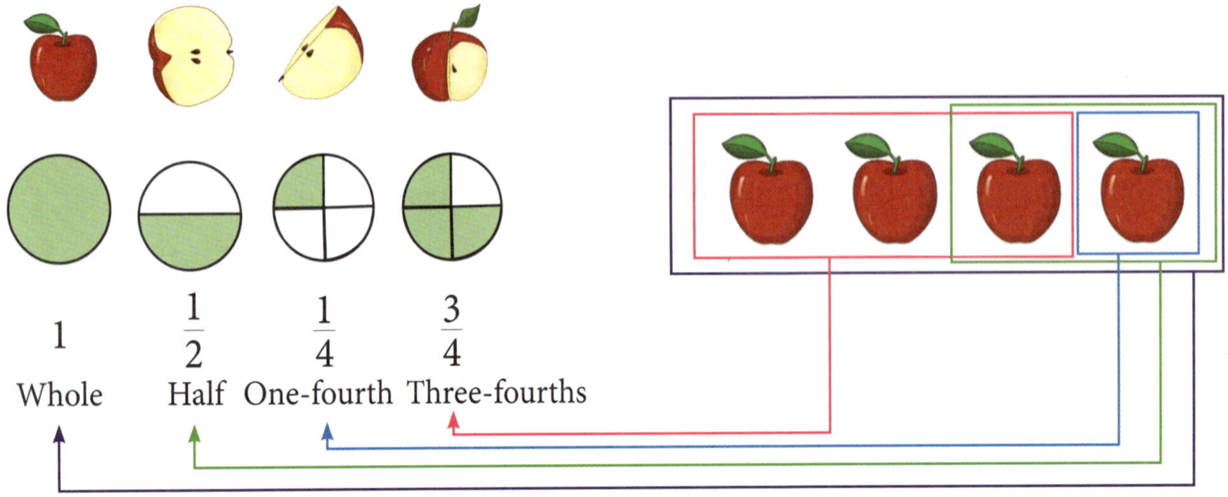

SIMPLEST FORM OF A FRACTION

A fraction is said to be in the simplest form if its numerator and denominator have no common factor except 1. In other words, there is no number apart from 1 which can divide both the numerator and the denominator.

SOLVED EXAMPLES

Example 1: Write the simplest form of $\frac{8}{10}$.

Solution:

$\frac{8}{10}$ Both 8 and 10 can be divided by 2. Dividing by 2, the numerator will become 4 and the denominator will become 5.

$\frac{\not{8}^{\,4}}{\not{10}_{\,5}}$

$\frac{4}{5}$ Now, there is no number apart from 1 which can divide 4 and 5. So, $\frac{4}{5}$ is the simplest form of $\frac{8}{10}$.

EQUIVALENT FRACTIONS

Equivalent fractions are the fractions that have the same value.

Look at the three circles given on the next page. Can you see that all the three circles have half portion shaded? The first one represents $\frac{1}{2}$, the second represents $\frac{2}{4}$ and the third represents $\frac{4}{8}$. These fractions have different numerators and denominators but they have the same value.

All the three fractions represent the same amount of shaded portion. Hence, these fractions are considered as equivalent fractions.

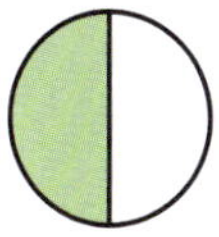 $\frac{1}{2}$ = 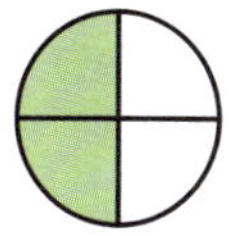 $\frac{2}{4}$ = 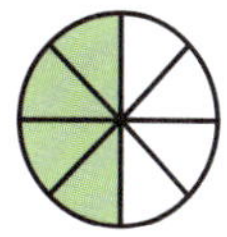 $\frac{4}{8}$

Finding an Equivalent Fraction

To find an equivalent fraction of a given fraction, multiply the numerator and the denominator of the given fraction by the same number.

SOLVED EXAMPLES

Example 2: Write two equivalent fractions of $\frac{2}{4}$.

Solution:

Multiplying the numerator and the denominator by 2 and 3, we get,

$$\frac{2}{4} = \frac{2 \times 2}{4 \times 2} = \frac{4}{8}; \quad \frac{2}{4} = \frac{2 \times 3}{4 \times 3} = \frac{6}{12}$$

Therefore, two equivalent fractions of $\frac{2}{4}$ are $\frac{4}{8}$ and $\frac{6}{12}$.

EXERCISE 6A

1. **Colour the figures for the given fractions.**

   a. $\frac{1}{4}$ 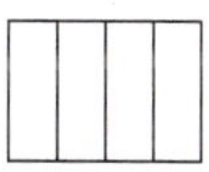   b. $\frac{1}{4}$ 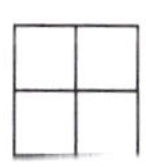   c. $\frac{3}{4}$ 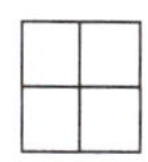

2. **Reduce the following fractions to the simplest form.**

   a. $\frac{9}{15}$ b. $\frac{12}{20}$ c. $\frac{15}{35}$ d. $\frac{24}{26}$

3. **Write five equivalent fractions of the following.**

   a. $\frac{1}{2}$ b. $\frac{2}{3}$ c. $\frac{4}{5}$ d. $\frac{3}{7}$

4. **Write a fraction equivalent to**

   a. $\frac{1}{3}$ with denominator 12.   b. $\frac{2}{5}$ with numerator 8.

5. **Solve the following word problems.**

   a. Out of 5 birds, 2 flew away. What is the fraction of the birds that flew away?

   b. Out of 11 boys, 5 can not swim. What fraction of boys can not swim?

   c. Out of 13 girls, 6 love to play football. What fraction of girls play football?

TYPES OF FRACTIONS

Depending on the relationship and values of the numerators and denominators, fractions are of four types: unit, proper, improper and mixed.

Unit Fractions

Fractions that have 1 as their numerator are called unit fractions.

Examples: $\frac{1}{2}, \frac{1}{15}, \frac{1}{32}, \frac{1}{493}$

Proper Fractions

Fractions in which the numerator is smaller than the denominator are called proper fractions.

Examples: $\frac{2}{3}, \frac{5}{7}, \frac{19}{23}, \frac{48}{165}$

Improper Fractions

Fractions in which the numerator is greater than or equal to the denominator are called improper fractions.

Examples: $\frac{5}{2}, \frac{11}{6}, \frac{129}{47}, \frac{8}{8}, \frac{53}{53}, \frac{247}{247}$

Mixed Fractions

A mixed fraction is a combination of a whole number and a proper fraction.

Examples: $1\frac{2}{3}, 5\frac{6}{7}, 8\frac{4}{5}, 9\frac{1}{8}$

Converting Improper Fractions into Mixed Fractions

In an improper fraction, the numerator is bigger than the denominator. So, the numerator can be divided by the denominator. Thus, to change an improper fraction into a mixed fraction, divide the numerator by the denominator. The quotient becomes the whole number and the remainder becomes the new numerator. The denominator remains the same.

SOLVED EXAMPLES

Example 3:

a. Convert $\frac{9}{2}$ into a mixed fraction.

Solution:

a.

$$\begin{array}{r|l} & \quad 4 \leftarrow \text{whole number part} \\ \text{denominator} \rightarrow 2 & \quad 9 \\ & -8 \\ \hline \text{numerator} \rightarrow & \quad 1 \end{array}$$

Thus, $\frac{9}{2} = 4\frac{1}{2}$

b. Convert $\frac{7}{3}$ into a mixed fraction.

b.

$$\begin{array}{r|l} & \ \ 2 \\ \hline 3 & \ \ 7 \\ & -6 \\ \hline & \ \ 1 \end{array}$$

Thus, $\frac{7}{3} = 2\frac{1}{3}$

Example 4: Convert $\frac{130}{12}$ into a mixed fraction.

Solution:

Method 1:

To convert an improper fraction that is not in its lowest term into a mixed fraction, first reduce the improper fraction to its lowest term and then convert it into a mixed fraction.

Step 1: First, reduce $\frac{130}{12}$ to its lowest term.

$$\frac{130}{12} = \frac{\cancel{130}^{65}}{\cancel{12}_{6}} = \frac{65}{6}$$

Step 2: Now, convert into a mixed fraction.

$$\begin{array}{r|l} & \ \ 10 \\ \hline 6 & \ \ 65 \\ & -6 \\ \hline & \ \ 05 \end{array}$$

Thus, $\frac{130}{12} = 10\frac{5}{6}$

Method 2:

In case you forgot to first simplify the improper fraction to its lowest term, then first convert the fraction into a mixed fraction and then simplify the fractional part to its lowest term.

$$\begin{array}{r|l} & \ \ 010 \\ \hline 12 & \ \ 130 \\ & -12 \\ \hline & \ \ \ \ 10 \end{array}$$

$$10\frac{\cancel{10}^{5}}{\cancel{12}_{6}} = 10\frac{5}{6}$$

Converting Mixed Fractions into Improper Fractions

To convert a mixed fraction into an improper fraction, multiply the denominator of the fraction with its whole number part and then add the numerator to the product. Write the sum in the numerator. The denominator remains the same.

SOLVED EXAMPLES

Example 5: Convert $2\frac{1}{3}$ into an improper fraction.

Solution:

$$2\frac{1}{3} = 2\overset{+}{\underset{\times}{}}\frac{1}{3} = \frac{(2 \times 3) + 1}{3} = \frac{6+1}{3} = \frac{7}{3}$$

Example 6: Convert $1\frac{3}{5}$ into an improper fraction.

Solution:

$$1\frac{3}{5} = 1\overset{+}{\underset{\times}{}}\frac{3}{5} = \frac{(1 \times 5) + 3}{5} = \frac{5+3}{5} = \frac{8}{5}$$

EXERCISE 6B

1. **Sort the following into unit, proper, improper and mixed fractions.**

   a. $\frac{2}{3}$ b. $\frac{1}{7}$ c. $\frac{5}{9}$ d. $\frac{23}{20}$ e. $8\frac{5}{9}$ f. $\frac{15}{11}$ g. $19\frac{3}{9}$

2. **Convert the following improper fractions into mixed fractions.**

   a. $\frac{5}{3}$ b. $\frac{19}{2}$ c. $\frac{141}{6}$ d. $\frac{173}{7}$

3. **Convert the following mixed fractions into improper fractions.**

   a. $9\frac{1}{3}$ b. $11\frac{1}{7}$ c. $13\frac{2}{5}$ d. $19\frac{3}{8}$

COMPARING FRACTIONS

Comparing Like Fractions

If the denominators of both the fractions are the same, then compare the numerators of the fractions. The fraction with the bigger numerator is the bigger fraction.

Consider the fractions $\frac{4}{8}$ and $\frac{5}{8}$. Let us find out which one is smaller.

In both the fractions, the denominator is the same. So, compare the numerators.

$$4 < 5 \qquad \text{Therefore, } \frac{4}{8} < \frac{5}{8}.$$

Comparing Unlike Fractions

Unlike Fractions with the same numerator

If the numerators of both the fractions are the same, then the fraction with the smaller denominator is the bigger fraction.

Consider the fractions $\frac{5}{2}$ and $\frac{5}{8}$. Both the fractions have the same numerator. So, compare the denominators.

$$8 > 2 \qquad \text{Therefore, } \frac{5}{2} > \frac{5}{8}.$$

Unlike Fractions with different numerators

If the numerators of both the fractions are different, then to find the greater fraction, write both the fractions and cross-multiply. For example, to find the greater fraction between $\frac{2}{3}$ and $\frac{5}{7}$, cross-multiply as given below.

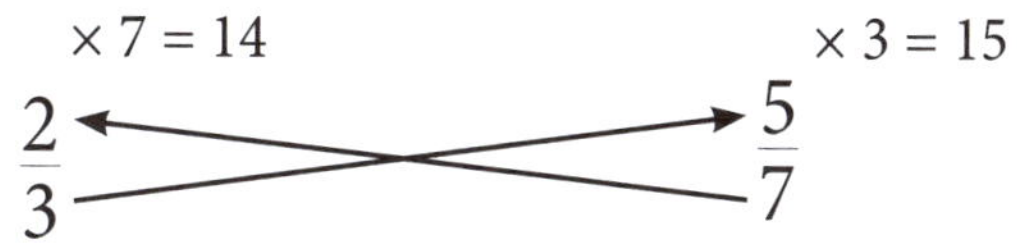

15 is bigger than 14 and 15 is on the right side, so the fraction on the right side, that is, $\frac{5}{7}$ is bigger. Therefore, $\frac{5}{7} > \frac{2}{3}$.

Comparing Mixed Fractions

To compare mixed fractions, first check the whole numbers. The fraction whose whole number part is bigger is the bigger fraction. Compare $4\frac{1}{3}$ and $5\frac{3}{7}$. Checking the whole numbers, we find that 4 < 5.

Therefore, $4\frac{1}{3} < 5\frac{3}{7}$.

GO EASY!

Compare $4\frac{2}{3}$ and $4\frac{5}{7}$.

Here, the whole number is the same and $\frac{2}{3} < \frac{5}{7}$ as shown in the previous example.

Therefore, $4\frac{2}{3} < 4\frac{5}{7}$.

Ordering of Fractions

To arrange fractions in ascending or descending order, first convert the fractions into like fractions.

SOLVED EXAMPLES

Example 7: Write $\frac{2}{3}, \frac{1}{6}, \frac{4}{12}$ in ascending and descending order.

Solution: To convert the fractions into like fractions, first find out the least common multiple (LCM) of all the denominators.

LCM of 3, 6 and 12 = 12

Multiples of 3 = 3, 6, 9, 12, 15, 18, 21, 24, ...

Multiples of 6 = 6, 12, 18, 24, ...

Multiples of 12 = 12, 24, 36, ...

- In the first fraction $\frac{2}{3}$, the denominator 3 should be multiplied by 4 to get the LCM 12. Therefore, multiply the numerator 2 also by 4.

$$\frac{2\times4}{3\times4}, \frac{1\times2}{6\times2}, \frac{4}{12} = \frac{8}{12}, \frac{2}{12}, \frac{4}{12}$$

- In the second fraction $\frac{1}{6}$, the denominator 6 should be multiplied by 2 to get the LCM 12. Therefore, multiply the numerator 1 also by 2.
- In the third fraction $\frac{4}{12}$, the denominator is already equal to the LCM, so leave that fraction as it is.
- Now, we arrange the like fractions from the smallest to the greatest.

$$\frac{2}{12} < \frac{4}{12} < \frac{8}{12}$$

- Then write the corresponding original fractions.

$$\frac{1}{6} < \frac{4}{12} < \frac{2}{3}$$

Therefore, the fractions in ascending order are $\frac{1}{6} < \frac{4}{12} < \frac{2}{3}$.

The fractions in descending order are $\frac{2}{3} > \frac{4}{12} > \frac{1}{6}$.

Exercise 6C

1. Fill in the boxes with > or <.

a. $\frac{3}{4}$ ☐ $\frac{2}{5}$ b. $\frac{5}{6}$ ☐ $\frac{1}{7}$ c. $\frac{2}{9}$ ☐ $\frac{3}{5}$ d. $\frac{3}{7}$ ☐ $\frac{3}{5}$ e. $\frac{3}{7}$ ☐ $\frac{4}{5}$

2. Arrange the following fractions in ascending order.

a. $\frac{3}{5}, \frac{1}{2}, \frac{3}{10}$ b. $\frac{7}{12}, \frac{5}{6}, \frac{1}{4}$ c. $\frac{7}{8}, \frac{1}{12}, \frac{5}{24}$

3. Arrange the following fractions in descending order.

a. $\frac{1}{10}, \frac{4}{5}, \frac{6}{20}$ b. $\frac{3}{5}, \frac{1}{4}, \frac{7}{20}$ c. $\frac{2}{9}, \frac{5}{6}, \frac{7}{18}$

ADDITION OF FRACTIONS

Adding Like Fractions

To add like fractions, first add the numerators. Then, place the sum over the common denominator. Finally, convert the fraction to its lowest term, if required.

SOLVED EXAMPLES

Example 8: Add $\frac{2}{8}$ and $\frac{5}{8}$.

Solution:

$$\frac{2}{8} + \frac{5}{8} = \frac{2+5}{8} = \frac{7}{8}$$

Example 9: Add $\frac{8}{5}$ and $\frac{7}{5}$.

Solution:

$$\frac{8}{5} + \frac{7}{5} = \frac{8+7}{5} = \frac{\cancel{15}^{3}}{\cancel{5}_{1}} = 3$$

COMMON ERRORS

$\frac{2}{4} + \frac{3}{4} = \frac{5}{4}$ ✓

$\frac{2}{4} + \frac{3}{4} = \frac{5}{8}$ ✗

MENTAL MATHS

Arrange these fractions in descending order.

$\frac{2}{3}, \frac{1}{6}, \frac{1}{3}$

Adding Unlike Fractions

To add unlike fractions, first find the LCM of the denominators. Then, convert the fractions into like fractions with the LCM as the common denominator. Finally, add the like fractions.

SOLVED EXAMPLES

Example 10: Add $\frac{2}{8}$ and $\frac{5}{12}$.

Solution:

Multiples of 8 = 8, 16, 24, 32, ...

Multiples of 12 = 12, 24, 36, ...

LCM of 8 and 12 = 24.

$$\frac{2^{\times 3}}{8^{\times 3}} + \frac{5^{\times 2}}{12^{\times 2}} = \frac{6}{24} + \frac{10}{24} = \frac{6+10}{24} = \frac{\cancel{16}^{2}}{\cancel{24}_{3}} = \frac{2}{3}$$

Adding Mixed Fractions

First, convert the mixed fractions into improper fractions. Then, convert the improper fractions into like fractions. Then, add the like fractions. Finally, if the result is an improper fraction, convert it into a mixed fraction.

SOLVED EXAMPLES

Example 11: Add $2\frac{1}{5}$ and $3\frac{2}{5}$.

Solution:

First convert the mixed fractions to improper fractions.

$$2\frac{1}{5} + 3\frac{2}{5} = \frac{11}{5} + \frac{17}{5}$$

Here, the fractions are already like fractions. So, the fractions can be added directly.

$$\frac{11}{5} + \frac{17}{5} = \frac{11+17}{5} = \frac{28}{5} = 5\frac{3}{5}$$

EXERCISE 6D

Solve the following and write the answers in the simplest form.

1. $\frac{2}{5}+\frac{1}{5}$
2. $\frac{3}{7}+\frac{2}{7}$
3. $\frac{1}{8}+\frac{5}{8}$
4. $\frac{7}{15}+\frac{3}{15}$
5. $\frac{1}{2}+\frac{1}{6}$
6. $\frac{2}{5}+\frac{3}{12}$
7. $3\frac{1}{4}+5\frac{1}{4}$
8. $5\frac{1}{7}+6\frac{2}{7}$
9. $4\frac{2}{5}+3\frac{1}{5}$
10. $3\frac{1}{6}+4\frac{2}{9}$
11. $9\frac{1}{3}+5\frac{7}{12}$
12. $7\frac{1}{2}+5\frac{3}{4}$

SUBTRACTION OF FRACTIONS

Subtracting Like Fractions

To subtract like fractions, first subtract the numerators. Then, place the answer over the common denominator. Then, convert the fraction to its lowest term, if required.

Subtraction of fractions follows exactly the same method as addition. The only difference is that we subtract instead of adding.

For example, subtract $\frac{1}{4}$ from $\frac{5}{4}$.

$$\frac{5}{4}-\frac{1}{4}=\frac{5-1}{4}=\frac{\cancel{4}^{1}}{\cancel{4}_{1}}=1$$

Subtracting Unlike Fractions

To subtract unlike fractions, first take the LCM of the denominators. Then, convert the fractions into like fractions with the LCM as common denominator. Finally, subtract the like fractions.

For example, subtract $\frac{1}{4}$ from $\frac{5}{8}$.

$$\frac{5}{8}-\frac{1}{4}=\frac{5^{\times 1}}{8^{\times 1}}-\frac{1^{\times 2}}{4^{\times 2}}=\frac{5-2}{8}=\frac{3}{8}$$ (LCM of 8 and 4 is 8.)

Subtracting Mixed Fractions

First, convert the mixed fractions into improper fractions. Then, convert the improper fractions into like fractions. Then, subtract the like fractions. Finally, if the result is an improper fraction, convert it into a mixed fraction.

For example, subtract $1\frac{1}{4}$ from $2\frac{3}{5}$.

$$2\frac{3}{5}-1\frac{1}{4}=\frac{13}{5}-\frac{5}{4}$$

$$=\frac{13^{\times 4}}{5^{\times 4}}-\frac{5^{\times 5}}{4^{\times 5}}$$

Multiples of 5 = 5, 10, 15, 20, 25, ...
Multiples of 4 = 4, 8, 12, 16, 20, 24, ...
LCM of 5 and 4 = 20

$$=\frac{52}{20}-\frac{25}{20}=\frac{52-25}{20}=\frac{27}{20}=1\frac{7}{20}$$

SOLVED EXAMPLES

Example 12: Arpana spent $\frac{1}{6}$ of her money to buy a doll and $\frac{2}{3}$ of her money to buy a dress. What fraction of her money did she spend on the doll and the dress altogether? What fraction of money is left with her?

Solution:

Fraction of Arpana's money spent to buy a doll and a dress $= \frac{1}{6} + \frac{2}{3}$

Multiples of 6 = 6, 12, 18, 24, ...

Multiples of 3 = 3, 6, 9, 12, ...

LCM of 6 and 3 = 6

$$\frac{1^{\times 1}}{6^{\times 1}} + \frac{2^{\times 2}}{3^{\times 2}} = \frac{1+4}{6} = \frac{5}{6}$$

NOTE

In fractions, the total is always taken as 1.

Arpana spent $\frac{5}{6}$ of her money to buy a doll and a dress.

Fraction of Arpana's money left $= 1 - \frac{5}{6} = \frac{6-5}{6} = \frac{1}{6}$.

EXERCISE 6E

1. **Solve the following.**

   a. $\frac{5}{8} - \frac{1}{4}$ b. $\frac{2}{3} - \frac{1}{9}$ c. $\frac{9}{5} - \frac{3}{10}$ d. $5\frac{2}{9} - 1\frac{1}{3}$ e. $8\frac{2}{7} - 5\frac{3}{4}$

2. **Seema walked $\frac{1}{5}$ of the distance to school and she took a bus for $\frac{2}{5}$ of the distance to school. What fraction of the total distance did she cover by walking and by bus?**

3. **Savita bought $7\frac{1}{2}$ m of cloth. She used $2\frac{1}{5}$ m out of it to make a dress. How many metres of cloth is left with her?**

Mental Maths

Find the value of △ + ⬠, if △ + ○ = $4\frac{1}{3}$, ○ + □ = $5\frac{1}{3}$ and □ + ⬠ = $9\frac{1}{3}$.

Maths Lab Activity

21 CS Critical Thinking, Creativity and Innovation | EL | AI | STEAM CHALLENGE

Aim: To transform a whole into fractions

Materials required: Four square sheets of paper, two rectangular sheets of paper, colour pencils

Procedure:

1. Take a square sheet of paper and fold it horizontally into two halves. Then, fold it again, this time vertically, to form four equal parts (Fig. A).

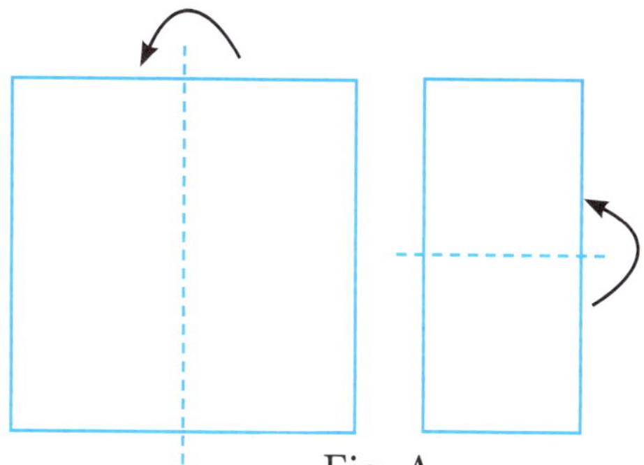

Fig. A

2. Unfold the paper and colour each part with four different colours as shown in Fig. B.
3. Take another square sheet of paper and fold it vertically three times (Fig. C). Colour the parts with different colours.
4. Think of other ways of folding the paper such that equal parts are formed (Fig. D and Fig. E).

Fig. B

Fig. C

Fig. D

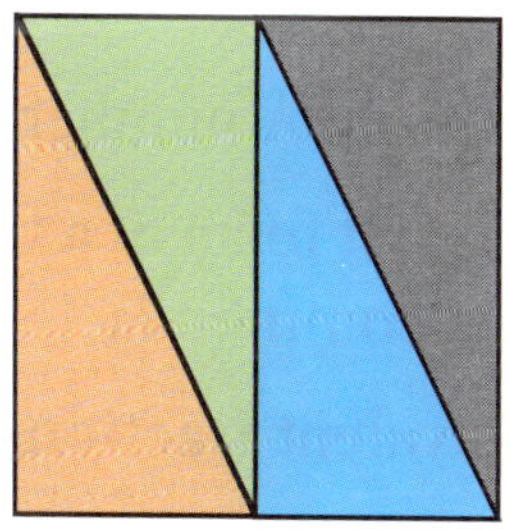

Fig. E

Observation: The square papers have been transformed into four square quarters, four rectangular quarters and four triangular quarters.

Conclusion: A fraction is a part of a whole. In this activity, each part of the fraction = $\frac{1}{4}$.

Work in pairs. Try forming other quarters using the rectangular sheets of papers.

Concept Map

Fractions

- Part of a whole or a group
- Types
  - Unit: $\frac{1}{2}$
  - Proper: $\frac{5}{7}$
  - Improper: $\frac{4}{4}$ and $\frac{9}{8}$
  - Mixed: $5\frac{1}{2}$
- Equivalent fractions
  Formed by multiplying or dividing both numerator and denominator by same numbers
  $$\frac{1}{2} = \frac{2}{4} = \frac{4}{8} = \frac{8}{16}$$
- Conversions:
  - Improper to mixed: divide the numerator by the denominator
  - Mixed to improper: multiply the whole number with the denominator and add the product with the numerator; write the sum over the original denominator
- Comparison:
  - Unlike fractions: cross-multiply and compare the product; greater the product, greater will be the fraction
  - Mixed fraction: fraction with greater whole number is the greater fraction
  - Ordering: first convert to like fractions for easy comparison

Key Concepts

- **Fraction:** A number that expresses a part of a whole object or a set of objects
- **Simplest form of a fraction:** The fraction whose numerator and denominator have no other common factor except 1
- **Equivalent fractions:** Fractions that have the same value
- **Unit fractions:** Fractions that have 1 as their numerator
- **Proper fractions:** Fractions where the numerator is smaller than the denominator
- **Improper fractions:** Fractions where the numerator is greater than or equal to the denominator
- **Mixed fractions:** A mixed fraction is a combination of a whole number and a proper fraction

Chapter Revision

A. Choose the correct option.

1. The ascending order of these fractions $\frac{7}{4}, \frac{1}{4}, \frac{3}{4}, \frac{5}{4}$ is ________.

   a. $\frac{5}{4}, \frac{1}{4}, \frac{7}{4}, \frac{3}{4}$ b. $\frac{1}{4}, \frac{3}{4}, \frac{5}{4}, \frac{7}{4}$ c. $\frac{7}{4}, \frac{5}{4}, \frac{3}{4}, \frac{1}{4}$ d. $\frac{3}{4}, \frac{7}{4}, \frac{5}{4}, \frac{1}{4}$

2. The simplest form of $\frac{32}{24}$ is ________.

   a. $\frac{32}{24}$ b. $\frac{24}{32}$ c. $\frac{3}{4}$ d. $\frac{4}{3}$

3. $5\frac{1}{6} + 2\frac{3}{4} =$ ________

   a. $5\frac{1}{6}$ b. $2\frac{3}{4}$ c. $7\frac{11}{12}$ d. $12\frac{7}{11}$

4. $9\frac{2}{5} - 3\frac{4}{5} =$ ________

   a. $9\frac{2}{5}$ b. $3\frac{4}{5}$ c. $2\frac{3}{5}$ d. $5\frac{3}{5}$

5. $\frac{2}{7}$ of the boys of a Sports Club went to play tennis and $\frac{4}{7}$ of the boys went to play cricket. What fraction of the boys went to play tennis and cricket?

   a. $\frac{2}{7}$ b. $\frac{6}{7}$ c. $\frac{4}{7}$ d. $\frac{1}{7}$

B. Fill in the blanks.

1. A unit fraction always has __________ as its numerator.
2. In a proper fraction, the __________ is always smaller than the __________.
3. In an improper fraction, the __________ is always bigger than or equal to the __________.
4. A number which has no denominator has the denominator __________.

C. Solve the following questions.

1. Write P for proper fraction, I for improper fraction, M for mixed fraction and U for unit fraction.

   a. $\frac{1}{8}$ b. $2\frac{3}{5}$ c. $\frac{19}{7}$ d. $\frac{2}{11}$

2. Write the following fractions in their simplest form.

   a. $\frac{6}{8}$ b. $\frac{12}{32}$ c. $\frac{18}{30}$ d. $\frac{20}{25}$

3. Convert as directed.

   a. $\frac{32}{7}$ into a mixed fraction b. $13\frac{2}{9}$ into an improper fraction

4. Write the following fractions in ascending order.

   a. $\frac{8}{9}, \frac{1}{3}, \frac{5}{18}$ b. $\frac{2}{5}, \frac{7}{10}, \frac{9}{20}$

5. Write the following fractions in descending order.

   a. $\frac{1}{5}, \frac{13}{15}, \frac{7}{30}$ b. $\frac{1}{5}, \frac{3}{4}, \frac{7}{10}, \frac{19}{20}$

D. Solve the following word problems.

1. Out of 25 students of Class IV, 7 were absent on Monday. Find the fraction of students who were absent and the fraction of students who were present on Monday.

2. Suman bought $\frac{3}{4}$ kg of sweets. She gave away $\frac{1}{2}$ kg of sweets to her friends. How many kilogram of sweets is left with her?

3. Vineet's weight was $45\frac{1}{2}$ kg. He reduced his weight by $2\frac{3}{4}$ kg. What is his weight now?

4. $\frac{1}{5}$ of the Class IV students come to school by bus and $\frac{2}{5}$ of the Class IV students come to school by car. What fraction of the students come to school by bus and by car?

5. Out of $7\frac{3}{4}$ kg of potatoes, $1\frac{1}{2}$ kg were used for cooking. How many kilograms of potatoes were left?

SKILL UP!

A. 21 CS Communication, Information Literacy | EL | CC Integration with Computer Science

Conduct a survey in your classroom. Find out what your classmates want to be in the future. Represent your data in an Excel sheet. Express your findings in fractions.

I want to be a	Number of classmates	Fractions
Mathematician		
Scientist		
Artist		
Chef		
Teacher		
(Add any other choice)		

B. 21 CS Critical Thinking, Life Skills | EL | CC Integration with Science

15 LIFE ON LAND

What are the different components of air? Find the fraction of each component present in the air. Have these fractions remained the same over time? Has any action of mankind affected these fractions?

C. 21 CS Critical Thinking, Creativity and Innovation

How would you express your name in fractions?

(*Hint:* Write down your name and find out the number of vowels and consonants.)

SUSTAINABLE DEVELOPMENT GOALS

Question B is in line with SDG 15 Life on Land. How does pollution affect air quality? List five states in India which are the least polluted?

Worksheet 6

21 CS Critical Thinking, Information Literacy | CC Integration with Science

15 LIFE ON LAND

Sheeba was expecting to have 50 flowers bloom in her garden. It seems the number of flowers that completely bloomed did not reach 50. Help her find out how many flowers have bloomed.

1. Fraction of flowers that bloomed
2. Fraction of flowers that did not bloom
3. Fraction of white flowers
4. Fraction of red flowers
5. Fraction of yellow flowers

7 Decimals

LEARNING OBJECTIVES

- To read and write decimals
- To express decimals in the expanded form
- To convert fractions into decimals
- To convert decimals into fractions
- To find equivalent decimals of a given decimal
- To compare decimals
- To add and subtract decimals

LET'S GET STARTED

21 CS Critical Thinking EL

Have you ever been to a restaurant? How is the cost of an item usually given in the food menu card?

In this menu card, the cost of a samosa is

₹6.50

This number looks a little different from the numbers you have learnt so far.

Give any two examples where you have seen this type of numbers.

A

B

Menu Card

Starters

Samosa	₹6.50
Pakora	₹6.50
Onion Bhaji	₹6.50
Paneer Aloo Tikka	₹8.50
Paneer Pakora	₹10.50

Main Course

Dal Fry	₹212.00
Butter Chicken	₹412.50
Kashmiri Dum Aloo	₹212.50
Shahi Paneer	₹258.50
Malai Kofta	₹318.50
Mixed Veg	₹212.00
Matar Mushroom	₹210.00

This type of number is called a decimal number. Let us learn about this number.

DECIMALS

Decimal numbers are a shorthand way to write fractions and mixed numbers with denominators that are multiples of 10, such as 10, 100, 1000, 10,000, etc. A decimal number contains two parts—whole number part and decimal part, separated by a dot called the decimal point.

A decimal point (.) separates the whole number part from the decimal number part. For example, 1.5 is a decimal number. The value of this decimal number in fraction is $1\frac{5}{10}$ or $1\frac{1}{2}$.

whole number part

↑

1.5 → decimal part

↓

decimal point

Decimal Place Values

Decimal places are places of the digits after the decimal point. The places where the digits are written on the right of the decimal point have specific names and values.

Fractions with denominator 10 are termed as **tenths**.

Fractions with denominator 100 are termed as **hundredths**.

Fractions with denominator 1000 are termed as **thousandths**.

Thousands	Hundreds	Tens	Ones	Decimal point	Tenths	Hundredths	Thousandths
1000 × 1	100 × 1	10 × 1	1	.	$\frac{1}{10}$	$\frac{1}{100}$	$\frac{1}{1000}$
					0.1	0.01	0.001

The number shown above = 1000 + 100 + 10 + 1 + 0.1 + 0.01 + 0.001 = 1111.111

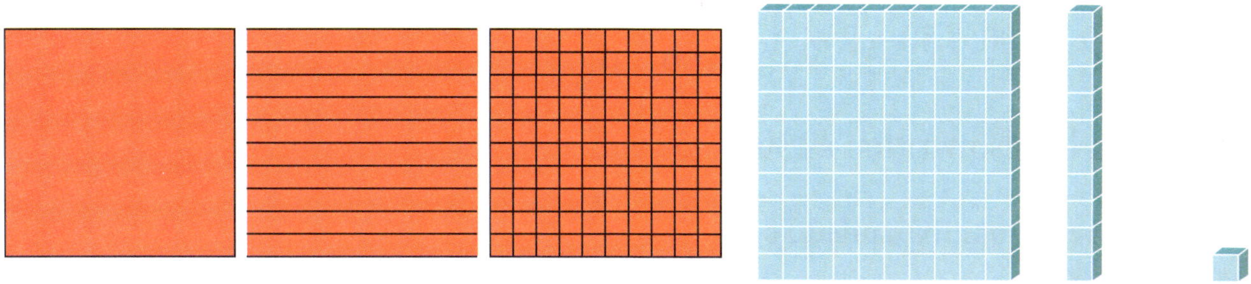

one tenths hundredths one tenths hundredths

Reading Decimal Numbers

There are two ways of reading number names of decimal numbers.

Method 1

Read the digits before the decimal point together as a number, but read the digits after the decimal point separately. The decimal itself is referred to as 'point'.

569.23 = Five hundred sixty-nine point two three

7218.410 = Seven thousand two hundred eighteen point four one zero

COMMON ERRORS

569.23

Read the digits after the decimal point as two three not twenty-three.

7218.410

Read the digits after the decimal point as four one zero not as four hundred ten.

Method 2

Decimals can also be read as their place value names.

Decimal number	Read as	Reason
1.9	One and nine tenths	9 falls in the tenth place
6.83	Six and eighty-three hundredths	83 together falls in the hundredth place
7136.428	Seven thousand one hundred thirty-six and four hundred twenty-eight thousandths	428 together falls in the thousandth place

Expanded Form

We know that the expanded form of 952 is 900 + 50 + 2.

Similarly, we can write the expanded form of a decimal number. The expanded form of

a. 741.826 is $700 + 40 + 1 + \frac{8}{10} + \frac{2}{100} + \frac{6}{1000}$

b. 352.1039 is $300 + 50 + 2 + \frac{1}{10} + \frac{0}{100} + \frac{3}{1000} + \frac{9}{10000}$

This can be also written as $300 + 50 + 2 + \frac{1}{10} + \frac{3}{1000} + \frac{9}{10000}$.

Writing Numbers from Expanded Forms

The expanded form of 185.693 is $100 + 80 + 5 + \frac{6}{10} + \frac{9}{100} + \frac{3}{1000}$.

If the expanded form is given, then we can write the decimal number as shown below.

$$100 + 80 + 5 + \frac{6}{10} + \frac{9}{100} + \frac{3}{1000} = 185.693$$

If the expanded form is $400 + 50 + 2 + \frac{7}{10} + \frac{8}{1000}$, then the decimal number is 452.708.

NOTE

We put 0 between 7 and 8 since there is no hundredth term in the expanded form.

EXERCISE 7A

1. **Write the place value of each digit in 7345.216.**
2. **Write the place value of digit 9 in each of the following decimal numbers.**

   a. 6289 b. 914.3 c. 254.91
   d. 593.24 e. 63.259
3. **Write the expanded form of each of the following decimal numbers.**

   a. 815 b. 937.2 c. 216.57 d. 953.481
4. **Write the decimal numbers from the following expanded forms.**

   a. $500 + 10 + 8 + \frac{3}{10}$ b. $400 + 70 + 1 + \frac{5}{10} + \frac{9}{100}$

   c. $600 + 80 + 2 + \frac{3}{10} + \frac{4}{100} + \frac{9}{1000}$
5. **Write the number name of each of the following decimal numbers.**

   a. 3.5 b. 2.47 c. 6.213 d. 29.5
   e. 51.83 f. 82.916 g. 176.9 h. 358.04

CONVERTING FRACTIONS INTO DECIMALS

Any number can be written in the decimal form by putting a decimal point at the extreme right of the number. Then by putting a zero, or any number of zeros, after the decimal point.

$$2 = 2.0 \text{ and } 5 = 5.0$$

Let us now see how fractions with denominators that are multiples of 10 such as 10, 100, 1000, etc. can be converted into decimals.

SOLVED EXAMPLES

Example 1: Convert the fraction $\frac{2}{10}$ into a decimal.

Solution: Here the numerator is 2 and, as explained above, we can write 2 in the decimal form as 2 = 2.0.

When we divide a number by 10, 100 or 1000, the decimal point moves to the left. It will move to the left as many times as there are zeros in the denominator. Therefore, in this case, the decimal point will move **once** to the left because the denominator 10 has only one zero.

$$\frac{2.}{10} = .2 \text{ or } 0.2$$

Example 2: Convert $\frac{3}{100}$ into a decimal.

Solution: The decimal point is after 3. When we divide a number by 100, the decimal point moves two places to the left because 100 has two zeros.

$\frac{3.}{100}$ Move the decimal point once to the left. It will come before 3. Again move the decimal point to the left one more time. As there is no number, we put a 0 there, preceded by the decimal point, that is, between 3 and the decimal point.

Thus, $\frac{3}{100} = .03$ or 0.03.

Example 3: Convert $\frac{15}{100}$ and $\frac{239}{1000}$ into a decimal.

Solution: $\frac{15.}{100} = .15$ or 0.15 $\quad \frac{239.}{1000} = .239$ or 0.239

Converting Mixed Fractions into Decimal Numbers

To convert a mixed fraction into a decimal, first separate the whole number from the fractional part and write it down on the side. Then, on its right, write the fractional part converted into a decimal.

Consider the mixed fraction $2\frac{3}{10}$. Here, the whole number is 2.

The fractional part = $\frac{3}{10}$

$\frac{3}{10}$ converted into a decimal = .3

Thus, $2\frac{3}{10} = 2.3$

SOLVED EXAMPLES

Example 4: Convert $3\frac{1}{10}$ into a decimal number.

Solution: $3\frac{1.}{10} = 3.1$

Example 5: Convert $2\frac{59}{10}$ into a decimal number.

Solution: $2\frac{59.}{10} = 2 + 5.9 = 7.9$

MENTAL MATHS

Convert the following into decimals.

1. $3\frac{1}{100}$
2. $3\frac{1}{1000}$

NOTE

1	×	100	=	100
2	×	50	=	100
4	×	25	=	100
5	×	20	=	100
10	×	10	=	100
20	×	5	=	100
25	×	4	=	100
50	×	2	=	100
100	×	1	=	100

Converting Fractions which do not have Multiples of 10 as Denominators into Decimals

If the denominators are not multiples of 10, then first try to convert the denominators into 10, 100, 1000, etc.

SOLVED EXAMPLES

Example 6: Convert $\frac{2}{5}$ into a decimal.

Solution:

The denominator 5 can be multiplied by 2 to make it 10. If we multiply the denominator by 2, then we must multiply the numerator also by 2.

$$\frac{2\times 2}{5\times 2} = \frac{4}{10}$$

Now, $\frac{4}{10}$, can be represented as 0.4 in decimal form. So, $\frac{2}{5} = 0.4$

Example 7: Convert $\frac{1}{2}$ into a decimal.

Solution:

2 can be multiplied by 5 to make 10. So, $\frac{1\times 5}{2\times 5} = \frac{5}{10} = 0.5$

Example 8: Convert $\frac{11}{20}$ into a decimal.

Solution:

The denominator 20 cannot be converted to 10 since 10 is smaller than 20. The number 20 can be converted to 100 by multiplying it by 5.

So, $\frac{11 \times 5}{20 \times 5} = \frac{55}{100} = 0.55$

EXERCISE 7B

1. **Convert the following into decimals.**

   a. $\frac{2}{100}$ b. $\frac{7}{10}$ c. $\frac{19}{1000}$ d. $\frac{5621}{10}$ e. $\frac{347}{100}$

2. **Convert the following mixed fractions into decimals.**

   a. $1\frac{2}{10}$ b. $5\frac{37}{100}$ c. $7\frac{159}{100}$ d. $2\frac{53}{100}$

   e. $12\frac{3}{1000}$ f. $19\frac{24}{1000}$ g. $3\frac{147}{1000}$ h. $8\frac{43}{10}$

3. **Convert the following into decimals.**

   a. $\frac{2}{5}$ b. $\frac{1}{2}$ c. $\frac{3}{4}$ d. $\frac{7}{50}$

   e. $\frac{1}{4}$ f. $\frac{3}{5}$ g. $\frac{6}{10}$ h. $\frac{9}{20}$

   i. $\frac{8}{20}$ j. $\frac{19}{25}$ k. $\frac{13}{50}$ l. $\frac{7}{4}$

CONVERTING DECIMAL NUMBERS INTO FRACTIONS

Follow the steps given below to convert a decimal number into a fraction.

Step 1: Write down the decimal number.

Step 2: Count the number of digits after the decimal point. In the denominator, write 1 with as many zeros as there are digits after the decimal point. Then, rewrite the number without the decimal point as the numerator.

Step 3: A fraction is usually written in its lowest form. So, reduce the resulting fraction in its lowest form.

GO EASY!

If the number of digits after the decimal point is two, then divide by 100.

If the number of digits after the decimal point is three, then divide by 1000.

SOLVED EXAMPLES

Example 9: Convert 0.7 into a fraction.

Solution:

In 0.7, there is one digit after the decimal point. Therefore, in the denominator, write 1 with **one** zero, that is, 10.

$$0.7 = \frac{7}{10}$$

Example 10: Convert 0.75 into a fraction in its lowest term.

Solution:

In 0.75, there are 2 digits after the decimal point. Therefore, in the denominator, write 1 with **two** zeros, that is, 100.

$$0.75 = \frac{\cancel{75}^{\cancel{15}^{3}}}{\cancel{100}_{\cancel{20}_{4}}} = \frac{3}{4}$$

Example 11: Convert 0.002 into a fraction.

Solution:

In 0.002, there are 3 digits after the decimal point. Therefore, in the denominator, write 1 with **three** zeros, that is, 1000.

$$0.002 = \frac{\cancel{2}^{1}}{\cancel{1000}_{500}} = \frac{1}{500}$$

Converting Decimals into Mixed Fractions

If the whole number part of the decimal number is other than 0, then write the whole number part as it is and convert the decimal number part into fraction.

SOLVED EXAMPLES

Example 12: Convert 5.1 into a fraction.

Solution: After the decimal point, there is one digit. Therefore, the denominator will be 1 with one 0, which is, 10.

$$5.1 = 5\frac{1}{10}$$

Example 13: Convert 6.14 into a fraction.

Solution: In this case, after the decimal point, there are 2 digits. Therefore, the denominator will be 1 with two zeros, which is, 100.

$$6.14 = 6\frac{14}{100}$$

Example 14: Convert 4.812 into a fraction.

Solution: The denominator here will be 1000.

$$4.812 = 4\frac{812}{1000}$$

MENTAL MATHS

Convert the following decimals into fractions.

1. 0.7 = ____________ 2. 2.8 = ____________

3. 0.321 = ____________ 4. 1.83 = ____________

EXERCISE 7C

1. Convert the following decimal numbers into fractions in their lowest terms.

a. 0.2 b. 0.7 c. 0.29 d. 0.31

e. 0.52 f. 0.894 g. 0.625 h. 0.001

2. Convert the following decimal numbers into fractions in their lowest terms.

a. 2.4 b. 5.8 c. 17.4 d. 3.1

e. 6.32 f. 9.56 g. 12.08 h. 15.64

i. 9.412 j. 11.503 k. 8.592 l. 1.204

EQUIVALENT DECIMALS

Equivalent decimals are the decimal numbers which have the same value.

0.2 is a decimal number where the place value of 2 is tenth.

To represent 0.2 as hundredths, we need to add zeros till the hundredth position. So, 0.2 as hundredth is 0.20.

DO YOU KNOW?

Adding zeros after the decimal point does not change the value of the number.

To represent 0.2 as thousandths, we need to add zeros till the thousandth position. So, 0.2 as thousandth is 0.200.

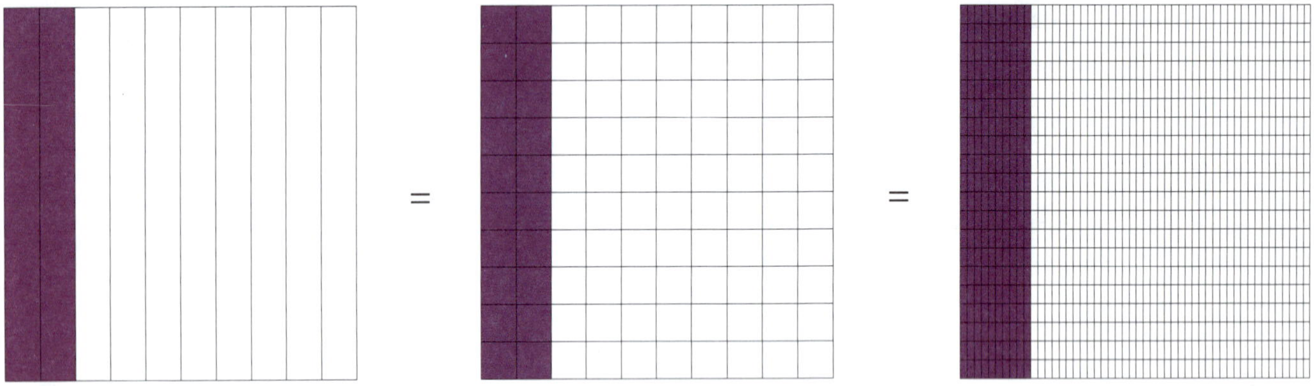

Here, 0.2, 0.20 and 0.200 are equivalent decimals.

$\frac{2}{10}$ $\frac{20}{100}$ $\frac{200}{1000}$

LIKE DECIMALS AND UNLIKE DECIMALS

Like decimals are decimal numbers that have the same number of decimal places.

Unlike decimals are decimal numbers that have different numbers of decimal places.

Like decimals	**Example:** 14.9 7.3 586.2	**Example:** 53.69 1.28 574.36	**Example:** 1.285 93.474 65.917
Number of decimal places	One	Two	Three

Unlike decimals with unequal number of decimal places	**Example:** 24.5 6.791 25.3846

Converting Unlike Decimals into Like Decimals

To convert unlike decimals into like decimals, check which decimal number has the greatest number of decimal places. Then make the decimal places of the other numbers same by adding zeros.

SOLVED EXAMPLES

Example 15: Convert 1.9, 2.753 and 827.24 into like decimals.

Solution: We find that the second number has the greatest number of decimal places, that is, 3. So, we complete the other two numbers too to three decimal places by adding zeros. We get 1.900, 2.753 and 827.240. These are like decimals.

Comparison of Decimals

To check which decimal number is greater, first check the whole number part of the decimals. Decimal with greater whole number part is greater. If the whole number part is the same, check the digits after the decimal point (start from the digit at the tenths place). The number that has the bigger digit is the bigger number. If the digit at the tenths place is also the same in both the numbers, then compare the digit at hundredths place. This process will continue till we find the greater digit in a number.

In a decimal number, zeros at the end have no value. We can remove them.

In 2.780000, we can remove the last four zeros. Therefore, 2.780000 = 2.78

SOLVED EXAMPLES

Example 16: Which of the following numbers is greater: 538.642 or 472.999?

Solution:

538 is greater than 472.
Therefore, 538.642 > 472.999

Example 17: Which of the following numbers is greater?

187.295 or 187.501

Solution:

Before the decimal point, both the numbers are the same, that is, 187. After the decimal point, the tenth digit of the first number is 2 while it is 5 in the second number. So, the second number is greater than the first one.

$$187.\underline{2}95 < 187.\underline{5}01$$

Example 18: Write the following numbers in ascending order.

1.35, 1.451, 1.456, 2.65, 1.055

Solution:

To arrange the numbers in ascending order, we need to arrange the numbers from the smallest to the greatest.

As the decimal numbers are unlike decimals, first convert them to like decimals by adding zeros at the right as required.

So, converting them to like decimals, the numbers become 1.350, 1.451, 1.456, 2.650 and 1.055. Now it becomes easier for us to arrange them in ascending order.

$1.055 < 1.350 < 1.451 < 1.456 < 2.650$

The given numbers arranged in ascending order are 1.055, 1.35, 1.451, 1.456, 2.65.

Example 19: Write the following numbers in descending order.

3.45, 2.45, 3.456, 4.65, 3.455

Solution:

To arrange the numbers in descending order, we need to arrange the numbers from the greatest to the smallest.

In this case also, first convert the numbers to like decimals and then arrange.

4.650 > 3.456 > 3.455 > 3.450 > 2.450

The given numbers arranged in descending order are 4.65, 3.456, 3.455, 3.45, 2.45.

Exercise 7D

1. **Which of the following groups of numbers are like decimals?**

   a. 15.32, 9.64, 278.13 b. 26.7, 5.892, 153.47 c. 5.682, 4.197, 1249.735

2. **Convert the following unlike decimals into like decimals.**

   a. 5.78; 25.193; 14.6 b. 29.3; 4.78; 63.152

3. **Write >, < or =.**

   a. 53.8 ☐ 294.6 b. 716.8 ☐ 9.1342 c. 68.9 ☐ 68.9

4. **Write the following decimals in ascending order.**

   a. 82.17 82.9 82.003 82.478 82.560

   b. 569.814 569.299 569.1432 569.6849

5. **Write the following decimals in descending order.**

   a. 468.3 25.7 9182.1 7.9999

   b. 273.006 273.4007 273.8 273.25

ADDING OR SUBTRACTING DECIMAL NUMBERS

Follow the steps given below to add or subtract decimal numbers.

Step 1: Write the decimal numbers one below the other in such a way that the decimal points are in a vertical line, that is, exactly one below the other.

$$\begin{array}{r} 1.43 \\ +\ 3.21 \\ \hline \\ \hline \end{array} \qquad \begin{array}{r} 9.3 \\ -\ 2.1 \\ \hline \\ \hline \end{array}$$

Step 2: Write the decimal point in the answer right below the other decimal points.

$$\begin{array}{r} 1.43 \\ +\ 3.21 \\ \hline . \\ \hline \end{array} \qquad \begin{array}{r} 9.3 \\ -\ 2.1 \\ \hline . \\ \hline \end{array}$$

Step 3: Add or subtract as you usually do.

$$\begin{array}{r} 1.43 \\ +\ 3.21 \\ \hline 4.64 \\ \hline \end{array} \qquad \begin{array}{r} 9.3 \\ -\ 2.1 \\ \hline 7.2 \\ \hline \end{array}$$

MENTAL MATHS

1. 6.07 + 3 = ______
2. 3.5 + 9.41 = ______
3. 12.44 + 6 = ______

SOLVED EXAMPLES

Example 20: Add 234.76, 12.093, 142 and 1.3.

Solution:

Step 1: Arrange the decimals as shown below.

$$\begin{array}{r} 234.76 \\ 12.093 \\ 142 \\ +\ \ \ 1.3 \\ \hline \\ \hline \end{array}$$

Step 2: Add zeros to the right to convert them into like decimals.

$$\begin{array}{r} 234.760 \\ 12.093 \\ 142.000 \\ +\ \ \ 1.300 \\ \hline \\ \hline \end{array}$$

Step 3: Add the decimal numbers as usual.

$$\begin{array}{r} 234.760 \\ 12.093 \\ 142.000 \\ +\ \ \ 1.300 \\ \hline 390.153 \\ \hline \end{array}$$

NOTE

If there is no decimal point in a number, then the decimal point is put at the end of the number on the right. The decimal point should appear one below the other in a vertical line.

Example 21: Subtract 4.13 from 49.9.

Solution:

Arrange the decimals as shown. Write zeros at the end and make like decimals.

$$\begin{array}{r} 8\ 10 \\ 4\ 9\ .\ \not{9}\ \ \not{0} \\ -\ \ \ \ 4\ .\ 1\ \ 3 \\ \hline 4\ 5\ .\ 7\ \ 7 \\ \hline \end{array}$$

Example 22: The height of a shelf is 5.3 m and the height of a chest of drawers is 3.7 m. By how much is the shelf taller than the chest of drawers?

Solution:

	4 13
Height of the shelf	~~5~~ . ~~3~~ m
Height of the chest of drawers	− 3 . 7 m
	1 . 6 m

The shelf is 1.6 m taller than the chest of drawers.

Example 23: I bought 2.560 kg of apples, 3.750 kg of oranges and 5.450 kg of bananas. How much would all the fruits weigh?

Solution:

	1 1
Mass of apples	2 . 5 6 0 kg
Mass of oranges	3 . 7 5 0 kg
Mass of bananas	+ 5 . 4 5 0 kg
	11 . 7 6 0 kg

The fruits would weigh 11.760 kg.

MENTAL MATHS

Fill in the boxes with >, < or =.

1. 1.700 ☐ 1.70
2. 6.78 ☐ 7.68
3. 78.902 ☐ 78.908
4. 345.891 ☐ 345.819

EXERCISE 7E

1. **Arrange the following in columns and add.**

   a. 35.6 + 12.5 + 72.8
   b. 183.47 + 295.18 + 300.76
   c. 3549.6 + 862.5 + 47.8
   d. 621.95 + 2586.74 + 5000.39
   e. 2964.87 + 573.02 + 8.1
   f. 7.5 + 249.03 + 56.001

2. **Arrange the following in columns and subtract.**

   a. 578.9 – 132.6
   b. 3541.6 – 873.9
   c. 840 – 359.7
   d. 1923 – 87.6
   e. 6293.725 – 1728.64
   f. 8000 – 259.736

3. **Solve the following word problems.**

   a. Suman weighs 35.7 kg. Renu weighs 29.8 kg. How much would both of them weigh?
   b. Bag A contains 4.2 kg of potatoes and 3.5 kg of onions. Bag B contains 3.6 kg of potatoes and 6.3 kg of onions. How much would both the bags weigh? Which bag would weigh more and by how much?
   c. I had ₹5750.75 in the bank. If I saved ₹985.25 more, how much money would I have in the bank?

MATHS LAB ACTIVITY

21 CS Critical Thinking, Collaboration | AI | HQ Happiness My Goal

Aim: To compare decimals through a decimal card game

Materials required: Chart papers, colour pencils

Procedure:

1. Cut the chart papers into small equal-sized pieces (4 cm × 3 cm each).
2. Create decimal cards with decimal numbers from 1 to 20. You can just write random decimal numbers.
3. You can even draw funny faces or cartoons on the cards as shown.
4. After all your cards are ready, shuffle the cards.
5. Divide the cards evenly between 2 students. (You will need to make more cards for more students.)
6. Place the cards face down in front of each student.
7. Then, open the first card. The student with the greater decimal number scores 1 point.
8. Continue playing till all the cards are picked.
9. The student with the maximum score wins the game.

Concept Map

Decimals

Place value

Thousands	Hundreds	Tens	Ones	Decimal point	Tenths	Hundredths	Thousandths
1000 × 1	100 × 1	10 × 1	1	.	$\frac{1}{10}$	$\frac{1}{100}$	$\frac{1}{1000}$
					0.1	0.01	0.001

Reading decimals

Methods	Decimal number	Read as
Method 1	569.23	Five hundred sixty-nine point two three
Method 2	1.9	One and nine tenths
	6.83	Six and eighty-three hundredths

Converting fractions into decimals

$\frac{2}{5} = \frac{4}{10} = 0.4$

Converting decimals into fractions

$0.004 = \frac{4}{1000} = \frac{1}{250}$

Like decimals:
24.5000 6.7910 25.3846

Unlike decimals:
24.5 6.791 25.3846

Comparing decimals: Check the whole number part. The one with the greater whole number part is greater.

Add or subtract decimals:
1. Write the decimals one over the other such that the decimal points of all decimals should come in a vertical line.
2. Write the decimal point in the answer right below the other decimal points.
3. Add or subtract as you usually do.

Key Concepts

- **Decimal:** A fraction that is written in the form of a dot followed by one or more digits
- **Decimal point:** The point (.) that separates the whole number part from the decimal number part
- **Tenths:** Fractions with denominator 10
- **Hundredths:** Fractions with denominator 100
- **Thousandths:** Fractions with denominator 1000
- **Equivalent decimals:** Decimal numbers that have the same value
- **Like decimals:** Decimal numbers that have the same number of decimal places
- **Unlike decimals:** Decimal numbers that have different numbers of decimal places

Chapter Revision

A. Choose the correct option.

1. $\frac{5869}{100}$ as a decimal is ________.

   a. 5.869 b. 58.69 c. 586.9 d. 0.5869

2. $12\frac{7}{1000}$ as a decimal is ________.

   a. 12.07 b. 12.70 c. 12.007 d. 12.700

3. 1.75 as a fraction in its lowest term is ________.

   a. $\frac{175}{10}$ b. $\frac{7}{4}$ c. $\frac{4}{7}$ d. $\frac{100}{175}$

4. 249.65 can be read as ________.

   a. Two hundred forty-nine and sixty-five

   b. Two hundred forty-nine and sixty-five hundredths

   c. Two hundred forty-nine and sixty-five hundreds

   d. Two hundred forty-nine and sixty-five thousands

5. 3.9 + 700 + 42.64 is equal to ________.

   a. 374.64 b. 742.64 c. 342.64 d. 746.54

6. Out of 7.95 m of cloth, the tailor uses 2.35 m. How much cloth will be left?

   a. 2.35 m b. 7.95 m c. 5.60 m d. 5.60 cm

B. Convert the following fractions into decimals.

1. $9\frac{7}{10}$ 2. $\frac{2}{10}$ 3. $15\frac{13}{100}$ 4. $36\frac{478}{1000}$ 5. $79\frac{27}{1000}$

C. Convert the following decimals into fractions in their lowest term.

1. 0.4 2. 0.62 3. 0.31 4. 2.6

D. Answer the following questions.

1. What is the numeral for the following?

   a. Two hundred ninety-five and seven tenths

   b. Five hundred twenty-eight point three nine four

2. Write in words the value of digit 7 in each decimal number.

   a. 12.78 b. 12.87 c. 12.807

3. Write the following decimal numbers in descending order.

   7.9 4.382 5.8 1.9999 8.003

4. Add the following.

   5.9 700 163.48 65.3

5. Ashok has ₹527.29 and Sunita has ₹796.13. Who has more money and by how much?

6. Anjali bought a pen for ₹12.75 and a notebook for ₹4.50. She gave the shopkeeper ₹20. How much money did the shopkeeper give back to her?

7. I walked around a rectangular field with length 39.5 m and breadth 25.75 m. How much distance did I cover when I went around the field once and then two times?

SKILL UP!

A. 21 CS Critical Thinking, Information Literacy AI

Use colour pencils to make a place value chart in your notebook or a chart paper. Look for any five numbers in a newspaper or a magazine. Then create a chart for each number as shown here.

Decimal Place Value

Hundreds	Tens	Ones	Tenths	Hundredths	Thousandths
4	5	2	4	5	

Ways to Write a Decimal:

Standard Form: 452.45

Word Form: Four hundred fifty-two and forty-five hundredths

Expanded Form: $4 \times 100 + 5 \times 10 + 2 \times 1 + 4 \times 0.1 + 5 \times 0.01$

B. 21 CS Critical Thinking, Life Skills HQ Knowing My Needs

Sheeba and Rageshree get the same monthly allowance from their parents. Sheeba has used $\frac{5}{8}$ of her allowance. Rageshree has used 0.425 of her allowance. Who has used more of the monthly allowance? Should we try to save from what we receive? Give reason for your answer.

C. 21 CS Critical Thinking

Sunita moves 10.2 m straight. Then, she moves 11.5 m straight back.
What is the distance between her original position and where she is standing now?

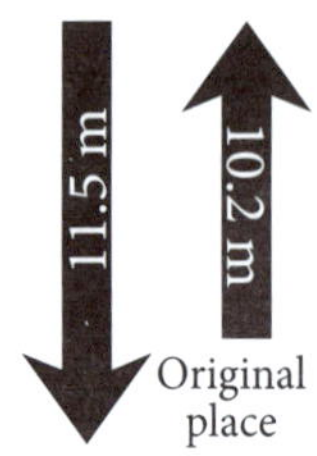

SUSTAINABLE DEVELOPMENT GOALS

Question B is in line with SDG 12 Responsible Consumption and Production. Do you save money from your pocket? What are the three reasons for saving money?

Worksheet 7

21 CS Critical Thinking, Information Literacy | HQ Happiness My Goal

The last race of the sports event is almost over. The scores for all the other sports events are also in. The scoreboard looks a little different from the usual one.

Find the students who will be in the top three. Who is the all rounder?

First ______

Second ______

Third ______

All rounder ______

Scoreboard

Student/ Sports	Sack race	100 m race	Long jump	Shot put throw
Josh	9.8		8.8	7.9
Karim	7.8		6.8	6.6
Suhana	8.8		8	8.6
Kriti	9.9		9	5.5
Mansi	8.6	5.6	7	6.4
Aditya	6.4	3.4	6.9	8.6
Rahul	7.0	2.4	4.5	6.9

8 Measurement

Learning Objectives

- To understand and use different units of length, mass and capacity
- To write measurements using decimals
- To solve word problems on length, mass and capacity
- To estimate measures

Let's Get Started

21 CS Critical Thinking, Information Literacy | CC Integration with Science

The students of Class IV are doing some experiments in the Science lab while measuring various objects. Which statements do you think are correct? Give reasons for your answer.

MEASUREMENT OF LENGTH

Various units for the measurement of length are kilometre, hectometre, decametre, metre, decimetre, centimetre and millimetre. The basic unit for measuring length is **metre**. A few examples from real life where measurement of length occurs are:

- The distance (the measurement of length between two points or locations) between any two cities is measured in kilometres.
- The length of a pencil is approximately 16 centimetres.

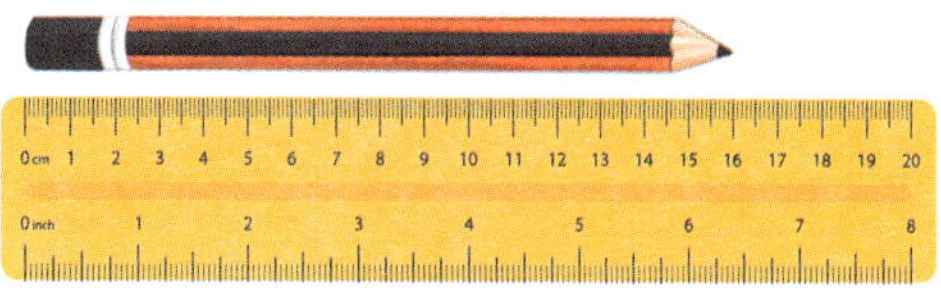

Conversion of Units of Length

Centimetre and millimetre are smaller units of measurements. These units are commonly used for measuring smaller lengths. Bigger units can be converted to smaller and smaller units can be converted to bigger units as shown below.

To convert a bigger unit to a smaller unit: multiply the bigger unit by 10 or multiples of 10

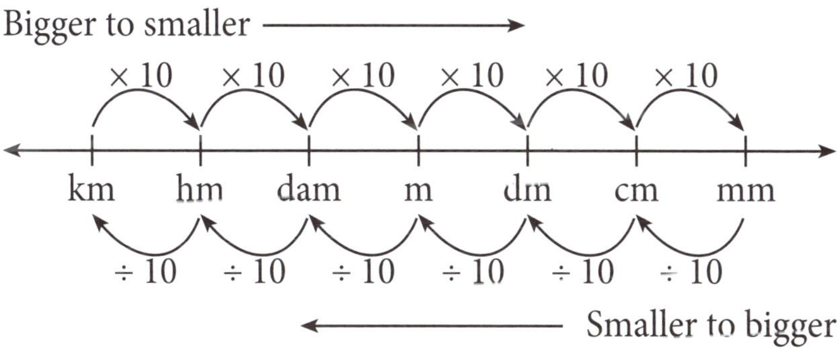

Multiples	**kilo**metre	km
	hectometre	hm
	decametre	dam
	metre	m
Submultiples	**deci**metre	dm
	centimetre	cm
	millimetre	mm

To convert a smaller unit to a bigger unit: divide the smaller unit by 10 or multiples of 10

SOLVED EXAMPLES

Example 1: Convert 2 dam to dm.

Solution: In the chart given above, between dam and dm, there are two multiplications by 10 (dam to m and m to dm). So, we multiply with $10 \times 10 = 100$.

Therefore, 2 dam = $2 \times 100 = 200$ dm.

Example 2: Find $\frac{1}{4}$ of 9 m in cm.

Solution: 1 m = 10 × 10 cm = 100 cm

$$\frac{1}{4} \times 9 \text{ m} = \frac{1}{\cancel{4}_{\cancel{2}_1}} \times 9 \times \cancel{100}^{\cancel{50}^{25}} = 225 \text{ cm}$$

Therefore, $\frac{1}{4}$ of 9 m = 225 cm.

Example 3: 8 km 2 hm 5 dam 9 m = _____ m

Solution: 8 km = 8 × 1000 = 8000 m

2 hm = 2 × 100 = 200 m

5 dam = 5 × 10 = 50 m

9 m = 9 × 1 = 9 m

Therefore, 8 km 2 hm 5 dam 9 m = 8000 m + 200 m + 50 m + 9 m = 8259 m.

Go Easy!

1 km = 1000 m

$\frac{1}{2}$ km = 500 m

$\frac{1}{4}$ km = 250 m

$\frac{3}{4}$ km = 750 m

Exercise 8A

1. Fill in the blanks with the correct unit.

a. The length of my eraser is about 2 ____________________.

b. The height of a table is approximately 1 ____________________.

2. Solve the following.

a. 4 km = ___ m

b. $\frac{1}{2}$ of 6 m = ___ cm

c. $\frac{3}{4}$ of 16 dm = ___ mm

d. 5 km 23 m = ___ m

e. 7 m 25 cm = ___ cm

f. 3 m 4 cm = ___ cm

g. 7 km 3 dam 2 m = ___ m

h. 5629 m = ___ km ___ m

MEASUREMENT OF MASS AND WEIGHT

The **mass** of an object is the amount of matter that the object has. The **weight** of an object is the measure of the heaviness of the object.

Kilogram, hectogram, decagram, gram, decigram, centigram and milligram are various units for the measurement of mass and weight of objects. The basic unit for measuring mass is **gram**.

	Unit	Symbol
Multiples	**kilo**gram	kg
	hectogram	hg
	decagram	dag
→	gram	g
Submultiples	**deci**gram	dg
	centigram	cg
	milligram	mg

A few real-life examples where measurement of mass and weight occurs are:

- the spices used in the kitchen are usually measured in milligrams or grams
- fruit and vegetables are normally measured in grams or kilograms
- a teaspoon of salt is around 5 g
- a tablespoon of salt is around 15 g
- the weight of a Class IV boy would be around 30 kg

Conversion of Units of Mass

To convert a bigger unit to a smaller unit, multiply by 10 or multiples of 10.

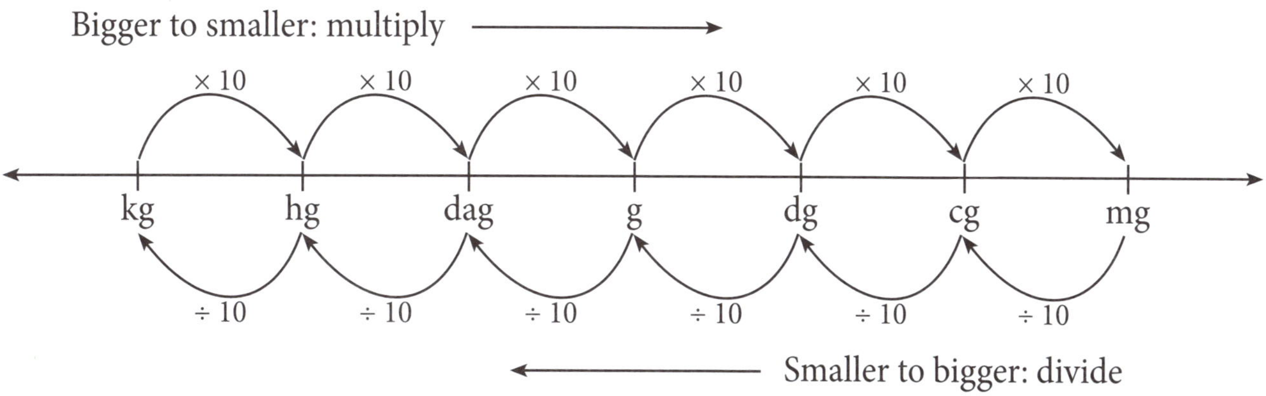

To convert a smaller unit to a bigger unit, divide by 10 or multiples of 10.

SOLVED EXAMPLES

Example 4: Convert 5 kg to g.

Solution: To convert a bigger unit to a smaller unit, we multiply. In the chart given above, between kg and g, there are three multiplications by 10 (kg to hg, hg to dag and dag to g). So, we multiply with $10 \times 10 \times 10 = 1000$.

So, 1 kg = 1000 g

Therefore, $5 \text{ kg} = 5 \times 1000 = 5000$ g.

Example 5: Find $\frac{2}{5}$ of 6 kg in g.

Solution: $\frac{2}{5}$ of 6×1000 (To convert kg to g, multiply by 1000.)

$$= \frac{2}{\cancel{5}} \times 6 \times \overset{200}{\cancel{1000}} = 2400 \text{ g}$$

Therefore, $\frac{2}{5}$ of 6 kg = 2400 g.

Example 6: Solve 25 g 7 cg = ______ cg

Solution: 25 g = 25 × 100 = 2500 cg (To convert g to cg, multiply by 100.)

Now, 2500 cg + 7 cg = 2507 cg

So, 25 g 7cg = 2507 cg.

COMMON ERRORS

25 g 7 cg = 2507 cg ✓

25 g 7 cg = 257 cg ✗

EXERCISE 8B

1. Fill in the blanks.

a. I bought 3 ____ apples from the market.

b. 7 kg = ____ g

c. 3 kg 275 g = ____ g

d. $\frac{1}{3}$ of 4 kg = ____ g

e. $\frac{1}{5}$ of 9 kg = ____ g

f. 5 kg 2 hg 1 dag 3 g = ____ g

g. 8 kg 9 hg 3 g = ____ g

h. 2350 g = ____ kg ____ g

i. 2359 g = ____ kg ____ g

MEASUREMENT OF CAPACITY

Kilolitre, hectolitre, decalitre, litre, decilitre, centilitre and millilitre are various units of measuring capacity. The basic unit for measuring capacity is **litre**.

	Unit	Symbol
Multiples	**kilo**litre	kℓ
	hectolitre	hℓ
	decalitre	daℓ
→	litre	ℓ
Submultiples	**deci**litre	dℓ
	centilitre	cℓ
	millilitre	mℓ

A few real-life examples where measurement of capacity occurs are:

- A bottle contains around 1 ℓ of water.
- A glass contains approximately 200 mℓ of water.
- A bucket contains 15 ℓ of water.
- Measuring spoons are used to measure ingredients while baking of cookies and cakes.

Conversion of Units of Capacity

Follow the chart given below to convert the units of measurement of capacity.

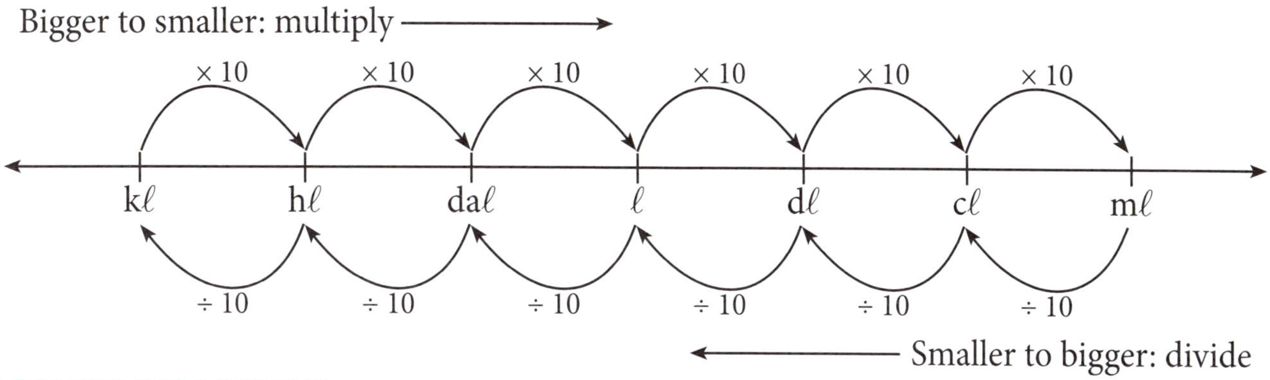

SOLVED EXAMPLES

Example 7: Convert 4 ℓ to mℓ.

Solution: Based on the chart for the units of capacity, to move from ℓ to mℓ, we need to multiply by 10 three times. So, we multiply with $10 \times 10 \times 10 = 1000$.

1 ℓ = 1000 mℓ

4 ℓ = 4×1000 = 4000 mℓ

EXERCISE 8C

1. Fill in the blanks.

a. This jar contains about __________ of milk.

b. A glass contains approximately __________ mℓ of water.

c. 9 kℓ = __________ ℓ

d. 6700 ℓ = __________ kℓ __________ ℓ

e. $\frac{1}{5}$ of 4 kℓ = __________ ℓ

f. 6701 ℓ = __________ kℓ __________ ℓ

g. $\frac{1}{4}$ of 5 hℓ = __________ mℓ

h. 9 kℓ 2 hℓ 3 ℓ = __________ ℓ

UNDERSTANDING MEASURES IN DECIMALS

Consider a case where 38.579 kg is to be expressed in kg, hg, dag and g.

- The number before the decimal, that is, 38 will be kg.
- The first digit after the decimal, that is, 5 will be hectogram.
- The next digit 7 will be decagram and the digit 9 will be gram.

Therefore, 38.579 kg = 38 kg 5 hg 7 dag 9 g.

NOTE

The units should be in the same order as in the charts.

Mental Maths

1. Express 98 km 4 m in km.

____

2. Express 30 g 9 dg 5 mg in grams.

____

Do you know?

In ancient times, people used body parts as units of measurement. The length of a foot, the width of a finger and the distance of a step were some of the units of measurement.

SOLVED EXAMPLES

Example 8: Express 739.209 km in km, hm, dam and m.

Solution: 739.209 km = 739 km 2 hm 0 dam 9 m

Example 9: Express 231.587 ℓ in ℓ, dℓ, cℓ and mℓ.

Solution: 231.587 ℓ = 231 ℓ 5 dℓ 8 cℓ 7 mℓ

Example 10: Express 162 g 9 dg 6 cg 1 mg in grams.

Solution: Following the same pattern used above, but in the reverse order, we get

162 g 9 dg 6 cg 1 mg = 162.961 g

Example 11: Express 162 ℓ 9 dℓ 1 mℓ in litres.

Solution: 162 ℓ 9 dℓ 1 mℓ = 162.901 ℓ

Example 12: Express 13 km 8 hm 5 dam 3 m in km.

Solution: 13 km 8 hm 5 dam 3 m = 13.853 km

Example 13: Express 52 g 7 mg in g.

Solution: 52 g 7 mg = 52.007 g

Exercise 8D

1. **Express the following in hg, dag and g.**
   a. 25.726 kg   b. 9.31 kg   c. 482.305 kg
2. **Express the following in hm, dam and m.**
   a. 35.763 km   b. 296.14 km   c. 5.009 km
3. **Express the following in hℓ, daℓ and ℓ.**
   a. 19.68 kℓ   b. 5.247 kℓ   c. 625.803 kℓ

4. **Fill in the blanks.**

a. 26 g 5 dg 7 cg 1 mg = ________ g

b. 35 ℓ 8 dℓ 2 cℓ 1 mℓ = ________ ℓ

c. 82 km 7 hm 3 dam 2 m = ________ km

d. 6 kg 9 hg 4 dag 1 g = ________ kg

e. 249.361 ℓ = ________ ℓ ________ dℓ ________ cℓ ________ mℓ

WORD PROBLEMS ON MEASUREMENTS

Let us now look at some examples from real life where measurements take place.

SOLVED EXAMPLES

Example 14: Vibhav bought 3 kg 250 g of apples, 2 kg of mangoes, 350 g of grapes and 30 g of mint leaves. What is the total mass of all the items that Vibhav bought?

Solution:

		kg
		1
Apples	=	3.250
Mangoes	=	2.000
Grapes	=	0.350
Mint leaves	=	0.030
		5.630

2 kg will be written like this

30 g will be written like this

The total mass of all the items is 5 kg 630 g.

Example 15: Ram travelled 15 km 270 m by car, 12 km by cycle and 825 m by foot. What was the total distance travelled by Ram?

Solution:

	km	m
	1	
	15	270
	12	000
+	00	825
	28	**095**

825 m will be written like this.

12 km will be written like this.

The total distance travelled by Ram is 28 km 95 m.

Example 16: Out of 5 ℓ 270 mℓ of water in a bucket, Seema used 1 ℓ 8 mℓ of water. How much water was left in the bucket?

Solution:

	ℓ	mℓ
		6 10
	5	2 ~~7~~ ~~0~~
−	1	0 0 8
	4	**2 6 2**

8 mℓ will be written like this.

4 ℓ 262 mℓ of water was left in the bucket.

EXERCISE 8E

Solve the following word problems.

1. The weights of Ajay, Vijay and Sumit are 46 kg 375 g, 51 kg 7 g and 49 kg 25 g, respectively.
   a. Who is the heaviest among these three boys?
   b. Who is the lightest among these three boys?
   c. What is the total weight of these three boys?
2. Bharat bought 10 kg 200 g of mangoes. Later he bought 5 kg 150 g of more mangoes. What is the total mass of mangoes that he bought?
3. A tank had 35 ℓ 750 mℓ of water. The gardener used up 7 ℓ 200 mℓ of water. How much water is left in the tank?
4. Out of a distance of 49 km 105 m, Krishna covered 11 km 795 m. How much distance is left to be covered?
5. Farha bought 5 m 75 cm of a red cloth and 18 m 6 cm of a blue cloth. What is the total length of the clothes that she bought?
6. Meher's weight is 49.750 kg and Zehra's weight is 32.520 kg. Whose weight is more and by how much?
7. The capacity of two buckets of water is 15 ℓ 275 mℓ. If the capacity of one bucket is 10 ℓ 195 mℓ, what is the capacity of the second bucket?
8. The distance from Mumbai to Lonavla is 82 km 725 m. The distance from Lonavla to Pune is 68 km 980 m. What is the total distance from Mumbai to Pune?
9. The mass of an empty box is 3 kg. If it is filled with toys, the mass becomes 12 kg 509 g. What is the mass of the toys?
10. Samira bought 3 ℓ 745 mℓ of orange juice, 4 ℓ 70 mℓ of guava juice and 5 ℓ 8 mℓ of pineapple juice. What is the total amount of juice that she bought?

ESTIMATION OF MEASUREMENTS

Instead of exact measurements, we sometimes estimate the length of objects, distance between different locations, weight or capacity. In such situations, the skill and knowledge of precise measurement can help in developing a good estimate. Also, comparing what you are trying to measure with a known measurement of a similar object, distance, weight or capacity would help in giving a close estimate. While estimating, decide which unit of measurement would be best suited for certain measurement.

Let us try to estimate the lengths, weights and capacities of certain objects and verify the actual measurement.

Estimation and verification of length			
Object	**Estimated length**	**Actual length**	**Variation**
1. Desk			
2. Door			
3. Window			
4. Maths book	20 cm	20 cm	Exact

Estimation and verification of distance			
Locations	**Estimated distance**	**Actual distance**	**Variation**
1. Your home and school			
2. Your classroom and the Principal's office			
3. Your class and the school canteen			
4. Your home and any nearby park			

Estimation and verification of weight			
Object	**Estimated weight**	**Actual weight**	**Variation**
1. Your school bag			
2. Your tiffin box			
3. Your water bottle	450 g	500 g	50 g less
4. Maths book			

Estimation and verification of capacity			
Object	**Estimated capacity**	**Actual capacity**	**Variation**
1. Your school bag			
2. Your tiffin box			
3. Your water bottle			
4. A water tank in your school campus			

Maths Lab Activity

21 CS Life Skills EL

Aim: To measure the length of any cuboidal shape using a thread

Materials required: A long thread (preferably white), a measuring tape or a ruler, marker pens, any object (book, pencil box, etc.)

Procedure:

1. Take your pencil box and a thread.
2. Place the tip of the thread at one corner of the pencil box. Then stretch it along the edge of the box till it reaches the next corner. Mark this length with a marker pen on the thread.
3. Now, measure the length of the marked thread with a measuring tape.

   This will give you the length of your pencil box.

   Using the same method, try measuring other objects in your bag or classroom.

Concept Map

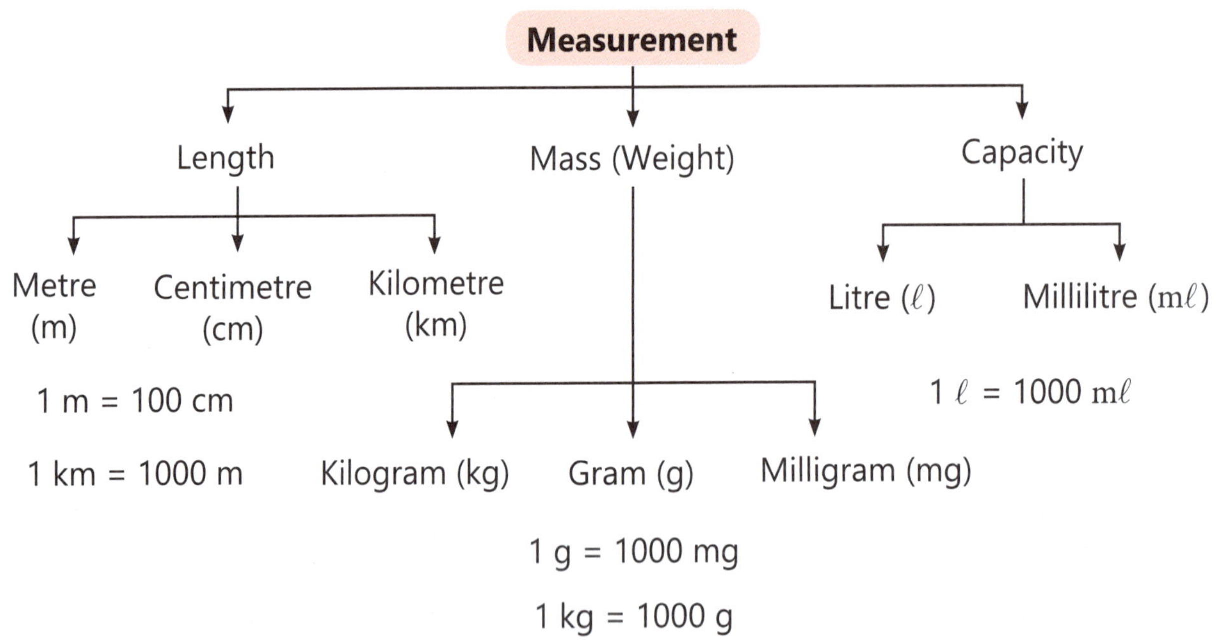

Key Concepts

- **Distance:** The measurement of length between two points or locations
- **Mass:** The amount of matter that an object has
- **Weight:** The measure of the heaviness of an object

A. Choose the correct option.

1. 27.81 km = ____________________.
   a. 27.81 m b. 278.1 m c. 27810 m d. 27081 m
2. $\frac{1}{5}$ of 18 m = ____________________.
   a. 360 cm b. 18 cm c. 5 cm d. 3.6 cm
3. 5 kg 5 g = ____________________.
   a. 5500 g b. 5050 g c. 5000 g d. 5005 g
4. 23 kℓ 7 ℓ = ____________________.
   a. 23007 ℓ b. 2307 ℓ c. 237 ℓ d. 23700 ℓ
5. 4 km 5 hm 8 m = ____________________.
   a. 4058 m b. 4580 m c. 45080 m d. 4508 m
6. 7234 g = ____________________.
   a. 72340 kg b. 7234 kg c. 7.234 kg d. 72.34 kg
7. 17.95 ℓ = ____________________.
   a. 17 ℓ 950 mℓ b. 1 ℓ 795 mℓ c. 179 ℓ 5 mℓ d. 1795 mℓ
8. 85.327 km = ________ km ________ hm ________ dam ________ m
   a. 85 km 3 hm 2 dam 7 m b. 8 km 53 hm 2 dam 7 m
   c. 8 km 5 hm 32 dam 7 m d. 8 km 5 hm 3 dam 27 m
9. 12 kg 725 g more than 125 kg 8 g = ____________________.
   a. 137 kg 8 g b. 138 kg 525 g c. 137 kg 733 g d. 138 kg 8 g
10. Anita bought 7 kg of apples and 1 kg 350 g of mangoes. How many more kg of apples did she buy than mangoes?
   a. 7.350 kg b. 5.650 kg c. 2.350 kg d. 1.750 kg

B. Fill in the blanks.

1. To convert kg to dg, multiply by ____________________.
2. To convert cm to hm, we ____________________ by 10,000.
3. 1 daℓ = ____________________ dℓ
4. 1 m = ____________________ cm
5. 1 glass contains 200 ____________________ of water.
6. The tailor needs 2 ____________________ of cloth to make my shirt.
7. Mother cooked 1 ____________________ of potatoes for lunch.
8. The school is about 3 ____________________ away from my house.

C. Solve the following.

1. Write the following in ascending order.
   2 kg,   5000 g,   250 hg,   10,000 dg
2. Raj weighs 59.7 kg. Aziz weighs 24.8 kg. Who weighs more and by how much?
3. Out of 20.750 kg of potatoes, 5.750 kg got spoiled. The rest of the potatoes were distributed among three families. How much did each family get?
4. Krishna's weight was 25.9 kg. His weight increased by 3.758 kg. What is Krishna's weight now?
5. A man travelled 347.5 km by train, 49.35 km by bus and 675 m by car. Find the total distance travelled by him.
6. Express 25.876 kℓ in hℓ, daℓ and ℓ.

SKILL UP!

A. 21 CS Collaboration, Information Literacy | EL | CC | Integration with Physical Education

3 GOOD HEALTH AND WELL-BEING

Measure and record the height and weight of each member in your class. Compare and find out who is the tallest, shortest, heaviest and lightest. Also, find out the amount of water consumed by each member during the day. Find out who among your classmates drinks the least and the most amount of water in a day.

B. 21 CS Critical Thinking, Life Skills | EL | CC | Integration with Science

15 LIFE ON LAND

Collect 10 leaves from any plant. Measure and record the length of each leaf. What is the length of the longest and shortest leaves? Is there more than one way of measuring the length of a leaf? Would you pluck leaves while collecting the leaves? Or would you rather pick up fallen leaves? Given reasons for your answer.

C. 21 CS Critical Thinking | CC | Integration with Science

Your mass would be the same on the Moon and the Earth. Find out the reason behind this.

SUSTAINABLE DEVELOPMENT GOALS

Question A is in line with SDG 3 Good Health and Well-Being. How much water should you drink in a day? Does it impact our health?
Question B is in line with SDG 15 Life on Land. Why is it important to plant trees? What are the benefits of planting trees?

Worksheet 8

21 CS Critical Thinking, Information Literacy | CC Integration with Physical Education

The score and the other details of a football match are given below.

The goalkeeper of France covered 612 m of distance in the whole match, while the goalkeeper of Italy covered 547 m of distance.

1. Which country's goalkeeper covered more distance and by how much?

____

2. Estimate how long a football field would be. Choose the correct option.

   a. 100 m – 110 m b. 100 cm – 110 cm c. 100 km – 110 km

3. What could be the mass of a football? Choose the correct option.

   a. 4 mg – 40 mg b. 410 g – 450 g c. 4000 g – 4110 kg

9 Time

Learning Objectives

- To read time to the exact minute
- To convert different units of time
- To understand the 12-hour and 24-hour time format
- To understand the difference between a.m. and p.m.
- To understand the relationship between timeline and duration
- To find the duration of familiar events
- To understand a calendar

Let's Get Started

21 CS Critical Thinking

Label the hands of the red-coloured clock.

In the clocks given below, the hour hand and the minute hand are missing. Draw the missing hands according to the time given for each clock.

1

2

5:30

3

2:45

4

3:10

READING TIME TO THE EXACT MINUTE

How would you read time to the exact minute? Look at any clock or a watch. On the face, the numbers 1 to 12 represent the hours. The two consecutive numbers are divided into 5 equal divisions. Each division represents a minute. When the minute hand moves by a division, then you can say 1 minute has passed.

Look at my dial!

SOLVED EXAMPLES

Do you know?
The face of a clock or a watch is called a dial.

Example 1: What is the time shown on the clock?

Solution:

1. First, look at where the hour hand is. It is in-between 4 and 5. So, it is after 4 o'clock.
2. Then, note the position of the minute hand. It is pointing at 6. So, its showing $6 \times 5 = 30$ minutes past 4.

   The time shown on the clock is 4:30 or 30 minutes past 4.

Example 2: What is the time shown on the clock?

Solution:

1. The hour hand is in-between 2 and 3. So, it is after 2 o'clock.
2. The minute hand is pointing at the fourth division after 1. So, its showing $1 \times 5 + 4 = 9$ minutes past 2.

   The time shown on the clock is 2:09 or 9 minutes past 2.

EXERCISE 9A

Write the time shown in each clock.

1. 

2. 

3. 

CONVERSION OF TIME

The second hand moves the fastest. When the second hand moves 60 times or completes one round of the dial, the minute hand moves one time or moves across one division.

When the minute hand moves 60 times or completes one round of the dial, the hour hand moves from one number to another consecutive number to its right.

NOTE

When the minute hand is between 12 and 6 on the right side of the clock, we write the time using 'minutes past'.

When the minute hand is between 6 and 12 on the left side of the clock, we write the time using 'minutes to'.

In mathematical terms,

1 minute = 60 seconds = 60 s

1 hour = 60 minutes = 60 min

1 hour = 3600 seconds = 3600 s

1 day = 24 hours = 24 h

1 week = 7 days

Seconds can also be written as s, minutes as min and hours as h.

GO EASY!

When converting a bigger unit into a smaller unit, always multiply.

When converting a smaller unit into a bigger unit, always divide.

The same rule applies for all the other conversions like hours to minutes or minutes to hours, days to hours or hours to days, etc.

Conversion Between Minutes and Seconds

To convert minutes into seconds, use the following relationship.

1 minute = 60 seconds

So, to convert minutes into seconds, multiply by 60.

To convert seconds into minutes, divide by 60.

SOLVED EXAMPLES

Example 3: Convert 2 minutes into seconds.

Solution: 1 min = 60 s

2 min = 2 × 60 s = 120 s. Therefore, 2 min = 120 s.

Example 4: Convert 360 seconds into minutes.

Solution:

$$1 \text{ minute} = 60 \text{ seconds}$$

$$1 \text{ second} = \frac{1}{60} \text{ minutes}$$

So,

$$360 \text{ seconds} = \frac{\overset{6}{\cancel{360}}}{\cancel{60}} = 6 \text{ minutes}$$

Thus, 360 seconds is equal to 6 minutes.

Conversion Between Hours and Minutes

To convert hours into minutes, use the following relationship.

1 hour = 60 minutes

So, to convert hours into minutes, multiply by 60.

To convert minutes into hours, divide by 60.

SOLVED EXAMPLES

Example 5: Convert 3 hours into minutes.

Solution:

1 hour = 60 minutes

Therefore, 3 hours = 3×60 minutes

= 180 minutes

So, 3 hours is equal to 180 minutes.

Example 6: Convert 240 minutes into hours.

Solution:

60 minutes = 1 hour

Therefore, 1 minute = $\frac{1}{60}$ hours

240 minutes = $\frac{\cancel{240}^{4}}{\cancel{60}}$ = 4 hours

So, 240 minutes is equal to 4 hours.

Conversion Between Hours and Seconds

To convert hours into seconds, use the following relationship.

1 hour = 60 minutes = 60×60 seconds = 3600 seconds

So, to convert hours into seconds, multiply by 3600.

To convert seconds into hours, divide by 3600.

SOLVED EXAMPLES

Example 7: Convert 21,600 seconds into hours.

Solution:

3600 seconds = 1 hour. Therefore, 1 second = $\frac{1}{3600}$ hours

21,600 seconds = $\frac{\cancel{21,600}^{\cancel{36}\,6}}{\cancel{3600}_{\cancel{6}\,1}}$ = 6 hours. So, 21,600 seconds is equal to 6 hours.

Example 8: Convert 2 hours 15 minutes 45 seconds into seconds.

Solution:

$$\begin{aligned} 2 \text{ hours} &= 2 \times 3600 &= 7200 \text{ s} \\ 15 \text{ min} &= 15 \times 60 &= 900 \text{ s} \\ 45 \text{ s} & &= +\ 45 \text{ s} \\ & & \overline{8145 \text{ s}} \end{aligned}$$

2 hours 15 minutes 45 seconds = 8145 seconds

Example 9: 5389 seconds = _____ hours _____ minutes _____ seconds

Solution:

First, divide 5389 seconds by 60.

60) 5 3 8 9 s (8 9 min
− 4 8 0
5 8 9
5 4 0
4 9 s

The remainder is 49 seconds and the quotient is 89 minutes. Since 89 minutes are more than 60 minutes, divide 89 by 60.

60) 8 9 min (1 h
− 6 0
2 9 min

We get 1 hour and 29 minutes.

5389 seconds = 1 hour 29 minutes 49 seconds.

EXERCISE 9B

Convert the following.

1. 3 h 25 min = __________ min
2. 1 h 40 min = __________ min = __________ s
3. 42 min 13 s = __________ s
4. 3 h 12 min = __________ s
5. 372 s = __________ min __________ s
6. 621 min = __________ h __________ min
7. 4392 s = __________ h __________ min __________ s
8. 5183 s = __________ h __________ min __________ s

12-HOUR CLOCK AND 24-HOUR CLOCK

There are 24 hours in one day. Each day begins at midnight and ends at midnight the next day.

The clock we normally use is called the **12-hour clock**. When the time is 12 at night, it is called midnight. When the time is 12 during the day, it is called noon.

In this clock, from 12:01 after midnight to 11:59 during the day we write **a.m.** with the time.

From 12:01 after noon till 11:59 at night, we write **p.m.** with the time.

After midnight, the next day starts and we again use a.m. with the time.

COMMON ERRORS

12 in the afternoon

noon ✓ 12 a.m. ✗

12 at night

midnight ✓ 12 p.m. ✗

NOTE

a.m. stands for ante meridiem in Latin. It means before noon.

p.m. stands for post meridiem. It means after noon.

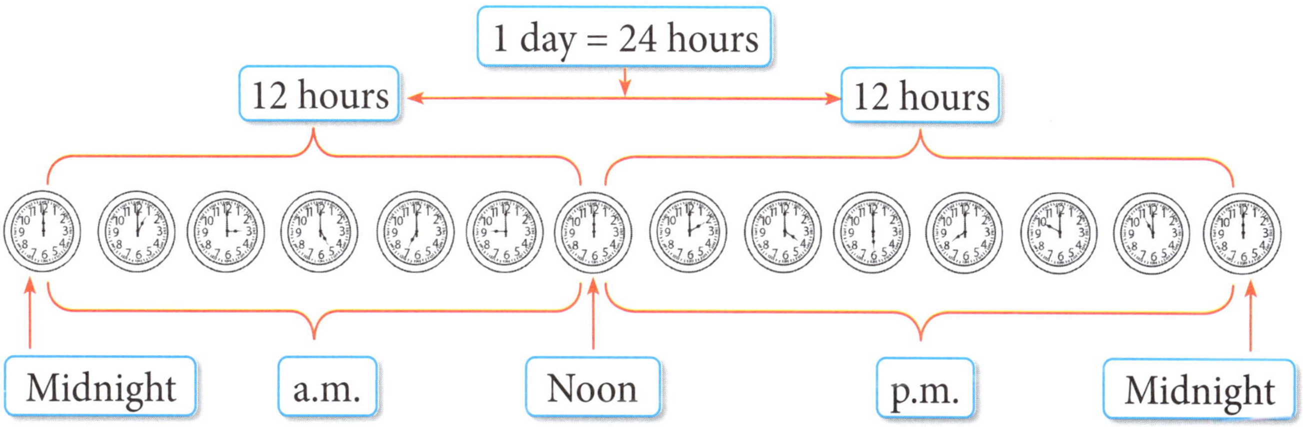

Time can also be read using the **24-hour clock**. In this clock, we do not use a.m. or p.m. with the time.

The day starts at midnight and is written as 00:00 followed by the hours passed from 1 to 23.

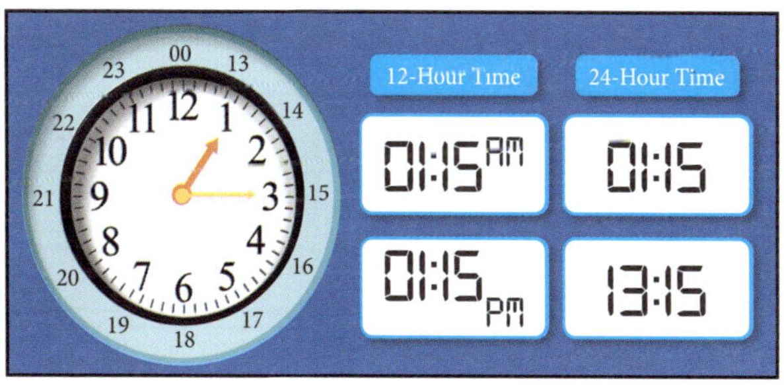

Sometimes you may see 00:00 written as 24:00. Both are acceptable. A table describing both the time has been given below.

24	00:00	01:00	02:00	03:00	04:00	05:00	06:00	07:00	08:00	09:00	10:00	11:00
a.m.	12:00	1:00	2:00	3:00	4:00	5:00	6:00	7:00	8:00	9:00	10:00	11:00
24	12:00	13:00	14:00	15:00	16:00	17:00	18:00	19:00	20:00	21:00	22:00	23:00
p.m.	12:00	1:00	2:00	3:00	4:00	5:00	6:00	7:00	8:00	9:00	10:00	11:00

Convert Time from 24-hour Clock to 12-hour Clock

To convert time from 24-hour clock to 12-hour clock, subtract 12 from the hour. The time 1300 hours in 24-hour clock becomes 1:00 p.m. in 12-hour clock.

13 – 12 = 1:00 p.m.

Example:

24-hour clock	12-hour clock
0100 hours	1:00 a.m.
1200 hours	noon
1259 hours	12:59 p.m.
1300 hours (13 – 12 = 1)	1:00 p.m.
1400 hours (14 – 12 = 2)	2:00 p.m.
1530 hours (15 – 12 = 3)	3:30 p.m.

Mental Maths

Write the following times in 24-hour clock.

1. 1:15 p.m. ________
2. 2:24 p.m. ________
3. 3:45 p.m. ________
4. 7:12 p.m. ________
5. 10:35 p.m. ________
6. 11:40 p.m. ________

Exercise 9C

1. Write a.m., p.m., noon or midnight for the following.

a. 3 at night
b. 6 in the morning
c. 10 in the morning
d. 11:55 in the morning
e. 12 during the day
f. 12:15 during the day
g. 1:25 during the day
h. 6:45 in the evening

2. Write the time in the 24-hour clock for the given timings.

12-hour clock	24-hour clock
4:35 a.m.	________
6:20 a.m.	________
10:50 a.m.	________

12-hour clock	24-hour clock
Noon	________
12:35 p.m.	________
12:57 p.m.	________

3. Write the time in the 12-hour clock for the given timings.

24-hour clock	12-hour clock
0320 hours	________
1410 hours	________

24-hour clock	12-hour clock
1150 hours	________
1245 hours	________

DURATION OF EVENTS

The duration of an event or an activity is the time during which it lasts. A duration has a start time and an end time. A few examples are given below.

Event/Activity	Start time	End time	Duration
Period 1	9 a.m.	9:45 a.m.	45 minutes
Final exam	10 a.m.	1 p.m. or 1300 hours	3 hours

When an event is arranged in an order, then it is called a **timeline**. Your classroom timetable is an example of a simple timeline.

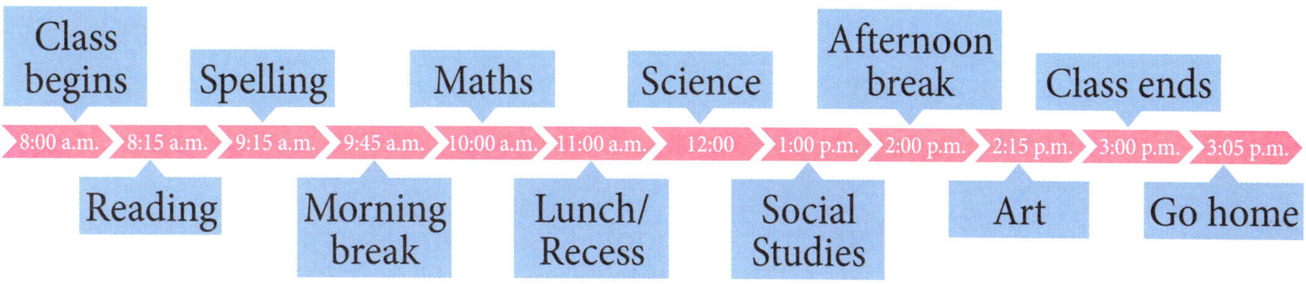

SOLVED EXAMPLES

Example 10: If Amy left her house at 1 p.m. and came back at 5 p.m., for how long was she away?

Solution:

Time at which Amy came back = 5 p.m.

Time at which Amy left = 1 p.m.

Number of hours (or duration) Amy was away = 5 – 1 = 4 hours

Thus, Amy was away for 4 hours.

We subtract the time of leaving from the time of returning. When we subtract, the time of returning is written on the top. Since both the timings are in p.m., we can subtract easily.

If one timing is in a.m. and one is in p.m., then convert the timings into 24-hour clock, and then subtract.

Example 11: Jack left at 11:45 a.m. for the park and came back at 5:30 p.m. It took him 1 hour 15 minutes to go and come back. How much time did he spend in the park?

Solution: First, we calculate the total time that Jack was away and then subtract the travelling time of 1 hour 15 minutes from it.

	h	min
	16	90
Time at which he came back	~~17~~	~~30~~
Time of leaving	− 11	45
Total time Jack was away	5	45
Travelling time	− 1	15
	4	30

When we borrow 1 hour, we get 60 minutes.

We add 60 and 30 and then subtract 45.

Therefore, Jack spent 4 hours 30 minutes in the park.

Example 12: Ira and John left for the school at 7:00 a.m. They took 45 minutes to go and come back. They spent 5 hours 30 minutes in the school. At what time did they come back home?

Solution:

	h	min
	7	00
		45
+	5	30
	12^{+1}	75
	13	15

$$\begin{array}{r|l} & 1\ \text{h} \\ 60 & 75\ \text{min} \\ & -60 \\ \hline & 15\ \text{min} \end{array}$$

Thus, Ira and John came back at 1:15 p.m.

Exercise 9D

Solve the following word problems.

1. Karan started cooking food at 9:25 a.m. He took 45 minutes to cook the food and spent 15 minutes to clean up the kitchen. What was the total time taken by Karan to finish cooking and cleaning?
2. A train left Jaipur at 12:25 p.m. and reached Delhi at 5:30 p.m. How long was the journey?
3. I go to school at 7:15 a.m. and come back at 2:30 p.m. I spend 20 minutes in travelling. How much time do I spend in school?
4. A potter took 4 hours 15 minutes to make earthen pots. If he started at 9.15 a.m., when did he finish making the pots?

CALENDAR

The calendar of a year consists of 12 months. All the months do not have the same number of days. The names of the 12 months with the number of days in each month are given below.

January	February	March	April	May	June
31 days	28 or 29 days	31 days	30 days	31 days	30 days

July	August	September	October	November	December
31 days	31 days	30 days	31 days	30 days	31 days

Converting years, months, weeks and days

Remember

1 week = 7 days

1 month = 30 days (or 28, 29 or 31 days)

1 year = 12 months

Look at the calendar of 2022.

October 1 is a Saturday. What will be the date on next Saturday?

Next Saturday will be after 1 week, that is, after 7 days. So, add 7 days to October 1.

$1 + 7 = 8$

Therefore, next Saturday will be on October 8.

Now, what will be the date after two weeks from July 5?

After two weeks, that is after 14 days from July 5, the date will be $5 + 14 = 19$. So, after two weeks, the date will be July 19.

DO YOU KNOW?

1 decade = 10 years
1 century = 100 years
1 millennium = 1000 years

SOLVED EXAMPLES

Example 13: Convert 3 years into months.

Solution:

$$1 \text{ year} = 12 \text{ months}$$

So, $3 \text{ years} = 3 \times 12 \text{ (As 1 year = 12 months)}$

$= 36 \text{ months}$

Thus, 3 years is equal to 36 months.

Example 14: Convert 4 weeks 5 days into days.

Solution:

$$\begin{aligned} 4 \text{ weeks} = 4 \times 7 = &\ \overset{1}{2}\,8 \text{ days} \quad \text{(As 1 week = 7 days)} \\ 5 \text{ days} = &\ \underline{+\,5 \text{ days}} \\ &\ 3\,3 \text{ days} \end{aligned}$$

Thus, 4 weeks 5 days is equal to 33 days.

Example 15: Convert 21 months into years and months.

Solution:

$$\begin{array}{r|l} & 1 \text{ year} \\ \hline 12 & 2\,1 \text{ months} \\ & -1\,2 \\ \hline & 9 \text{ months} \end{array}$$

[Divide by 12 because 1 year = 12 months]

Thus, 21 months is equal to 1 year 9 months.

Example 16: Convert 18 days into weeks and days.

$$\begin{array}{r|l} & 2 \text{ weeks} \\ \hline 7 & 1\,8 \text{ days} \\ & -1\,4 \\ \hline & 4 \text{ days} \end{array}$$

[Divide by 7 because 1 week = 7 days]

Thus, 18 days is equal to 2 weeks 4 days.

Leap Year

In a **calendar year**, there are 365 days with 28 days in February. After every four years, February has 29 days making the days count of that year 366. Such a year is called a **leap year**. Why is there an extra day in this year?

You know that the Earth takes $365\frac{1}{4}$ days to move around the sun. This is called a **solar year**. There is a difference of $\frac{1}{4}$ days between a solar year and a calendar year. The calendar year and the solar year need to be the same at some point to balance the difference of $\frac{1}{4}$ days.

Go Easy!

To identify a leap year, divide it by 4. If it is divisible by 4, it is a leap year. If a year ends with 00, then it has to be divisible by 400 to be a leap year.

Now, let us do some calculations.

$\frac{1}{4}$ of 1 day = 6 hours

6 hours × 4 = 24 hours = 1 day

This extra 6 hours get added up over a period of 4 years to make a day.

So every fourth year, 1 day gets added to make a **leap year**.

MENTAL MATHS

Is 2022 a leap year?

SOLVED EXAMPLES

Example 17: Is 1992 a leap year?

Solution: Check the divisibility of the number using the divisibility rule of 4.

The last two digits, that is 92 is divisible by 4, therefore, 1992 is divisible by 4.

Since 1992 is divisible by 4, it is a leap year.

Example 18: Is 1995 a leap year?

Solution: Checking the divisibility by 4,
1995 is not divisible by 4.

Therefore, 1995 is not a leap year.

Example 19: Is 2000 a leap year?

Solution: As the year ends with 00,
divide it by 400.

As 2000 is divisible by 400, it is a leap year.

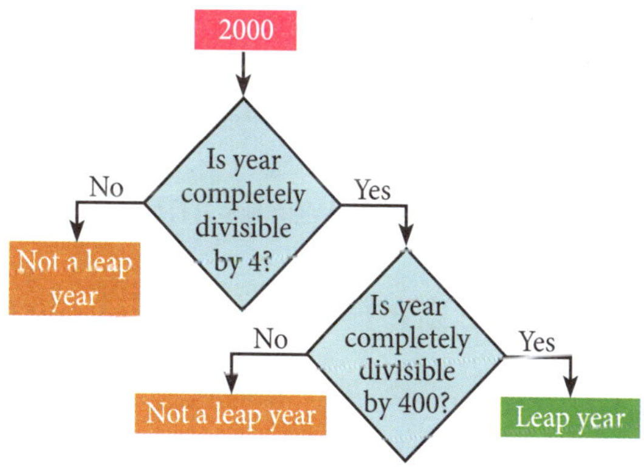

Example 20: Is 1900 a leap year?

Solution: Since 1900 is not completely divisible by 400, it is not a leap year.

WORD PROBLEMS ON TIME

To solve word problems on time, remember the following:

1 week = 7 days

1 month = 4 weeks (approx.)

1 year = 12 months

1 year = 365 days

1 leap year = 366 days

1 year = 52 weeks + 1 day

SOLVED EXAMPLES

Example 21: Out of my holiday of 2 weeks, I spent 3 days in Delhi and the remaining days at home. How many weeks and days did I spend at home?

Solution:

Weeks	Days
1	7
~~2~~	~~0~~
–	3
1	4

When we borrow 1 week, we get 7 days.
We add 7 to 0 and then subtract 3.

So, I spent 1 week and 4 days at home.

Example 22: I spent 8 days in Mumbai and 12 days in Nagpur. How many weeks and days did I spend in these two places?

Solution:

Days
8
+ 12
20

20 days is more than 7 days. So, divide by 7.

$$\begin{array}{r|l} & \text{2 weeks} \\ 7 & \text{2 0 days} \\ & -\text{1 4} \\ & \text{6 days} \end{array}$$

Thus, I spent 2 weeks and 6 days in Mumbai and Nagpur.

Example 23: How many days are there between March 16 and April 5?

Solution:

When we calculate the number of days between two dates, we do not include the first and the last date.

Total number of days in March = 31
– 16
15

Number of days between April 1 and April 5 = 5 – 1 = 4

Total number of days between March 16 and April 5 = 15 + 4 = 19

The number of days between March 16 and April 5 is 19.

Example 24: How many days are there from March 16 to April 5?

Solution: The first and the last date need to be included when the total number of days is to be calculated from a date to another date.

Number of days in March	= 31 – 16 15	Number of days from April 1 to April 5	= 5 – 1 4
We add 1 because the day is to be counted from March 16.	+ 1 16	We add 1 because the day is to be counted to April 5.	+ 1 5

Total number of days from March 16 to April 5 = 16 + 5 = 21.

The number of days from March 16 to April 5 is 21.

Example 25: How many days are there from January 2 to January 29?

Solution:

$$\begin{array}{r} 29 \\ -\ 2 \\ \hline 27 \\ +\ 1 \\ \hline 28 \end{array}$$

We add 1 because the day is to be counted from January 2.

There are 28 days from January 2 to January 29.

EXERCISE 9E

Answer the following questions.

1. Which of the following years are leap years?
   a. 2016 b. 1949 c. 1200 d. 2000 e. 2015
2. How many months, weeks and days are there in a year?
3. If July 4 is a Tuesday
   a. What is the date on next Tuesday? b. What is the date after 2 weeks?
4. Convert 35 months into years and months.
5. I spent 12 days in Delhi, 14 days in Mumbai and 5 days in Chennai. How many weeks and days did I spend in all these three places?
6. I spent 13 days studying english and 13 days studying maths before my exams. How many weeks and days did I spend studying english and maths altogether?
7. How many days are there between
   a. February 5 and February 23? b. August 23 and September 7?
8. How many days are there from
   a. March 6 to March 23? b. October 15 to November 6?

Maths Lab Activity

21 CS Critical Thinking, Life Skills · EL · HQ Harmony in The Self

Aim: To understand how to estimate and verify the duration of familiar events

Materials required: A chart paper, colour pencils

Procedure:

1. Make a table as shown below on the chart paper.
2. Make a list of activities that you do on Saturdays and Sundays.
3. Estimate how much time you would spend doing each activity.
4. Note down the actual start time and end time of each activity.
5. Then, find out on which activity did you spend the most time (find out the longest duration).

Estimation and verification of duration of different activities				
Activity	**Estimated duration**	**Start time**	**End time**	**Actual duration**
1. Playing a game of football				
2. Watching T.V.				
3. Studying				

Concept Map

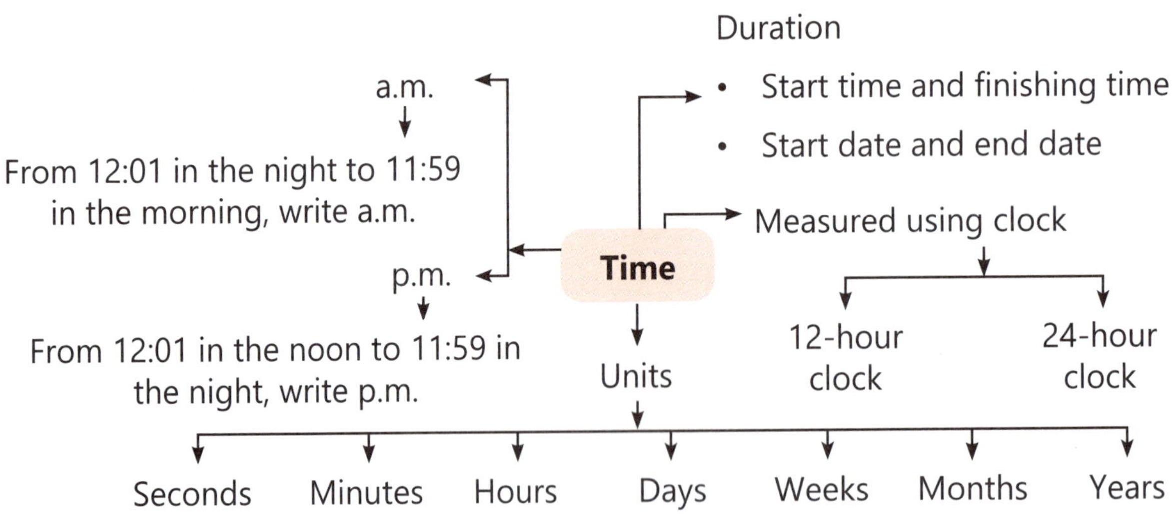

Key Concepts

- When the time is 12 at night, it is called midnight.
- When the time is 12 during the day, it is called noon.
- The calendar of a year consists of 12 months.

A. Choose the correct option.

1. 3 h 45 min = ________________ min

   a. 180 min b. 225 min c. 45 min d. 345 min

2. 47 min 9 s = ________________ s

   a. 2829 s b. 2820 s c. 479 s d. 4700 s

3. 2 days 5 hours 13 min = ________________ min

   a. 3195 min b. 2513 min c. 3119 min d. 3193 min

4. 4900 s = ________________ h ________________ min ________________ s

   a. 21 h 1 min 40 s b. 40 h 21 min 1 s

   c. 1 h 21 min 40 s d. 81 h 40 min 1 s

5. February 2016 had ________________ days.

   a. 28 b. 29 c. 30 d. 31

6. What will be the date 2 weeks after March 4?

   a. March 24 b. March 16 c. March 18 d. March 9

7. 7 years 3 months = ________________ months

   a. 87 b. 73 c. 84 d. 36

B. Fill in the blanks.

1. There are ________________ months in a year.
2. March always has ________________ days.
3. In a leap year, February has ________________ days.
4. If October 7 is a Friday, then the date on the next Friday will be ________________.
5. A leap year has ________________ days.
6. The number of days between September 2 and September 13 are ________________.

C. Write T for true and F for false.

1. 5:00 p.m. is five in the morning.
2. 7:20 a.m. in the 24-hour clock is written as 0720 hours.
3. 12:30 in the afternoon is written as 12:30 a.m.
4. The time duration from 6:15 a.m. to 6:30 a.m. is 15 minutes.

D. Solve the following word problems.

1. Ameeta went for a walk at 11:30 a.m. and came back at 1:10 p.m. How much time did she spend on the walk?

2. Govind left his house at 9:20 a.m. He took 25 minutes to go to the market. He spent 40 minutes at the market and another 25 minutes to come back home. At what time did he reach home?
3. If the first Tuesday of April is the 5th, then what is the date on
   a. the second Tuesday? b. the third Tuesday? c. the fourth Tuesday?
4. Raman is 6 years 5 months old. His sister is 3 years 7 months older than him. How old is his sister?
5. How many days are there between June 13 and July 4?

SKILL UP!

A. 21 CS Information Literacy, Technology Literacy | EL | CC Integration with Science

15 LIFE ON LAND

Plant some beans or peas in a flower pot. Record the growth with the help of a timeline chart. You can even measure and record the length of the plant.

B. 21 CS Information Literacy, Technology Literacy | EL | CC Integration with Computer Science

Find out what digital clocks are. Also, find out how different they are from the usual clocks that you use. Make a PowerPoint presentation on your findings.

C. 21 CS Critical Thinking, Life Skills | HQ Harmony in The Self

Jack's mother wakes him up at 6 a.m. every morning. He delays waking up by 5–10 minutes every day. Have you ever postponed waking up on time in the morning? By how many minutes do you delay waking up? Count how many hours you would have lost if you do this for a month.

D. 21 CS Information Literacy

Do you know that when we travel from India straight to other countries, we might lose or gain a day? Find out the name of any two such countries.

SUSTAINABLE DEVELOPMENT GOALS

Question A is in line with SDG 15 Life on Land. Trees greatly contribute to the environment by providing oxygen, supporting wildlife, improving air quality, conserving water, preserving soil and climate enhancement. Prepare a poster on the plantation of trees and display it in your class.

WORKSHEET 9

21 CS Critical Thinking, Life Skills | AI | CC Integration with Science

15 LIFE ON LAND

The students of Class IV took the responsibility of cleaning their school playground. The tasks that need to be done are shown in the table. Draw a timeline for this cleaning activity in the space provided below. (Note that the tasks given are not in order. Carefully look at the start time of each task to sort the tasks in order. Use colour pencils and different line styles to make the timeline attractive.)

How many hours did the students take to complete all the tasks?

	Task name	Start time
A	Clear trash	09:00 a.m.
B	Pull out weeds	09:30 a.m.
C	Put trash in the bag	1300 hours
D	Tend to the plants in the garden	1100 hours
E	Bring plants from the gardener	10:30 a.m
F	Take bags to the recycling bin	1:30 p.m.
G	Water plants	11:30 a.m.
H	Take a break	10:00 a.m.
I	Have lunch	Noon

Timeline

10 Money

Learning Objectives

- To convert rupees into paise
- To convert paise into rupees
- To add and subtract money
- To solve real-life problems involving money

Let's Get Started

21 CS Critical Thinking, Life Skills

Bhawna has been saving currency coins for a month. Help her count how much money she has saved.

50 coins

$10 \times \square = \square$

25 coins

$5 \times \square = \square$

Bhawna's mother said she will give her one 500-rupee note and one 200-rupee note in exchange for the coins. Bhawna said no, she would not exchange her coins for just two notes. Do you think Bhawna should exchange her coins for rupee notes or not? Give reasons for your answer.

CONVERSION OF MONEY

A few Indian rupees in the form of notes and coins are given below.

Notes			Coins

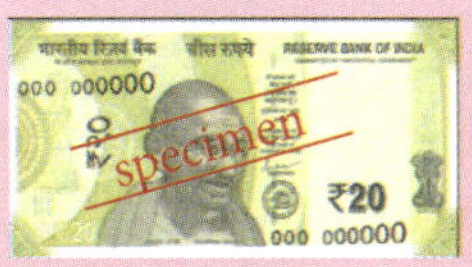		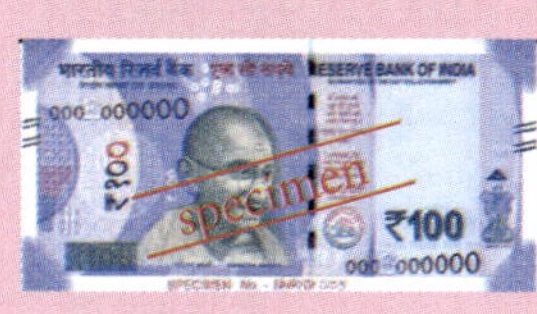	
			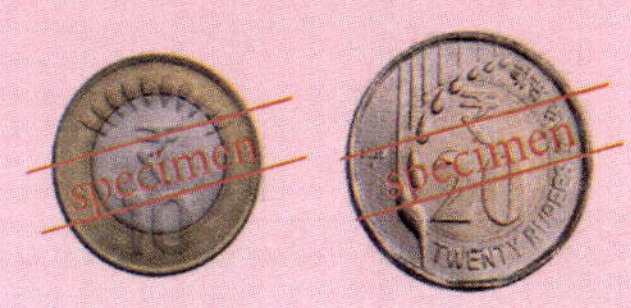

The plural of rupee is rupees and the plural of paisa is paise. The symbol for rupees is ₹ and the symbol for paise is **p**.

Converting Rupees into Paise

When converting rupees into paise, we multiply with 100, as ₹1 is equal to 100 paise.

₹1 = 100 paise

₹2.50 = 2 × 100 paise + 50 paise = 250 paise

₹9.70 = 9 × 100 paise + 70 paise = 970 paise

On the left of the dot are rupees and on the right of the dot are paise.

GO EASY!

A **shorter method** for converting rupees and paise into paise is to just remove the decimal point.

₹3.75 = 375 p

₹17.35 = 1735 p

SOLVED EXAMPLES

Example 1: Convert 3 rupees 75 paise into paise.

Solution: 3 rupees = 3 × 100 = 3 0 0 paise

75 paise = + 7 5 paise

3 7 5 paise

Thus, 3 rupees 75 paise is equal to 375 paise.

First, convert 3 rupees into paise and then add 75 paise to the answer.

Example 2: Convert 17 rupees 35 paise into paise.

Solution:

17 rupees = 17 × 100	=	1 7 0 0 paise
35 paise	= +	3 5 paise
		1 7 3 5 paise

Thus, 17 rupees 35 paise is equal to 1735 paise.

MENTAL MATHS

1. ₹2.50 = ________ p
2. ₹6.05 = ________ p
3. ₹17.30 = ________ p

Converting Paise into Rupees

When converting paise into rupees, we divide by 100, as 100 paise is equal to 1 rupee.

$$100 \text{ p} = ₹1$$

$$1 \text{ p} = ₹\frac{1}{100} = ₹0.01$$

SOLVED EXAMPLES

Example 3: Convert 200 paise into rupees.

Solution: To convert 200 paise into rupees, divide by 100.

$$200 \div 100 = 2.00 = ₹2$$

200 paise = ₹2

Example 4: Convert 43 paise into rupees.

Solution: 43 ÷ 100 = 0.43 = ₹0.43

43 paise = ₹0.43

Example 5: Convert 5 paise into rupees.

Solution: 5 ÷ 100 = 0.05 = ₹0.05

5 paise = ₹0.05

Example 6: Convert 2 rupees 45 paise into rupees.

Solution:

2 rupees = 2 × 100 =	2 0 0 p
45 paise =	+ 4 5 p
	2 4 5 p

So, moving the dot two places from the right, 245 paise = ₹2.45

2 rupees 45 paise = ₹2.45

COMMON ERRORS

To convert paise into rupees, leave two digits from the right and put the dot. Put the symbol of rupee at the beginning. Remember that there are always 2 digits for paise because 100 has 2 zeros.

5 paise = ₹0.05 👍
5 paise = ₹0.50 👎
8 paise = ₹0.08 👍
8 paise = ₹0.80 👎
10 paise = ₹0.10 👍
10 paise = ₹0.01 👎

MENTAL MATHS

1. 3 rupees 15 paise = ₹ ______
2. 26 rupees 45 paise = ₹ ______
3. 89 rupees 3 paise = ₹ ______
4. 129 rupees 8 paise = ₹ ______

EXERCISE 10A

1. Convert the following into paise.

a. ₹3 b. ₹7 c. ₹11 d. ₹23

e. ₹81 f. ₹500 g. ₹1400 h. ₹5003

i. ₹2.50 j. ₹13.25 k. ₹45.30 l. 13 rupees 50 paise

m. 24 rupees 75 paise

2. Convert the following into rupees.

a. 100 paise b. 700 paise c. 950 paise d. 825 paise

e. 430 paise f. 1450 paise g. 82 rupees 9 paise h. 11 rupees 50 paise

i. 2 rupees 30 paise

ADDITION AND SUBTRACTION OF RUPEES AND PAISE

Rupees and paise are added and subtracted just like numbers.

After adding or subtracting, remember to place the dot just before two places from the right. The dot separates the rupees part from the paise part. The left side of the dot specifies rupees. The right side of the dot specifies paise.

SOLVED EXAMPLES

Example 7: Solve the following.

a. ₹1000 + ₹200 + ₹5 b. ₹15.75 + ₹2.50

Solution: a.

$$\begin{array}{r} ₹ \\ 1000 \\ 200 \\ +\quad 5 \\ \hline 1205 \end{array}$$

The total is ₹1205.

b.

$$\begin{array}{r} ₹_{1}\ \ p \\ 15.75 \\ +\ \ 2.50 \\ \hline 18.25 \\ \hline \end{array}$$

The total is ₹18.25.

Example 8: Solve the following.

a. ₹695 – ₹174 b. ₹92.35 – ₹18.49

Solution: a.

$$\begin{array}{r} ₹ \\ 695 \\ -\ 174 \\ \hline 521 \\ \hline \end{array}$$

The difference is ₹521.

b.

$$\begin{array}{r} ₹\quad p \\ \scriptstyle 8\ 11\ \ 12\ 15 \\ \not{9}\not{2}.\not{3}\not{5} \\ -\ 18.49 \\ \hline 73.86 \\ \hline \end{array}$$

The difference is ₹73.86.

NOTE

1. If there is no paise, write 00 after the dot.
2. The number that contains the word 'from' is written on top in subtraction.

Exercise 10B

1. **Add the following.**

   a. ₹28.35, ₹13.68 and ₹72.40
   b. ₹460.40, ₹12.98 and ₹3.25
   c. ₹257.85, 46 p and ₹400
   d. ₹15.40, ₹207.35, ₹47.98 and ₹79.80

2. **Subtract the following.**

   a. ₹13.25 from ₹58.76
   b. ₹30.75 from ₹128.20
   c. ₹15.40 from ₹207.35
   d. ₹47.98 from ₹79.84

MONEY OPERATIONS AND ESTIMATION

The cost of something is the amount of money that is needed to buy things, do something or make something. In our day-to-day life, we come across many situations where we need to add, subtract, multiply or divide money. These operations are used when we need to know how to put together a given amount with the minimum number of notes and coins. When we go shopping, we sometimes need to estimate the total cost or **unit cost**. Unit cost is the cost of one thing.

Do you know?
The following countries use the name rupee (Rs) to represent their currency.
Sri Lanka Nepal Pakistan
Mauritius

SOLVED EXAMPLES

Example 9: If the unit cost of a sweet is ₹12, then what will be the cost of 6 such sweets?

Solution:

$$\begin{array}{r} 12 \\ \times\ 6 \\ \hline 72 \\ \hline \end{array}$$

Thus, six sweets will cost ₹72.

Example 10: If ₹875 is distributed among 7 people, how much will each person get?

Solution:

Based on the division given on the right, each person will get ₹125.

$$\begin{array}{r} 125 \\ 7\overline{)875} \\ -7 \\ \hline 17 \\ -14 \\ \hline 35 \\ -35 \\ \hline 00 \\ \hline \end{array}$$

Example 11: Pay ₹576 to a shopkeeper using the least number of currency notes.

Solution: Using the least number of currency notes, we get

$$
\begin{array}{rcr}
1 \times 500\text{-rupee note} & = & ₹500 \\
+ & & \\
1 \times 50\text{-rupee note} & = & ₹50 \\
+ & & \\
1 \times 20\text{-rupee note} & = & ₹20 \\
+ & & \\
1 \times 5\text{-rupee note} & = & ₹5 \\
+ & & \\
1 \times 1\text{-rupee note} & = & ₹1 \\
\hline
 & & ₹576 \\
\hline
\end{array}
$$

Example 12: If I need to pay a shopkeeper ₹352 and I give him a 500-rupee note, how much money will the shopkeeper return to me?

Solution:

$$
\begin{array}{rrrr}
 & {\scriptstyle 4} & {\scriptstyle 9} & {\scriptstyle 10} \\
 & \not{5} & \not{0} & \not{0} \\
- & 3 & 5 & 2 \\
\hline
 & 1 & 4 & 8 \\
\hline
\end{array}
$$

Thus, the shopkeeper will return ₹148 to me.

EXERCISE 10C

Solve the following word problems.

1. If a chocolate costs ₹25, how much will 7 such chocolates cost?
2. Shreya spent ₹349 on a doll and ₹58 on a toy. What is the total amount of money did Shreya spend?
3. Out of ₹729, Sachin spent ₹185. How much money is left with Sachin?
4. Shalini bought a pen for ₹35. How much will 8 such pens cost her?
5. Alice wants to buy a shirt for ₹350. She has only ₹275 with her. How much more money does she need?
6. Razia bought a pair of shoes for ₹925. She gave the shopkeeper a 2000-rupee note. How much money will the shopkeeper return to her?
7. To pay ₹100 to a shopkeeper, I can pay ________ 100-rupee note or ________ 50-rupee notes.
8. To pay ₹200 to a shopkeeper, I can pay ________ 100-rupee notes.
9. To pay ₹500 to a shopkeeper, I can pay ________ 500-rupee note.

Maths Lab Activity

21 CS Collaboration, Life Skills | EL | AI | HQ Cooperation and Collaborative Living

Aim: To organise a pop-up shop to raise funds for a charity of your choice

Materials required: Reusable toys, clothes, shoes, bags, books, crafts that students have created, music CDs, etc.

Procedure:

1. Organise a pop-up shop in your classroom.
2. Send out invitations to your school.
3. Bring some items from your home that you want to sell such as old books, toys, bags, clothes, music CDs, etc. You can use your creativity and make crafts that people can use such as pen holder and shopping bags from old clothes.
4. You can also bring in recyclable goods from home for this event.
5. Discuss with your classmates and set a price for each item.
6. Display your items at a specific place and open the pop-up charity shop.

   How much money did you collect?

   Donate the money to a charity of your choice.

Concept Map

Money

- Convert rupees into paise
  - ₹1 = 100 paise
  - ₹2.50 = 250 paise
  - ₹9.70 = 970 paise
- Convert paise into rupees
  - 100 p = ₹1
  - 1 p = ₹0.01
- Money operations and estimation
  - Selling and buying

Key Concepts

- **Cost:** The amount of money that is needed to buy things, do something or make something
- **Unit cost:** The cost of one thing

CHAPTER REVISION

A. Choose the correct option.

1. Lekha bought a pencil for ₹5 and a pen for ₹10. What should she do to find the total cost?

   a. Add b. Subtract c. Multiply d. Divide

2. John had a total of ₹500 with him. He spent ₹50 on his lunch. What should you do to find out how much money is left with him?

   a. Add b. Subtract c. Multiply d. Divide

3. Sheeba collected ₹500 each from 50 people in a charity event. How can you find the total amount of money collected?

   a. Add b. Subtract c. Multiply d. Both a and c

4. What is the unit cost of a pencil if a set of 12 pencils costs ₹120?

   a. ₹12 b. ₹10 c. ₹20 d. ₹120

5. A notebook costs ₹20. You bought four such notebooks. You gave a 100-rupee note to the shopkeeper. The shopkeeper returned some 5-rupee coins. How many 5-rupee coins will you get?

   a. 5 b. 4 c. 20 d. 10

B. Convert into paise.

1. ₹3
2. ₹17
3. ₹250
4. ₹6.70
5. ₹19.89

C. Convert into rupees.

1. 200 paise
2. 1900 paise
3. 3 rupees 47 paise
4. 18 rupees 35 paise

D. Add the following.

1. ₹100 + ₹20
2. ₹200 + ₹100 + ₹50
3. ₹2888.09 + ₹200.78
4. ₹1654.56 + ₹1000.43 + ₹312.24
5. ₹600 + ₹100 + ₹30
6. ₹700 + ₹40 + ₹10
7. ₹23.17 + ₹16.25 + ₹38.72
8. ₹624.65 + ₹42.26 + ₹10

E. Subtract the following.

1. ₹100 – ₹15
2. ₹200 – ₹130
3. ₹431 – ₹298
4. ₹1000 – ₹598
5. ₹29.50 from ₹82.35
6. ₹250.05 from ₹330
7. ₹542.11 from ₹730.22

F. Solve the following word problems.

1. Kavya wants to buy a dress for ₹565. She has only ₹420 with her. How much more money does she need?
2. Shazia had to pay the shopkeeper ₹382. She gave him ₹500. How much money should the shopkeeper return to her?

3. Sanjana bought a pair of shoes for ₹130, a pair of socks for ₹45.50 and a belt for ₹101.25. She gave the shopkeeper ₹500. How much money should the shopkeeper return to her?
4. Meena needed to give the shopkeeper ₹800. She gave him two 500-rupee notes. How much money should the shopkeeper return to her?

SKILL UP!

A. 21 CS Technology Literacy, Life Skills | EL | CC Integration with Computer Science

Find out how much money one spends on food in a day. Estimate the amount of money you generally spend starting from breakfast till dinner. Prepare a presentation on your findings.

Items	Estimate
Bread	₹25
Milk	
Eggs	
Jam	

B. 21 CS Critical Thinking, Life Skills

Collect some old newspapers or junks lying in your home. Sell these to the local scrap dealers (*kabadiwala*). How much money would you get? What would you do with that money? What do you think happens to the newspapers or junks? Find out.

C. 21 CS Critical Thinking | IF | CC Integration with Social Studies

Every country has its own currency, e.g., USA uses the Dollar, England uses the Pound and Japan uses the Yen. In India, we use rupees and paise. The notes used earlier are not in use these days. Find out the benefits and drawbacks of changing notes of a country.

SUSTAINABLE DEVELOPMENT GOALS

Question A is in line with SDG 12 Responsible Consumption and Production. Responsible consumption emphasizes the reduction of food wastage. This can be done by keeping track of items that you have bought and used. Do you know the reasons for food wastage?

Question B is in line with SDG 11 Sustainable Cities and Communities. Most developed countries have adopted recycling techniques to make their environment clean. Recycling of paper is the process by which waste paper is turned into new paper products. This helps reduce the quantity of litter.

Worksheet 10

21 CS Critical Thinking, Life Skills

Do you have enough money to buy the items? Draw a 🙂 if you can. Draw a 🙁 if you cannot.

	Items	Money with me	Buy or cannot buy
1.	 ₹ 550	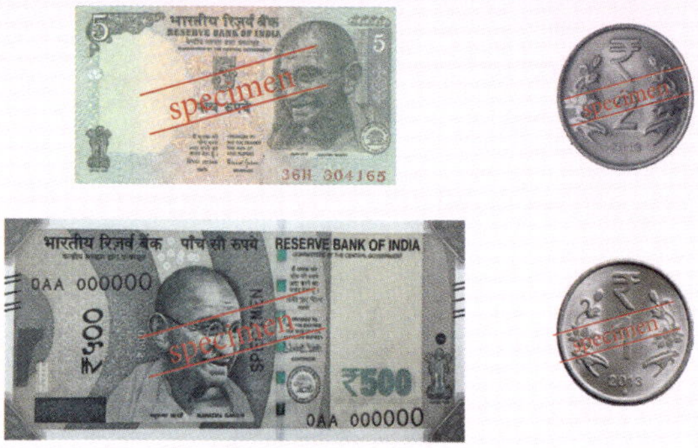	
2.	 ₹ 55		
3.	 ₹ 250		
4.	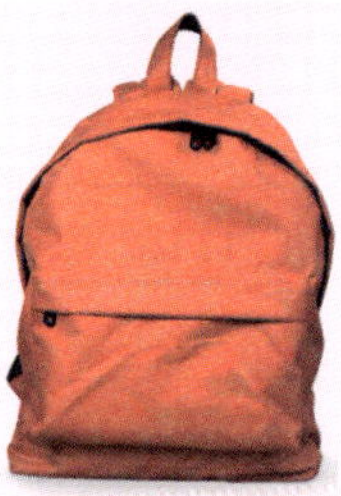 ₹ 200		

REASONING WORKSHEET 2

1. **What number should come next in this series: 1.5, 2.3, 3.1, 3.9, ____**

   a. 4.4 b. 4.2 c. 5.1 d. 4.7

2. **What number should come next in this series: 5.2, 4.8, 4.4, 4, ____**

   a. 3 b. 3.3 c. 3.5 d. 3.6

3. **What number should come next in this series: 2, 1, $\frac{1}{2}$, $\frac{1}{4}$, ____**

   a. $\frac{1}{8}$ b. $\frac{2}{8}$ c. $\frac{1}{16}$ d. $\frac{1}{3}$

4. **Find the missing number in the series: 0.15, 0.3, __, 1.2, 2.4, ...**

   a. 4.8 b. 0.006 c. 0.6 d. 0.9

5. **Identify the missing letter and number combination.**

   U32, V29, __, X23, Y20, ...

   a. W26 b. W17 c. Z17 d. Z26

6. **Which of the following is the heaviest?**

   a. 

   15 kg, 500 g, 1000 g, 700 g

   b. 

   10 kg, 1700 g, 1000 g

   c. 

   20 kg, 1400 g, 1700 g, 700 g

   d. 

   1900 g, 1400 g

7. **The given list shows the names of students who are in a music club. What fraction of names are starting with A?**

   a. $\frac{2}{6}$ b. $\frac{2}{8}$ c. $\frac{5}{18}$ d. $\frac{4}{18}$

Students in a music club		
Sodesh	Sailex	Polly
Mrinalini	Alex	Anuradha
Anisha	John	Kriti
Bhawna	Rahul	Sakshi
Lekha	Mansi	Hazel
Avinash	Ahmed	Farzan

8. **Find the values of W, X, Y and Z?**

W	X	Y	Z
Number of factors of 30	LCM of 24 and 216	HCF of 36 and 216	158421 is divisible by 3

	W	X	Y	Z
a.	5	216	3	True
b.	4	612	3	False
c.	8	216	36	True
d.	5	612	3	False

11 Geometry

Learning Objectives

- To draw and measure a line segment
- To identify different types of angles
- To define different parts of a circle
- To draw a circle by various methods
- To identify different types of polygons
- To understand mirror reflection and symmetry
- To understand tessellations

Let's Get Started

21 CS Critical Thinking, Information Literacy AI

Kriti's younger sister has created the picture given aside. How many lines, line segments, rays or flat shapes can you identify? Label the points using letters of English alphabet and write the name of the lines, line segments, rays or flat shapes in the space provided. One has been done for you.

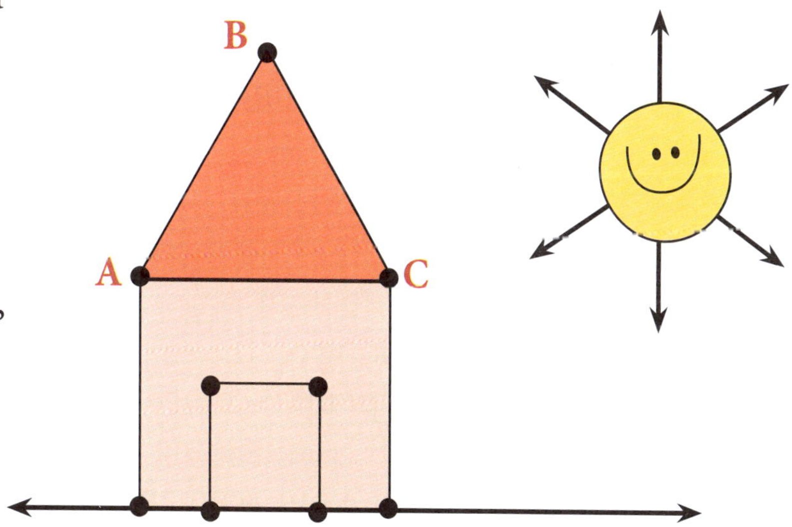

1. ABC: Triangle

DRAW AND MEASURE A LINE SEGMENT

To draw or measure a line segment, you need a ruler. A ruler, as shown below, has markings that denote different measurements of length.

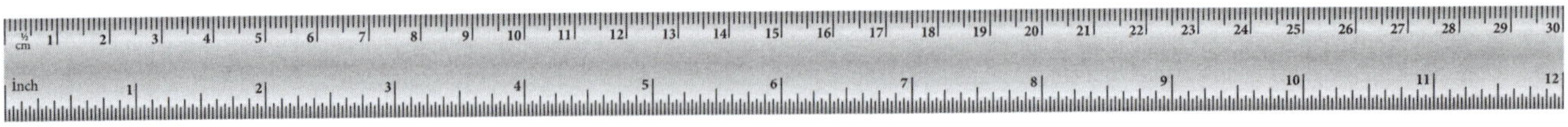

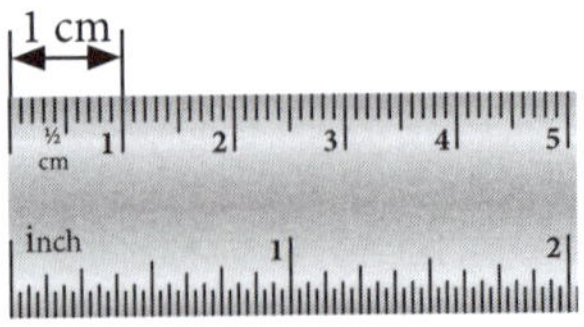

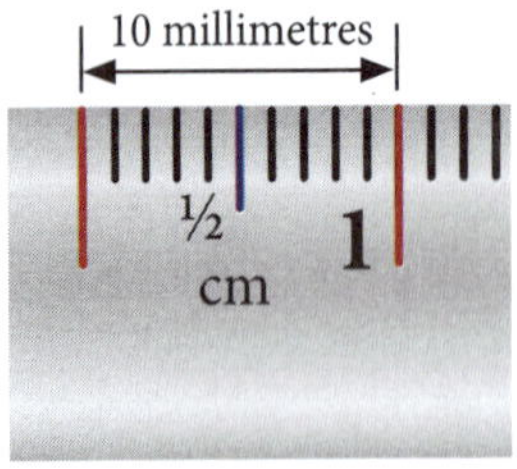

- 1 cm
- 0.5 cm
- 10 lines per centimetre

To draw a line segment of certain measurement, follow these steps.

- Place a ruler on the paper and with your pencil put a mark on point 0 cm and point 3 cm.
- Join both these points along the ruler.
- You will get a line equal to 3 cm.

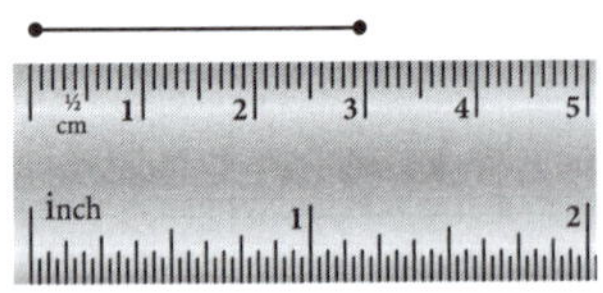

How would you compare two or more line segments? Can you identify the longer line segment?

To measure the length of these line segments and identify which one is longer or shorter, follow these steps.

- First, find out the exact length of each line segment.
- Place the ruler along the line segment AB such that the '0' mark of the ruler coincides with the endpoint A.
- Note down the marking on the ruler where the other endpoint B coincides.
- Observe that point B is coinciding with 3. Hence, the length of line segment AB is 3 cm. Similarly, measure the length of CD and compare it with AB.
- The length of line segment CD is 4.5 cm. Therefore, CD > AB.

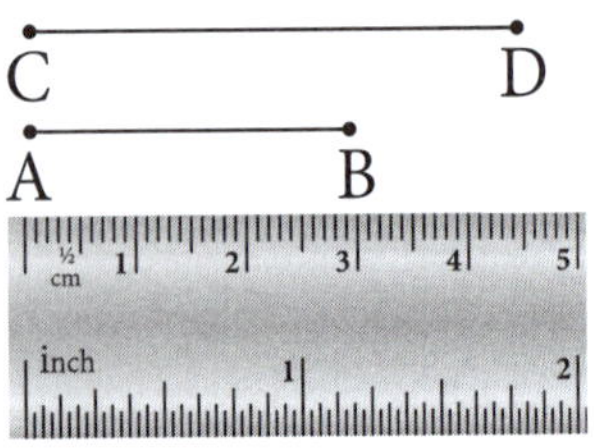

Common Errors

Take careful note where the endpoints coincide with the markings of the ruler.

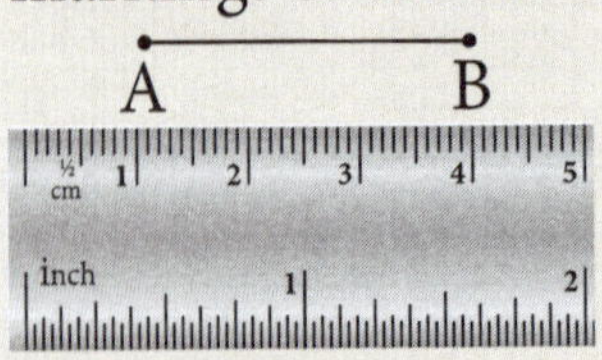

AB = 3 cm
AB = 4 cm

The length of AB = 3 cm because point A is at 1 cm.
So, AB = (4 – 1) cm = 3 cm.

ANGLES

An **angle** is formed when two rays meet at one point. The point where two rays meet is called the **vertex** of the angle.

The plural of vertex is vertices.

The rays are called the **arms** of the angle. An angle is represented by the symbol $\angle$.

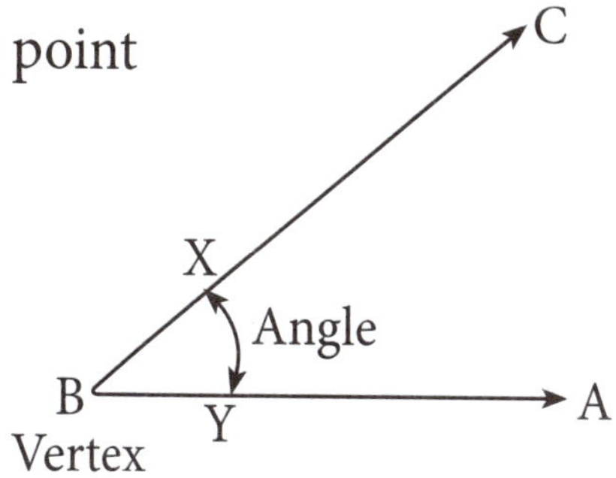

In the figure, the arms BA and BC meet at vertex B. The space between BA and BC (or amount of turn between BA and BC) is the angle.

Types of Angles

Different types of angles can be found in everyday life as shown in the pictures given below.

Right angle: An angle formed by a vertical line and a horizontal line is called a right angle.

Acute angle: An angle less than a right angle is an acute angle.

Obtuse angle: An angle greater than a right angle is an obtuse angle.

Straight angle: An angle formed by joining two right angles is a straight angle.

Straight angle

The minute and hour hands form a straight angle when the time is 6 o'clock.

EXERCISE 11A

1. **With the help of a ruler and a pencil, draw line segments of the following lengths.**

   a. 2 cm b. 3.5 cm c. 4.5 cm d. 5 cm e. 6.5 cm

2. **What is the length of the following line segments?**

   a. b.  c.

3. **In the given angle:**

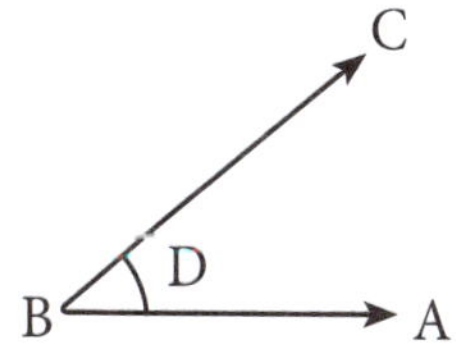

   a. Name the vertex of the angle.
   b. Name the arms of the angle.
   c. Name this angle in four different ways.
   d. Which type of angle is it?

CIRCLE

A circle is a round shape and looks like the given figures. It is a simple closed curve with no vertices.

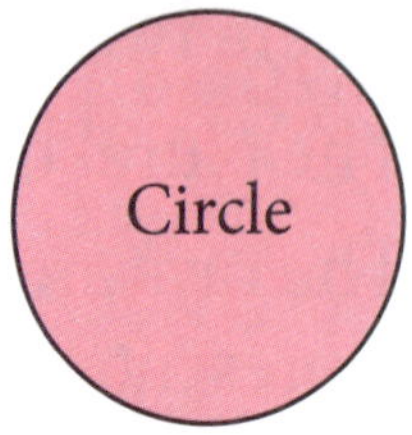

You can find many things around you whose shape is similar to a circle. For example, coins, buttons, plates, bangles, a tyre, wheels, a clock, most cookies and *rotis*.

Parts of a Circle

The different parts of a circle are given below.

Circumference: The boundary of the circle is called the circumference.

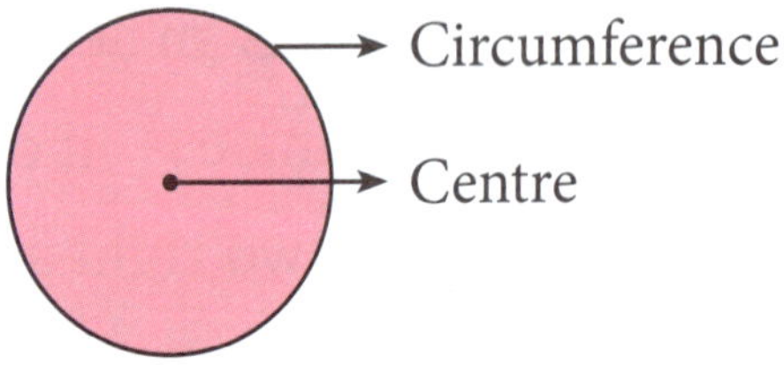

Centre: The point right in the middle of the circle is called the centre.

Radius: The distance from the centre to any point on the circumference is called the radius.

The plural of radius is **radii**.

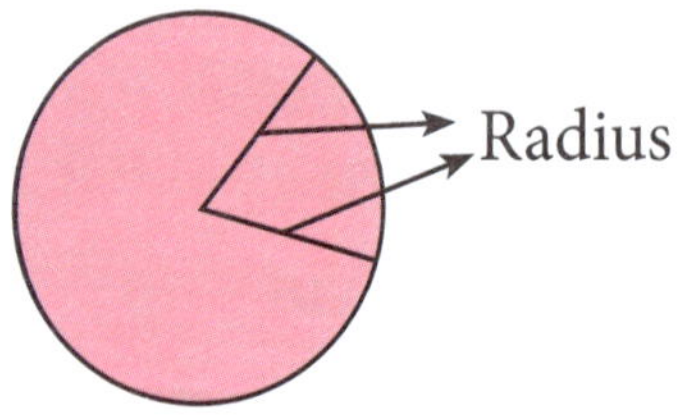

Diameter: A diameter is the straight line starting from any point on the circumference passing through the centre to another point on the circumference.

$$\text{Diameter} = \text{radius} + \text{radius}$$
$$= 2 \text{ radii}$$

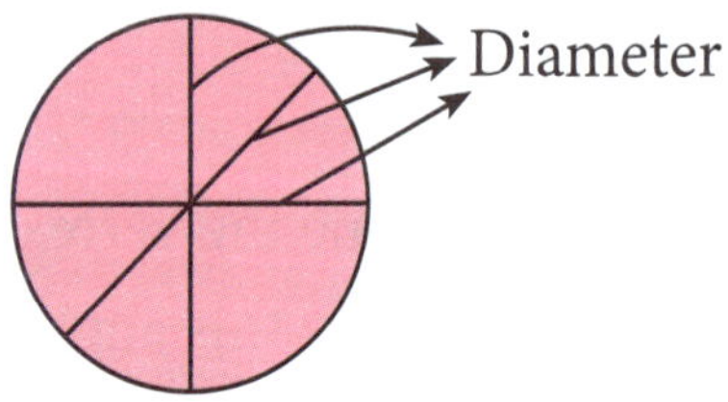

Drawing a Circle

The following methods can be used to draw a circle.

Method 1

Tracing the outline of circular objects such as a coin, bottle cap, bangle, glass tumbler, etc.

Method 2

Using a piece of a string and a pencil

Step 1: Take a piece of string and tie it to the end of a pencil.

Step 2: Fix the other end of the string to the paper with a pin.

Step 3: Hold the string tightly and rotate the pencil.

Method 3

Using a compass from your geometry box

Step 1: Fix a pencil inside the compass tightly. Adjust the pencil such that the compass needle and the pencil edge (pointed one) are at the same level.

Step 2: Fix the needle of the compass on the paper.

Step 3: Stretch the other arm of the compass which is holding the pencil.

Step 4: Rotate the pencil by rotating the compass to draw a circle. (Make sure the pencil is touching the paper.)

Method 1

Method 2

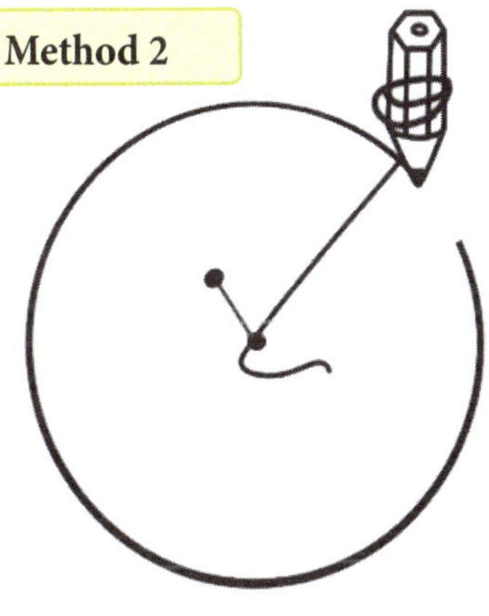

Method 3

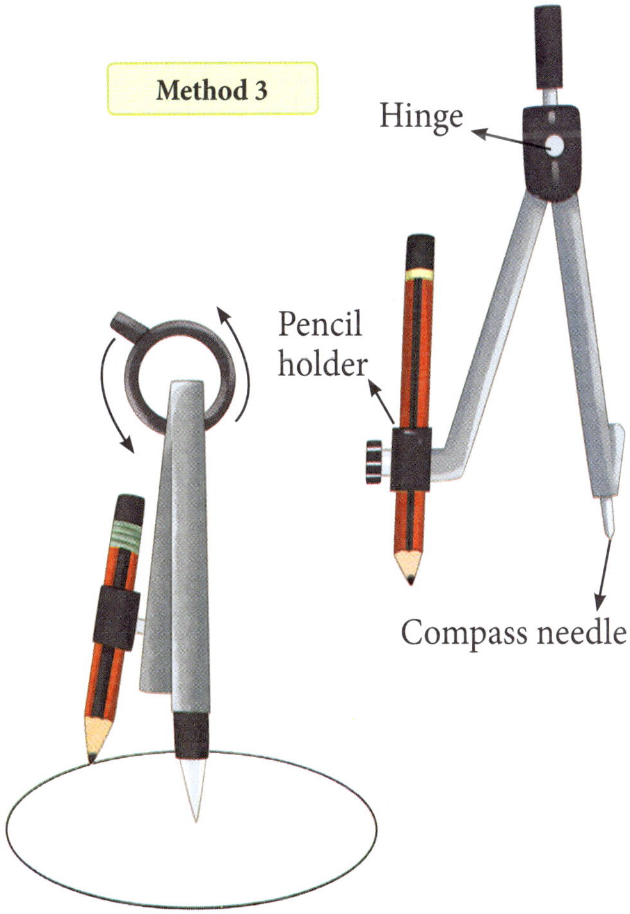

Exercise 11B

1. Fill in the blanks.

a. The point right in the middle of the circle is called the ______________.

b. The plural of radius is ______________.

c. The diameter is twice the length of the ______________.

2. In the given circle, name the following.

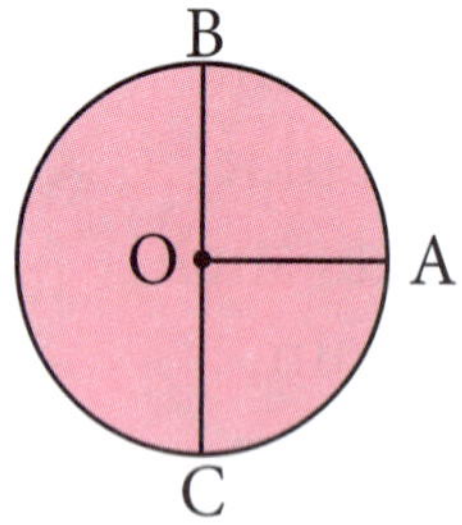

a. Circumference b. Centre

c. Radius d. Diameter

POLYGONS

A **polygon** is a closed figure made up of line segments. A polygon must have at least 3 sides for it to be a closed figure.

Closed Figures

The figure given alongside is made up of 4 line segments: AB, BC, CD and DA. It is a closed figure.

Open Figures

In the figure given alongside, the line segments AB, BC and CD are joined, but DA is not joined. So, it is an open figure.

If there is only one side, the figure will not be closed and thus, it is not a polygon.

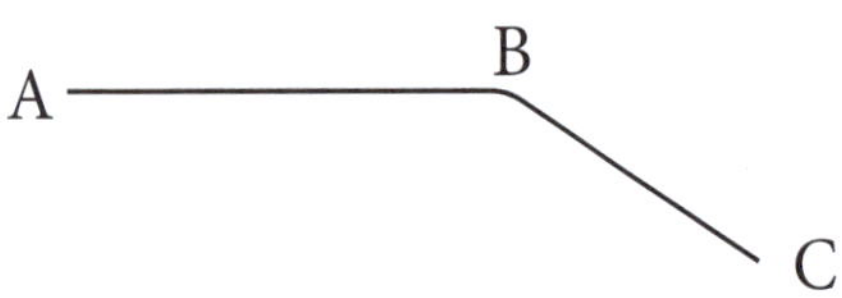

If the figure has only two sides, then it will not be closed and it is not a polygon.

Types of Polygons

Closed figures with three or more sides are called polygons. These polygons have specific names.

Number of sides	Name of the polygon	Figures
3	Triangle **Note:** Tri means 3.	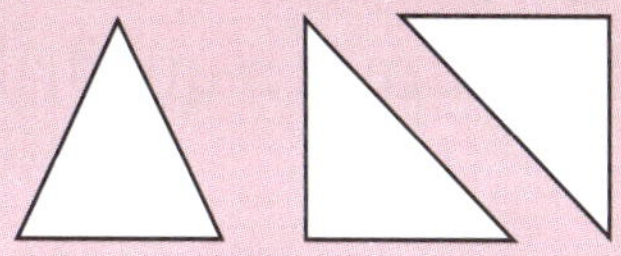
4	Quadrilateral **Note:** Quad means 4.	
5	Pentagon **Note:** Penta means 5.	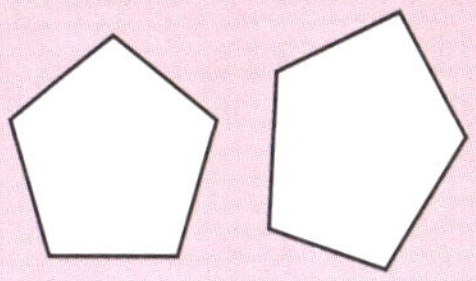

Triangle

A triangle is a polygon made up of 3 line segments.

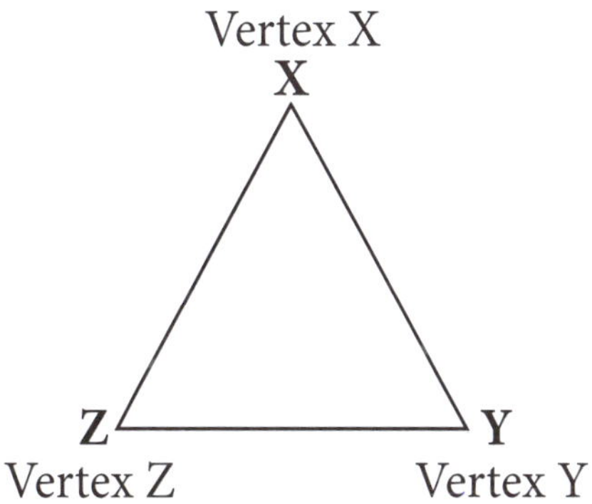

In the above triangle, the three line segments are XY, YZ and ZX. These are also called the sides of a triangle. There are 3 vertices in a triangle. In this triangle, the vertices are X, Y and Z. The symbol for a triangle is Δ. This triangle can be named as ΔXYZ, ΔXZY, ΔYXZ, ΔYZX, ΔZXY, ΔZYX.

Pyramids found in Egypt and mountains in hilly areas are triangular in shape.

Quadrilateral

A quadrilateral is a polygon made up of four line segments.
In this figure, the four sides are AB, BC, CD and DA. The four vertices are A, B, C and D. The quadrilateral can be named as ABCD, BCDA, DABC, ADCB, DCBA, CBAD or BADC.

Square: A square is a quadrilateral in which all the sides are equal.
AB = BC = CD = DA. Here, ABCD is a square.

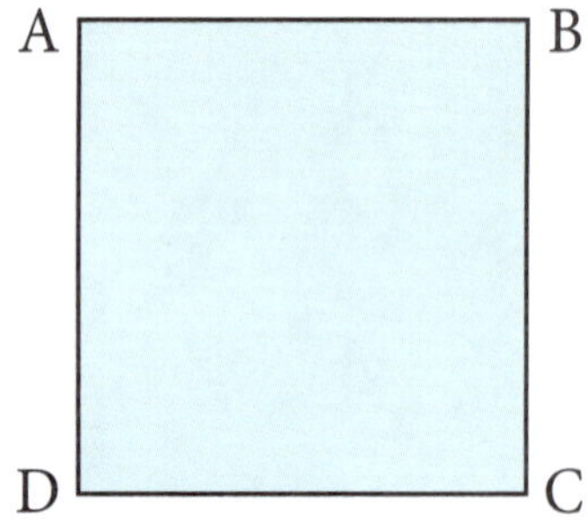

Rectangle: A rectangle is a quadrilateral in which the opposite sides are equal. In the rectangle given below, EF = HG and EH = FG.

Laptops and mobiles are quadrilaterals.

EXERCISE 11C

1. Fill in the blanks.

a. A polygon is a ______________ figure made up of line segments.

b. A polygon must have at least ______________ sides.

c. A triangle is a polygon made up of ______________ line segments.

d. A quadrilateral is a polygon made up of ______________ line segments.

e. A square is a quadrilateral in which all the four sides are ______________.

2. Which of the following shapes are polygons?

a. 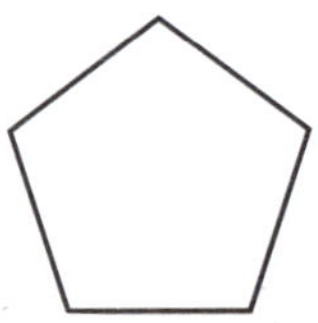

b. 

c. 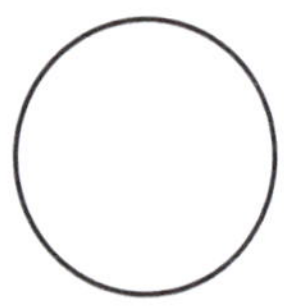

3. Write the names of the polygons with the given number of sides.

Number of sides	Name of the polygon
a. 3	______________
b. 4	______________

MIRROR IMAGE OR REFLECTION

An exact copy or the image that you can see in a mirror, glass or water is called **mirror image** or **reflection**.

Symmetry

When one-half of a figure is the reflection of the other half, the figure is called **symmetrical**. It means, if we divide a symmetrical shape from the middle, then one-half of the shape falls exactly on the other half. The line in the middle of the symmetrical shape is called the **line of symmetry**. Therefore, the line of symmetry divides a symmetrical shape into two equal halves.

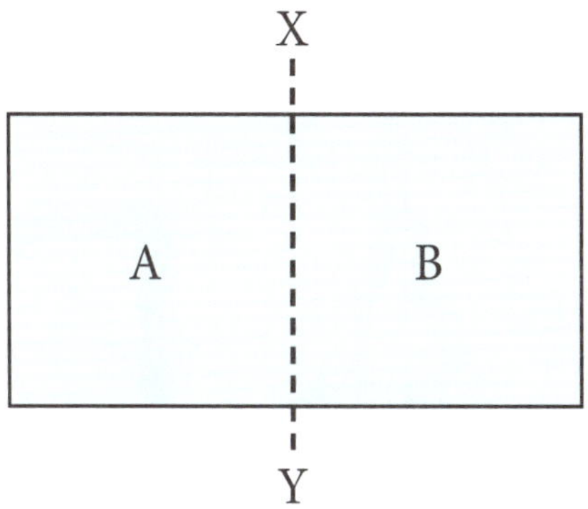

Line of symmetry

When we fold the rectangle from left to right, we find that part A of the rectangle falls exactly on part B of the rectangle.

Thus, the line XY along which the rectangle folds into two equal halves is called the line of symmetry. Shapes can have one or more lines of symmetry.

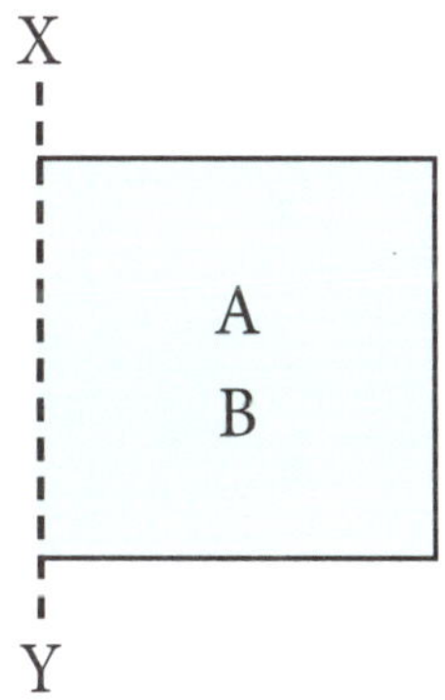

A rectangle has two lines of symmetry as shown below.

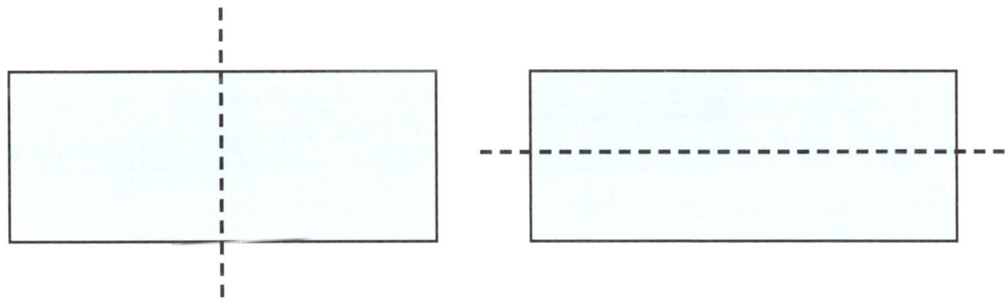

A square has four lines of symmetry.

A circle has infinite lines of symmetry.

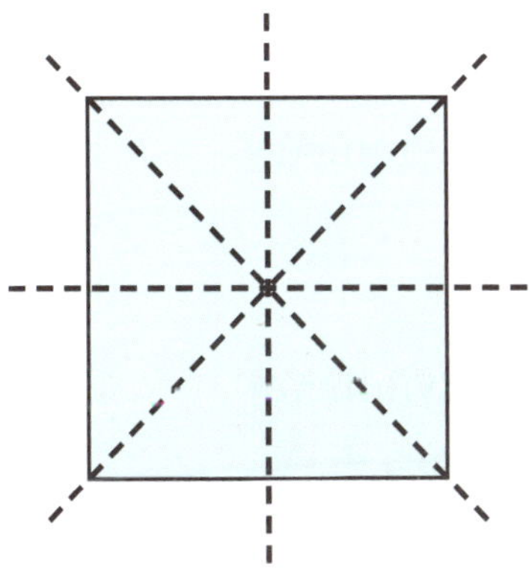

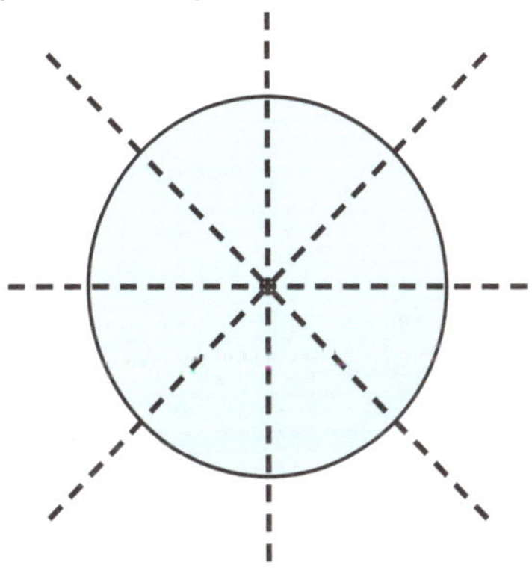

NOTE

Symmetry applies not only to geometric shapes but also to other things. A face is usually symmetrical.

Below are a few more examples showing line symmetry.

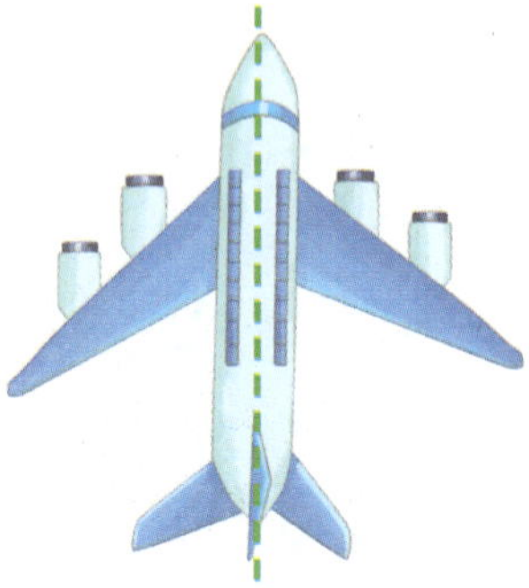

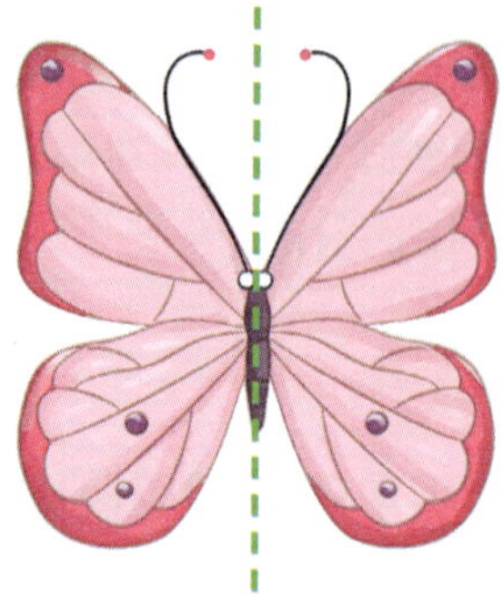

Lines of symmetry can be vertical, horizontal or diagonal. As the names suggest, these lines of symmetry divide the figures vertically, horizontally or diagonally. Some examples are given below.

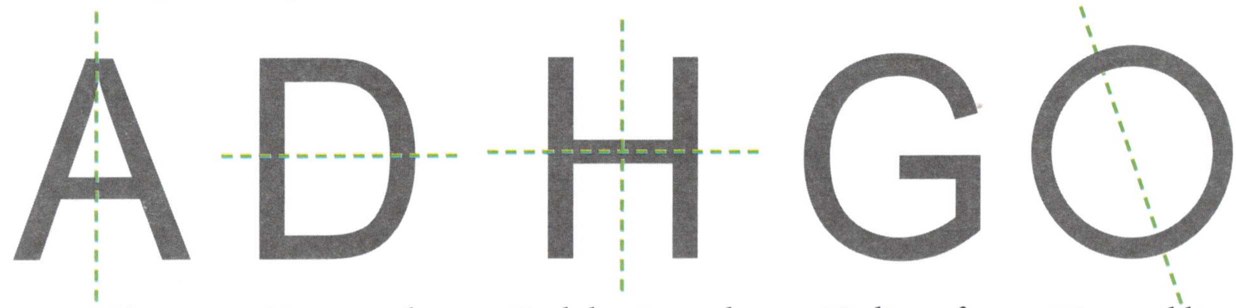

Vertical line of symmetry | Horizontal line of symmetry | Both horizontal and vertical line of symmetry | No line of symmetry | Diagonal line of symmetry

Exercise 11D

Draw the line(s) of symmetry for the shapes given below. Also, write the number of lines of symmetry for each shape. One has been done for you.

1. 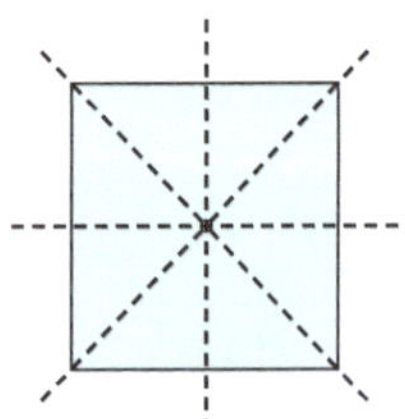 4 lines of symmetry

2. 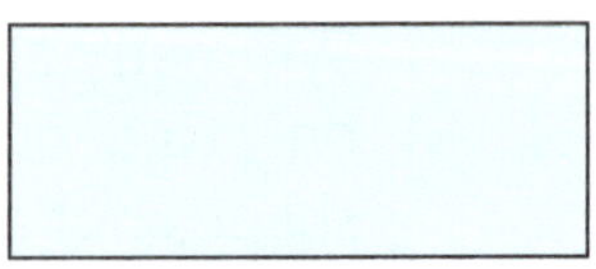 ________ lines of symmetry

3.  ________ lines of symmetry

TESSELLATIONS

A **tessellation** is a pattern created when a shape is repeated over and over again, covering a place without any gaps or overlaps. Tessellation can also be called **tiling**. Shapes that can be used for tiling are called **tiling shapes**.

Shapes that leave a gap cannot be used for tiling. Such shapes that cannot be used for tiling are called **non-tiling shapes**.

Tiling shapes

Non-tiling shapes

EXERCISE 11E

Colour and complete the tiling patterns.

1. 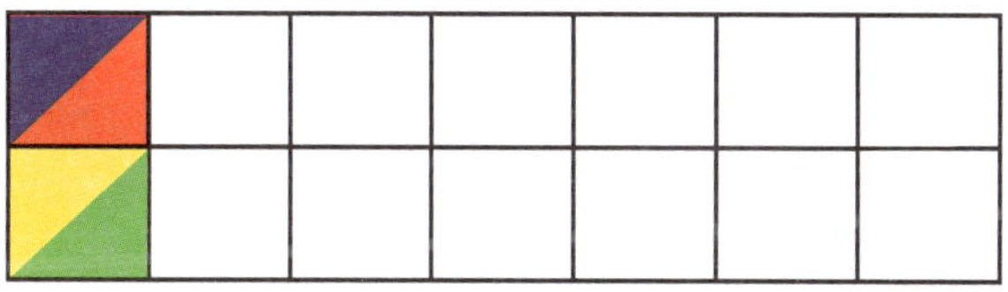

2. 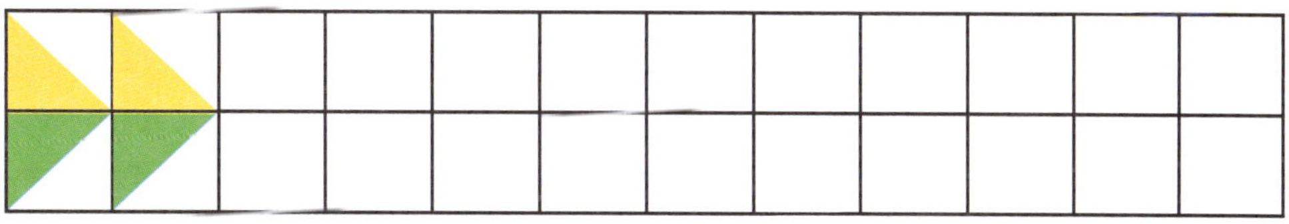

3. 

MATHS LAB ACTIVITY

21 CS Critical Thinking, Creativity and Innovation | AI | EL | STEAM CHALLENGE

Aim: To identify and create shapes and check whether the shapes can be used to tile or tessellate a place

Materials required: A chart paper, waste papers, scissors, glue stick, fallen leaves, petals of fallen flowers

Procedure:

1. Make groups of two students each.
2. Create or design different shapes.

3. Use the waste papers to make cut-outs of your designs.
4. Also, make cut-outs of circles, triangles, quadrilaterals and pentagons using the waste papers.
5. You can even collect fallen leaves and petals of flowers.
6. Now, draw two lines on a chart paper to divide the chart paper into four equal sections.
7. Select any one or two shapes and predict whether the shapes will tile a section of the chart paper.
8. Try to tile the section. Use the glue stick to paste the pieces of shapes onto the chart paper.
9. Repeat steps 7 and 8 to try and tile the remaining sections of the chart paper. Were you able to create any tiling pattern?
10. Recreate a table as shown below in your notebook and record your observations.

Shape	Predict: Will the shape/object tile the section of the chart paper?	Result: Does the shape/object tile the section of the chart paper?
Triangle		
Quadrilateral		
Pentagon		
Leaves		
Petals of flowers		
(Name of your design)		

Concept Map

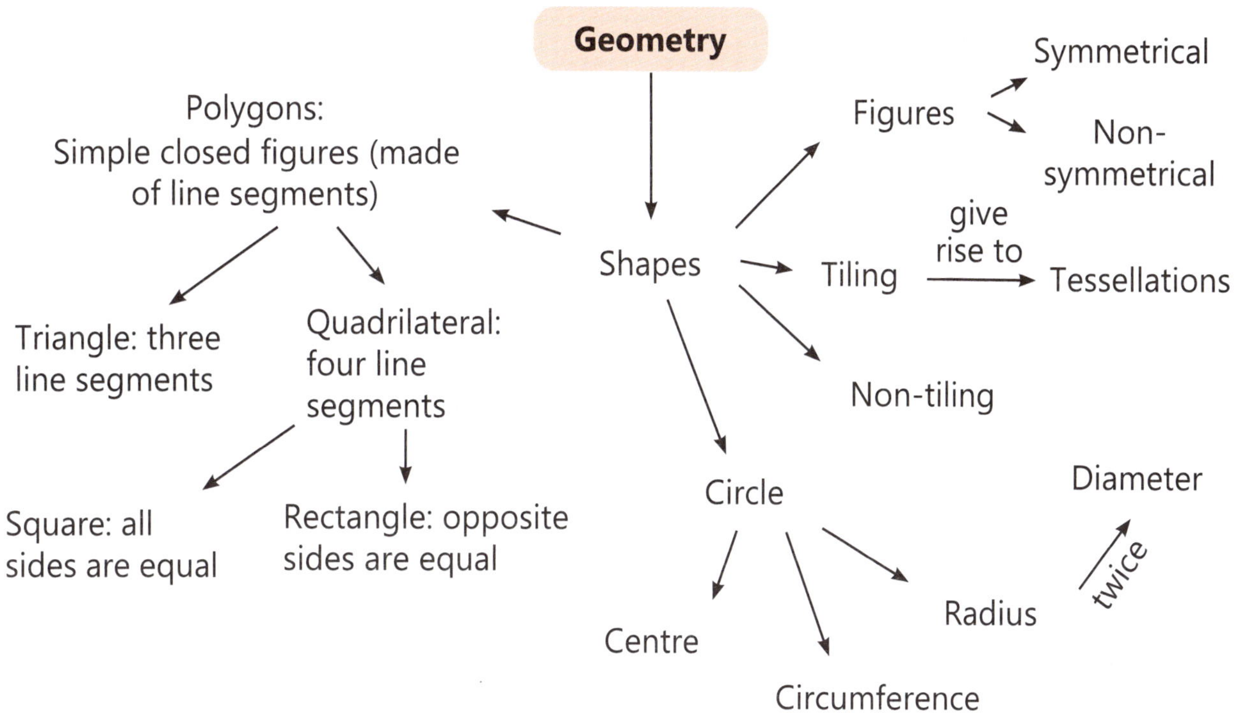

Key Concepts

- **Angle:** Formed when two rays meet at a common point
- **Vertex:** The point where two rays meet
- **Circumference:** The boundary of a circle
- **Centre:** The point right in the middle of the circle
- **Radius:** The distance from the centre to any point on the circumference
- **Polygon:** A closed figure made up of line segments
- **Triangle:** A polygon made up of three line segments
- **Quadrilateral:** A polygon made up of four line segments
- **Square:** A quadrilateral in which all the sides are equal
- **Rectangle:** A quadrilateral in which the opposite sides are equal
- **Mirror image or reflection:** An exact copy or the image that you can see in a mirror, glass or water
- **Symmetrical:** When one-half of a figure is the reflection of the other half
- **Line of symmetry:** The line in the middle of the symmetrical shape that divides the shape into mirror images
- **Tessellation:** A pattern created when a shape is repeated over and over again covering a place without any gaps or overlaps
- **Tiling shapes:** Shapes that can be used for tiling
- **Non-tiling shapes:** Shapes that leave a gap and cannot be used for tiling

Chapter Revision

A. Choose the correct option.

1. An angle formed by a vertical line and a horizontal line is called a/an

   a. acute angle   b. right angle   c. obtuse angle   d. straight angle

2. A simple closed curve with no vertices

   a. Triangle   b. Square   c. Circle   d. Rectangle

3. The diameter of a circle with radius 2 cm is

   a. 6 cm   b. 4 cm   c. 5 cm   d. 1 cm

4. A polygon with four equal sides

   a. Triangle   b. Square   c. Circle   d. Rectangle

5. A polygon with three sides

   a. Triangle   b. Square   c. Circle   d. Rectangle

6. A polygon with opposite sides are equal

   a. Triangle   b. Line   c. Circle   d. Rectangle

7. Which of the following letters has both vertical and horizontal lines of symmetry?

   a. A   b. C   c. D   d. H

B. Draw the following.

1. A line segment of length

   a. 4 cm   b. 6 cm   c. 5.5 cm   d. 8.4 cm

2. A circle with centre, radius and diameter clearly marked.

C. Does the dotted line on each shape represent a line of symmetry? Write Yes or No.

1.
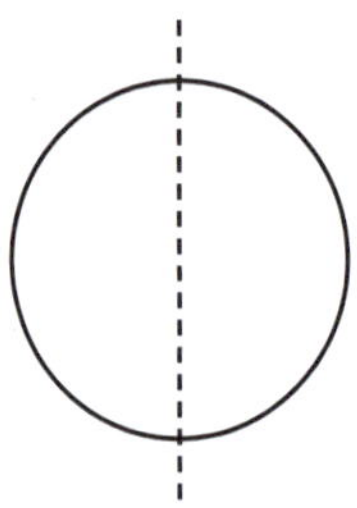

2.
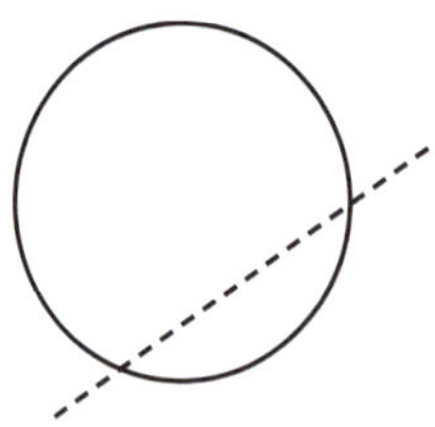

3.
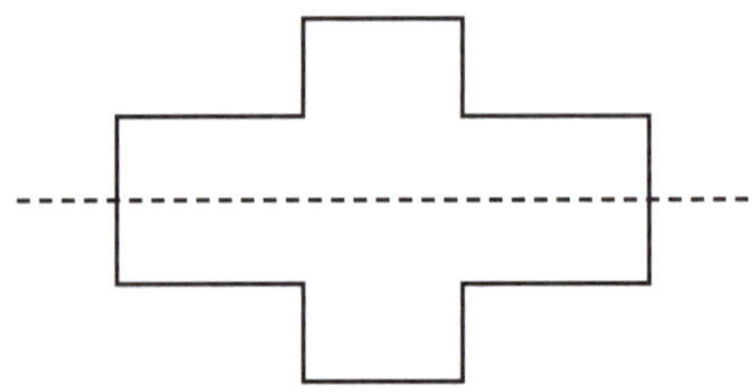

4.
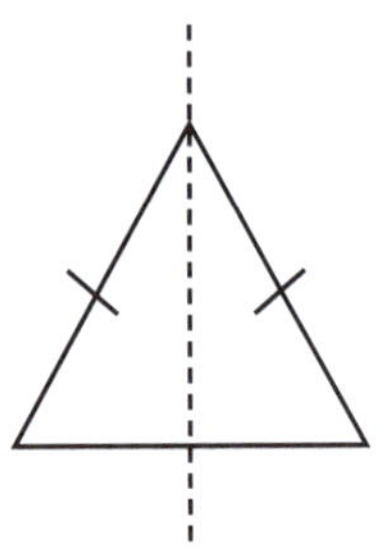

5.
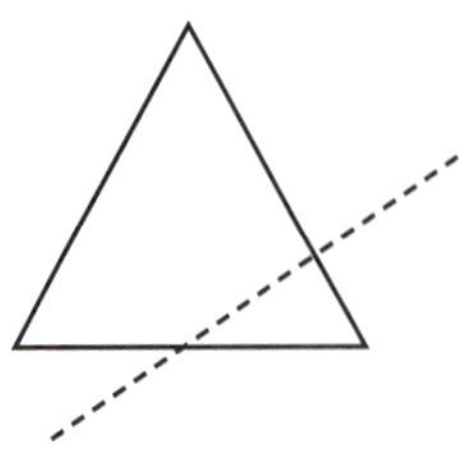

6.
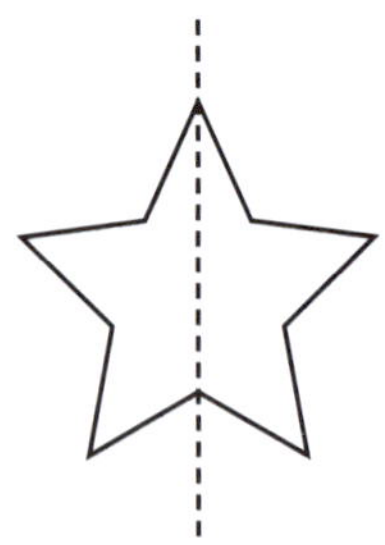

D. **If the dotted line is the line of symmetry for each shape given, then complete the shapes by drawing the other half.**

1. 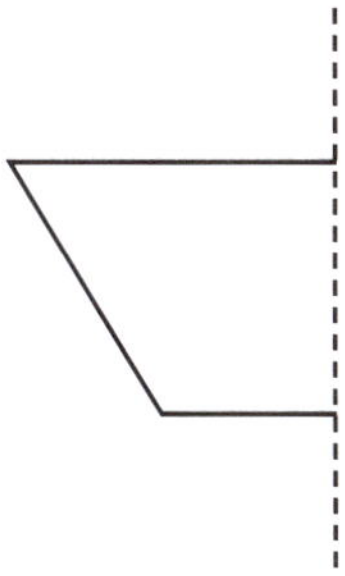

2. 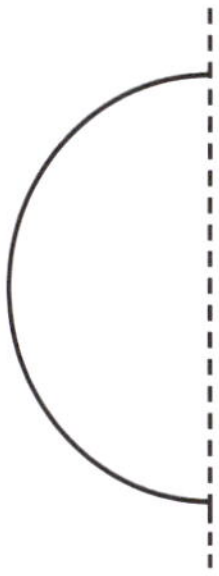

3. 

4. 

E. **Draw the line(s) of symmetry for the figures given below.**

1. 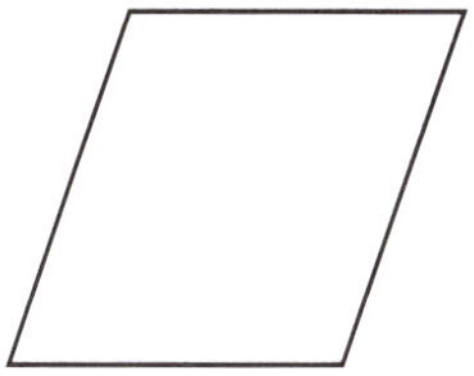

2. 

3. 

4. 

5. 

6. 

F. **Circle the image formed by tessellating shapes.**

1. 

2. 

3. 

4. 

5. 

6. 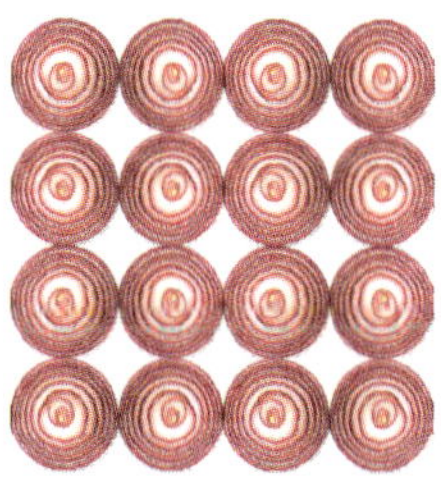

Skill up!

A. 21 CS Creativity and innovation, Technology Literacy | AI | STEAM Challenge

9 INDUSTRY, INNOVATION AND INFRASTRUCTURE

Geometric angles and shapes are used in the construction of buildings. Architects are those people who design buildings using angles and different shapes. Would you like to be an architect for a day? Design a house using different shapes and angles. Draw the design on a chart paper and display it in the class.

B. 21 CS Media Literacy | CC Integration with Social Studies and Computer Science

Find out any five famous monuments in the world. Identify the shapes used in constructing these monuments. Collect pictures if you can and make a presentation on your findings.

C. 21 CS Creativity and innovation, Life Skills | EL | AI | HQ Happiness My Goal

Mansi is designing a pattern for her mother's new saree. She wants to use a circle and polygons in the design and three different colours. Use a grid paper to create two different designs that Mansi might use. Colour your designs.

D. 21 CS Critical Thinking, Creativity and Innovation | EL | AI

Identify two different polygons that can be used together to create a tessellating pattern. Draw a tessellation on a grid paper using the two polygons. Can you create tessellations using free-hand drawings instead of polygons?

SUSTAINABLE DEVELOPMENT GOALS

Question A is in line with SDG 9 Industry, Innovation and Infrastructure. What is the strongest geometric shape used in construction? Why is it important to build a strong foundation while constructing a building or a house?

Worksheet 11

21 CS Collaboration, Communication | HQ Happiness My Goal

If you know the shapes, you can play this game. Two or three players can play this game. Use your eraser as your piece and then roll a dice. Move your piece based on the keys given below. (*Hint*: Suppose 1 comes in the dice, land your piece on the next circular image and so on.)

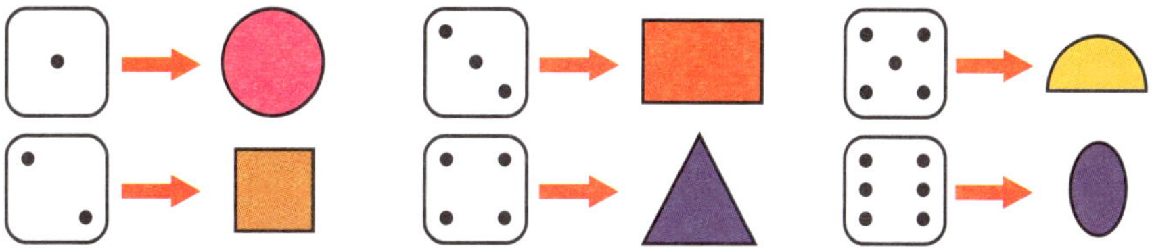

12 Perimeter and Area

Learning Objectives

- To find the perimeter of regular shapes
- To find the perimeter of irregular shapes
- To find the area of regular shapes
- To find the area of irregular shapes

Let's Get Started

21 CS Critical Thinking AI STEAM Challenge

The floor plan of a house is given below. The floor of the living room needs to be changed. Design a pattern of tiles for the room in the space given below. The available shapes of the tiles are  and .

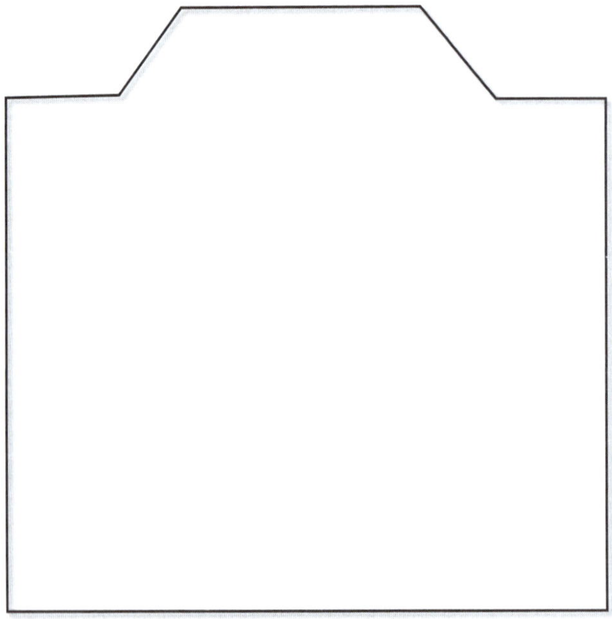

How can you find out how many tiles would be required? What measurements would you need to find out?

PERIMETER

Perimeter is the distance covered along the boundary of a polygon or a figure when you go around it once.

In other words, **perimeter** is the sum of all the sides of a polygon. Thus, to find the perimeter, add all the sides of a polygon.

Perimeter of a Square

A square has four equal sides. Therefore, to find its perimeter, multiply the measure of one side by 4.

P = side + side + side + side

P = 4 × side = $4s$

Each side of the clock = 50 cm

So, the perimeter = 50 cm + 50 cm + 50 cm + 50 cm

= 4 × 50 cm = 200 cm

Perimeter of a Rectangle

The opposite sides of a rectangle are equal. Therefore, to find the perimeter, use the following formula.

P = length + breadth + length + breadth

P = 2 × length + 2 × breadth

= 2(length + breadth)

= $2(\ell + b)$

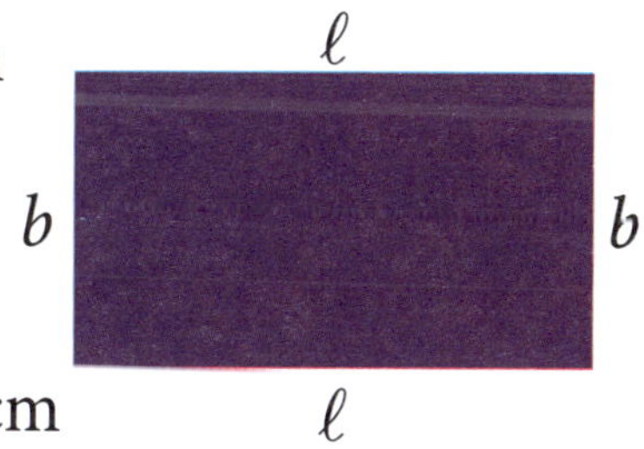

NOTE

The longer side of a rectangle is called the length (ℓ) and the shorter side of a rectangle is called the breadth (b) or width.

The length ℓ of the rectangle = 6 cm

The breadth b of the rectangle = 2 cm

So, the perimeter = 2(6 cm + 2 cm)

= 2 × (8 cm)

= 16 cm

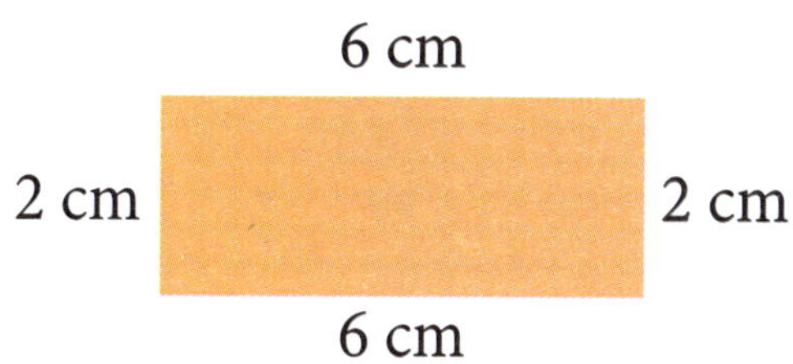

SOLVED EXAMPLES

Example 1: Find the perimeter of each figure.

Solution:

Perimeter of the triangle = 3 cm + 4 cm + 5 cm = 12 cm

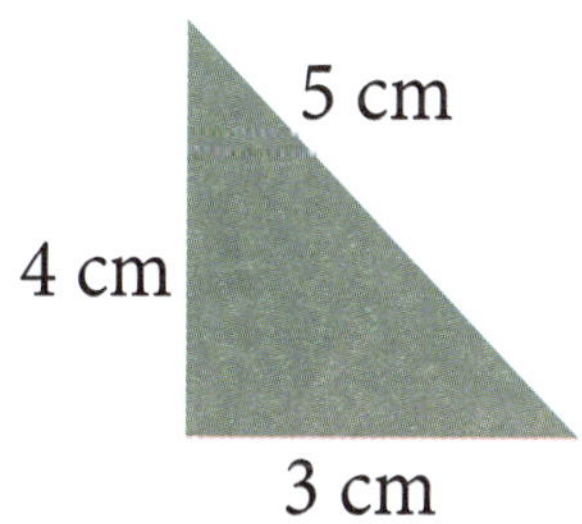

Perimeter of the square
$= 5 \text{ cm} + 5 \text{ cm} + 5 \text{ cm} + 5 \text{ cm}$
$= 4 \times 5 = 20 \text{ cm}$
Perimeter of the rectangle
$= 2 \text{ cm} + 6 \text{ cm} + 2 \text{ cm} + 6 \text{ cm}$
$= 2(6 + 2) = 2(8) = 16 \text{ cm}$
Perimeter of the pentagon
$= 4 \text{ cm} + 5 \text{ cm} + 5 \text{ cm} + 4 \text{ cm} + 6 \text{ cm}$
$= 24 \text{ cm}$

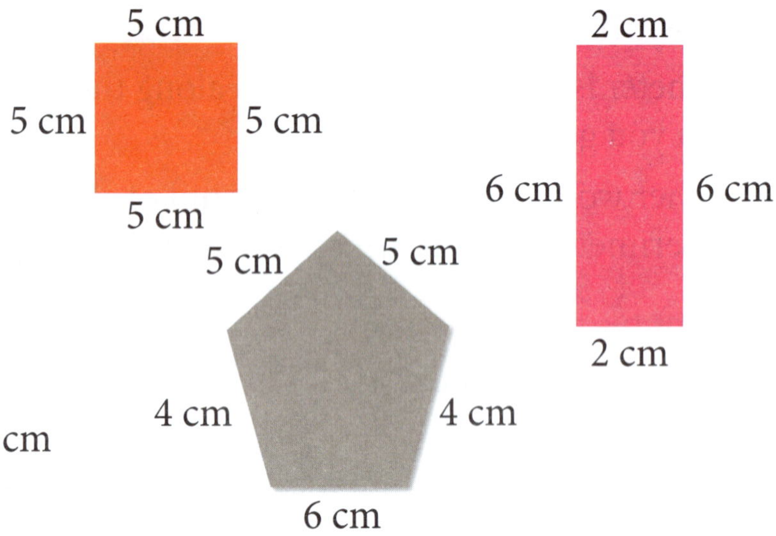

EXERCISE 12A

1. Find the perimeter of the following shapes.

a. 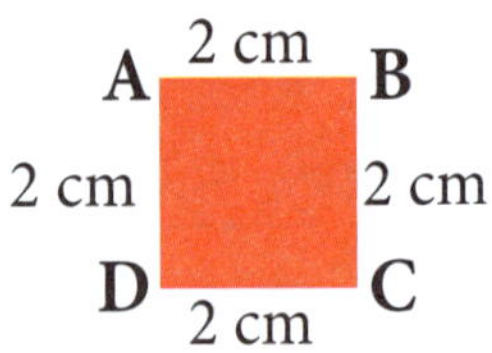

b. 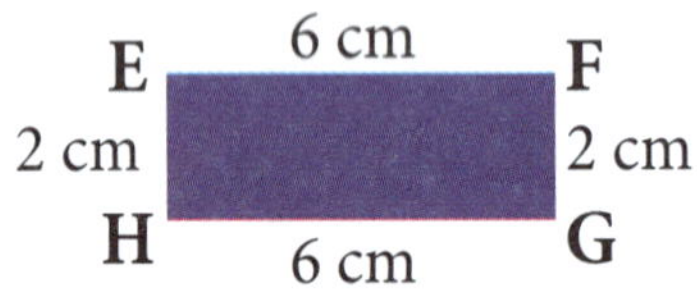

c. 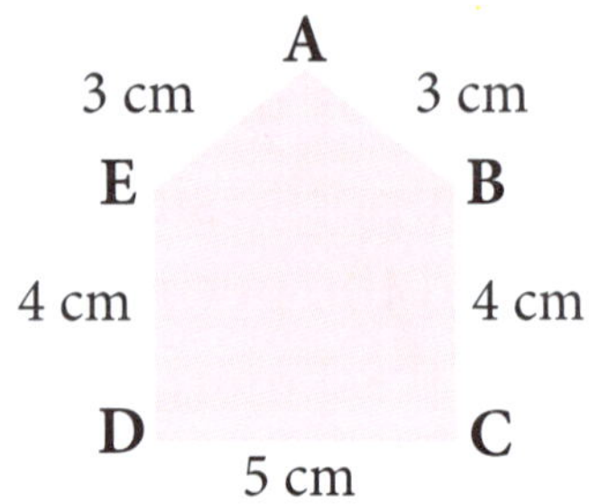

d. 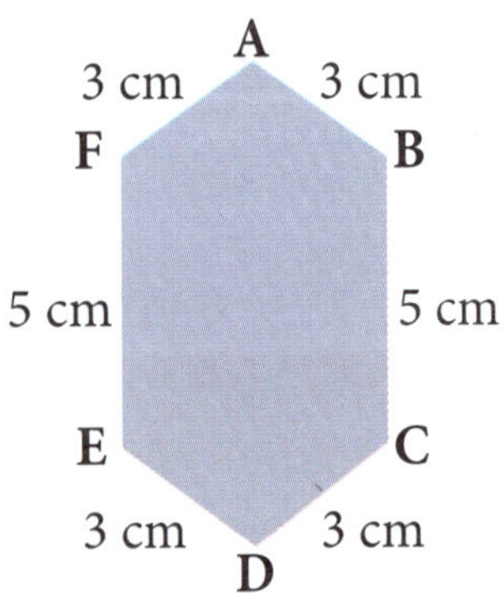

e. 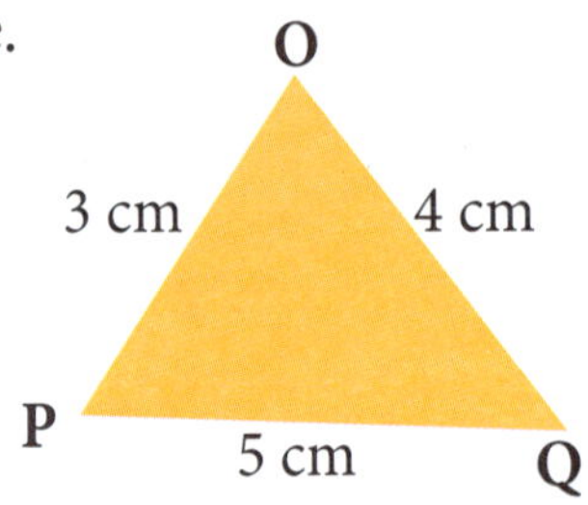

f. 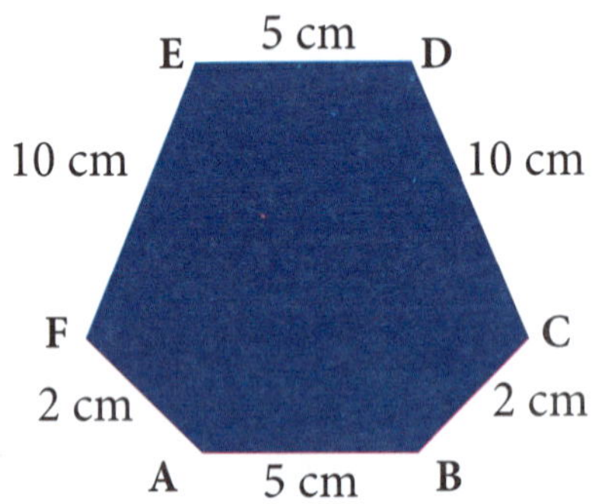

Finding the Side of a Square

A square has 4 equal sides. To find each side, divide the perimeter by 4.

$$P = 4 \times \text{side}$$

$$\text{So, } \frac{P}{4} = \text{side}$$

Finding the Length or Breadth of a Rectangle

We know, $P = 2(\ell + b)$

$$P = 2\ell + 2b$$

Case 1: When perimeter and breadth are known:

$$P - 2b = 2\ell$$

Therefore, $\ell = \dfrac{P - 2b}{2}$

Case 2: When perimeter and length are known:

$$P - 2\ell = 2b$$

Therefore, $b = \dfrac{P - 2\ell}{2}$

COMMON ERRORS

$P = 2(\ell + b)$ 👍

$P = 2(\ell \times b)$ 👎

$P = 2\ell \times b$ 👎

$P = \ell \times b$ 👎

$P = 2\ell + b$ 👎

SOLVED EXAMPLES

Example 2: The perimeter of a square is 20 cm. Find the length of each side.

Solution:

Each side $= \dfrac{P}{4} = \dfrac{20}{4} = 5$ cm

So, each side of the square is 5 cm.

Example 3: Find the length of a rectangle whose perimeter is 18 cm and breadth is 4 cm.

Solution: Here, perimeter = 18 cm and breadth = 4 cm

Using the formula, $\ell = \dfrac{P - 2b}{2}$

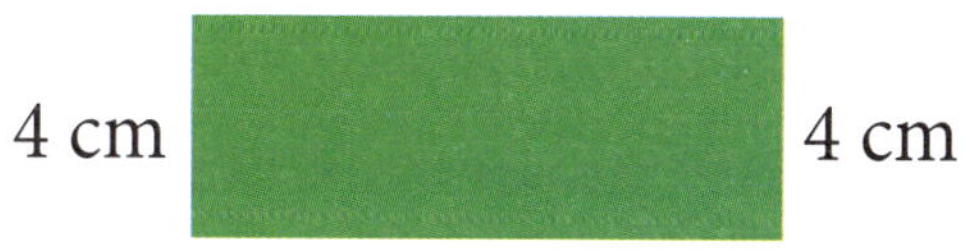

We get, $\ell = \dfrac{18 - 2(4)}{2} = \dfrac{18 - 8}{2} = 5$ cm

So, the length of the rectangle is 5 cm.

Example 4: Find the breadth of a rectangle whose perimeter is 24 cm and length is 10 cm.

Solution: Here, perimeter = 24 cm and length = 10 cm

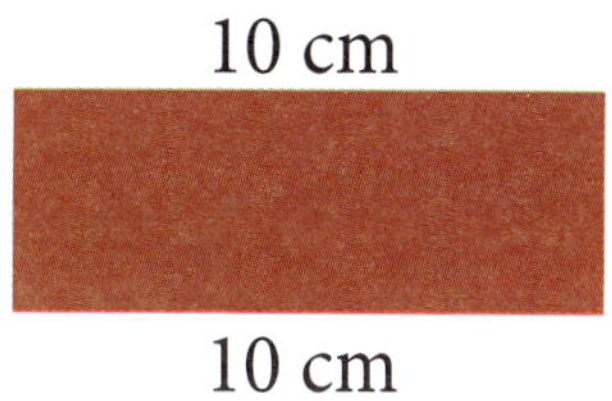

Using the formula, $b = \dfrac{P - 2\ell}{2}$

We get, $b = \dfrac{24 - 2(10)}{2} = \dfrac{24 - 20}{2} = 2$ cm

So, the breadth of the rectangle is 2 cm.

Measuring Perimeter of Irregular Shapes

There are different methods for measuring perimeter of irregular shapes, curves and even regular shapes. Some of these methods are mentioned below.

Using a Thread

To find the perimeter of irregular shapes such as leaves, place a thread along the boundary of the leaf. Then measure the length of the thread using a ruler. The length of the thread gives the perimeter of the figure.

Using a GeoBoard

Form different irregular figures on a geoboard using a rubber band. Take a thread and measure the lengths along the boundaries. The length of the thread will give the perimeter of the irregular shapes.

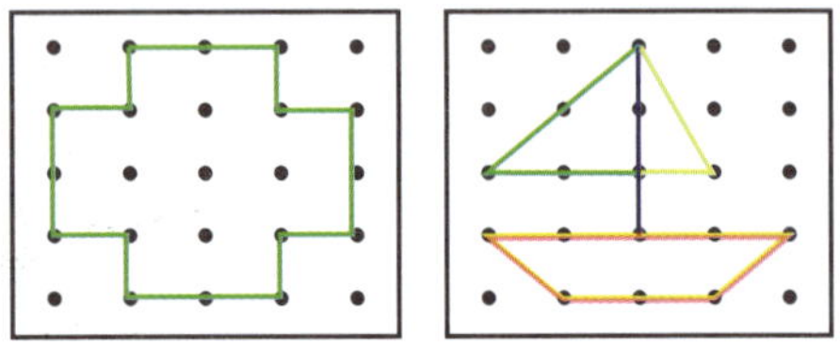

Using Square Grids

Each square in a square grid has a side of length 1 cm. The number of squares along each side of the figure gives the length of each side. Adding the lengths of all the sides gives the perimeter of the figure.

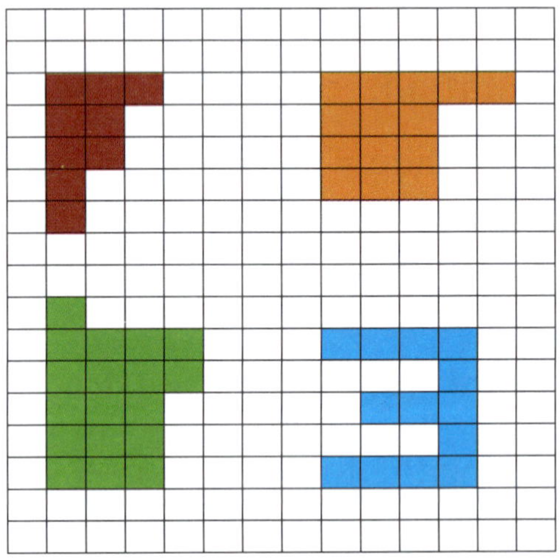

Perimeter of the brown figure = 3 cm + 1 cm + 1 cm + 2 cm + 1 cm + 2 cm + 1 cm + 5 cm = **16 cm**

Find out the perimeter of the other three figures.

Exercise 12B

1. Find the perimeter of the squares with the given sides.

a. 4 cm b. 6 cm c. 14 cm d. 18 cm

2. Find the perimeter of the rectangles with the given lengths and breadths.

a. Length = 5 cm, breadth = 2 cm
b. Length = 7 cm, breadth = 3 cm
c. Length = 9 cm, breadth = 5 cm
d. Length = 12 cm, breadth = 7 cm

3. Find the perimeter of the triangles with the given sides.

a. 5 cm, 4 cm, 3 cm
b. 8 cm, 9 cm, 12 cm
c. 11 cm each
d. 15 cm each

4. Find the side of the squares with the following perimeters.

a. 12 cm b. 20 cm c. 28 cm d. 52 cm

5. Find the length of the rectangles with the following perimeters and breadths.

a. Perimeter = 14 cm, breadth = 2 cm b. Perimeter = 20 cm, breadth = 4 cm

AREA

Area is the region covered inside the boundary of a figure or a polygon.

In the rectangle ABCD, perimeter is AB + BC + CD + DA. The area is the shaded region within the rectangle.

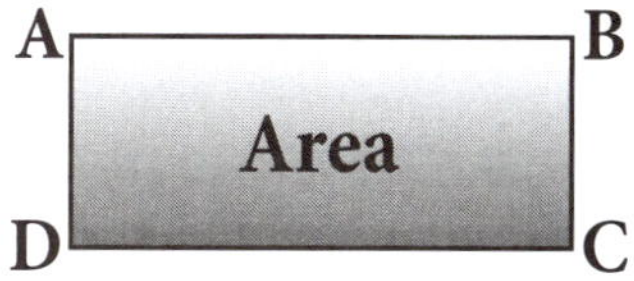

To fence a rectangular field, we need its perimeter. To find how much region is enclosed inside the fence, we need its area.

To find the area of a rectangle, use the following formula:

Area of a rectangle = length × breadth

$$A = \ell \times b$$

We can apply the same formula to find the area of a square. In case of a square, the length is equal to the breadth, that is, all the sides are equal. So, the same formula can be written as:

Area of a square = side × side

$$A = s \times s$$

Once the area is calculated, the units are written with it. For example, the area can be written in sq. cm or sq. m (read as square centimetre or square metre, respectively).

Measuring Area

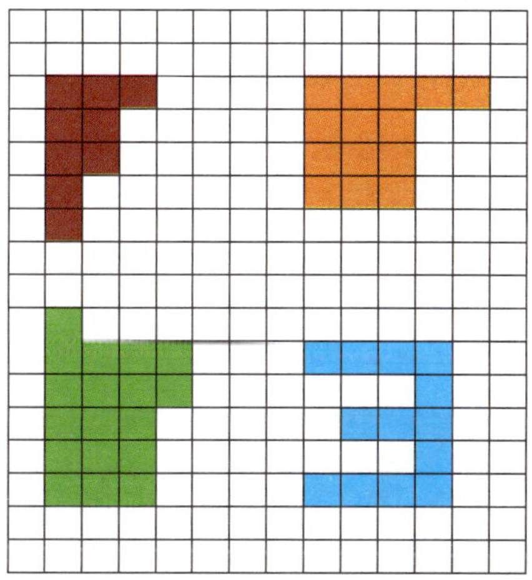

The area of shapes can be measured by using a square grid.

Figures with Completely Filled Squares

Count the number of squares in the brown figure. It gives the area covered by it. The figure is made of 9 squares. Therefore, it has an area of **9 square centimetres**. In short form, it is written as **9 sq. cm**.

Find out the area of the other three figures.

Figures with Half-Filled Squares

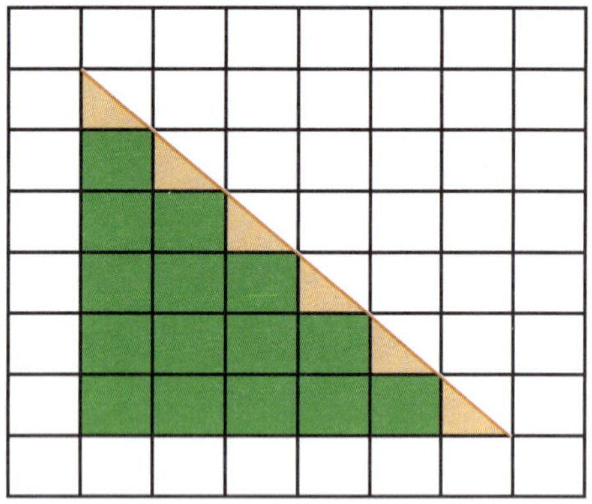

Some figures cover not only complete squares but also half squares.

In such cases, count the number of completely filled squares. Then count the half-filled squares.

In the given figure, there are 15 completely filled squares (green squares) and 6 half-filled squares (orange squares). Six half-filled squares is equal to 3 completely filled squares.
The area covered by the triangle = 15 + 3 = 18 squares.
Therefore, it has an area of 18 sq. cm.

Area of Irregular Shapes

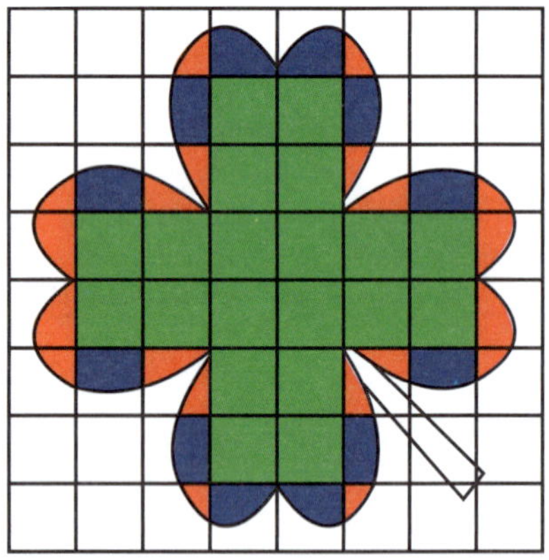

To find the area of irregular shapes, count more than half-filled square as one complete square.

Ignore less than half-filled squares.

In this figure, there are 20 completely filled squares (green-shaded squares), 0 half-filled squares, 12 more than half-filled squares (blue-shaded squares) and 20 less than half-filled squares (red-shaded squares).
The area covered by the figure is given by
20 + 12 = 32 squares.
Therefore, it has an area of 32 sq. cm.

SOLVED EXAMPLES

Example 5: Find the area of a rectangle with length 10 cm and breadth 5 cm.

Solution: Area of a rectangle = length × breadth

Area = 10 cm × 5 cm

= 50 sq. cm [Note that the unit is sq. cm]

Thus, the area of the rectangle is 50 sq. cm.

Common Errors

$A = \ell \times b$ 👍
$A = s \times s$ 👍
$A = 2(\ell \times b)$ 👎
$A = 2\ell \times b$ 👎
$A = \ell + b$ 👎
$A = 2\ell + b$ 👎

Example 6: Find the area of a square with side equals to 7 m.

Solution: Area of a square = side × side

Area = 7 m × 7 m

= 49 sq. m [Note that the unit is sq. m.]

Thus, the area of the square is 49 sq. m.

Exercise 12C

1. Find the area of the rectangles with the given lengths and breadths.

a. Length = 5 cm, breadth = 3 cm
b. Length = 8 cm, breadth = 5 cm
c. Length = 13 cm, breadth = 7 cm
d. Length = 19 cm, breadth = 8 cm
e. Length = 20 cm, breadth = 10 cm
f. Length = 24 cm, breadth = 6 cm

2. Find the area of the squares with the given sides.

a. 5 cm b. 8 cm c. 15 cm d. 24 cm e. 32 cm

3. Find the area of the following figures.

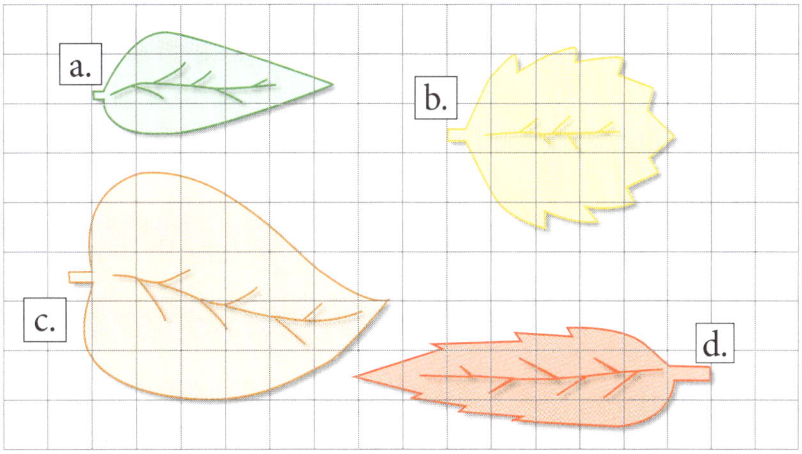

Maths Lab Activity

21 CS Creativity and Innovation, Collaboration | EL | AI | STEAM CHALLENGE

Aim: To understand how to find perimeter and area of shapes that can be tiled

Materials required: The chart paper and the shapes used in the maths lab activity of Chapter 11

Procedure:

1. Make groups of 2 students each.
   Select a shape from the shapes you have created.
2. Arrange the shape on the chart paper so that no gap is left.
3. Find out the answers to the following questions.
   a. Which shape can be used to cover the chart paper completely?
   b. Which shape can be used in the least number to cover the chart paper completely?
   c. Which shape can be used in the maximum number to cover the chart paper completely?
4. Find out the perimeter and area of each shape used to tile the chart paper. Then, find the total perimeter and area of all the shapes used. Finally, find out the perimeter and area of the chart paper.
5. Compare your results with other groups.

Concept Map

Shapes

- Perimeter
  - Distance along the boundary of an object
  - Perimeter of square
    = side + side + side + side
    = 4 × side = 4*s*
  - Perimeter of rectangle
    = length + breadth + length + breadth
    = 2(length + breadth)
    = $2(\ell + b)$
  - Measure
    - Using a thread
    - Using a geoboard
    - Using a square grid
- Area
  - Region covered inside the boundary of a figure
  - Area of square
    = side × side
  - Area of rectangle
    = length × breadth
    = $\ell \times b$
  - Measure
    - Using a square grid

Key Concepts

- **Perimeter:** The distance covered along the boundary of a polygon or a figure when you go around it once
- **Area:** The region covered inside the boundary of a figure or a polygon
- When a figure is placed on a square grid paper, the number of squares along each side of the figure gives the length of each side.
- The area can be written in sq. cm or sq. m (read as square centimetre or square metre, respectively).
- To find the area of irregular shapes, count more than half-filled square as one complete square. Ignore less than half-filled squares.

Chapter Revision

A. Choose the correct option.

1. The perimeter of a square with side 5 cm is __________.
   a. 5 cm b. 20 cm c. 15 cm d. 25 cm
2. The perimeter of a rectangle with length 10 cm and breadth 4 cm is __________.
   a. 40 cm b. 16 cm c. 28 cm d. 14 cm
3. The perimeter of a triangle with sides 5 cm, 7 cm and 9 cm is __________.
   a. 21 cm b. 15 cm c. 20 cm d. 27 cm
4. If the perimeter of a rectangle is 24 cm and the breadth is 5 cm, then the length is __________.
   a. 5 cm b. 7 cm c. 24 cm d. 29 cm
5. If the side of a square is 15 cm, then its area is __________.
   a. 15 sq. cm b. 60 sq. cm c. 30 sq. cm d. 225 sq. cm
6. The area of a rectangle with length 15 cm and breadth 12 cm is __________.
   a. 180 sq. cm b. 150 sq. cm c. 120 sq. cm d. 100 sq. cm

B. Fill in the blanks.

1. To find the perimeter of a square, multiply the side of the square with ____________.
2. To find the area of a rectangle, multiply the length of the rectangle with its ____________.
3. The formula to find the perimeter of a rectangle is ____________.
4. To find the area of a square, multiply the ____________ of the square with itself.
5. To find the perimeter of a polygon, ____________ all the sides.

C. Find the perimeter of the following figures.

1.

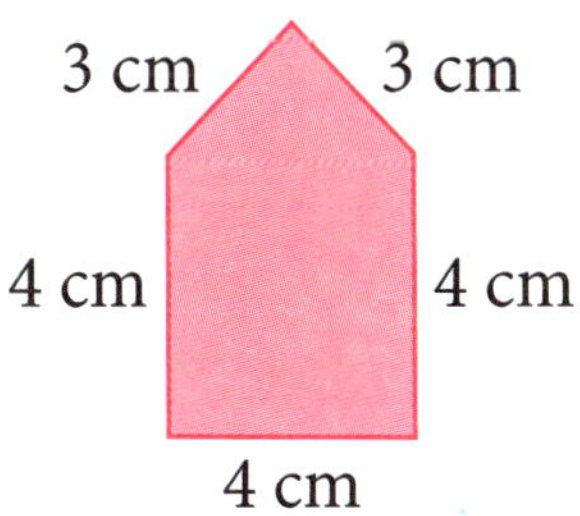

2.

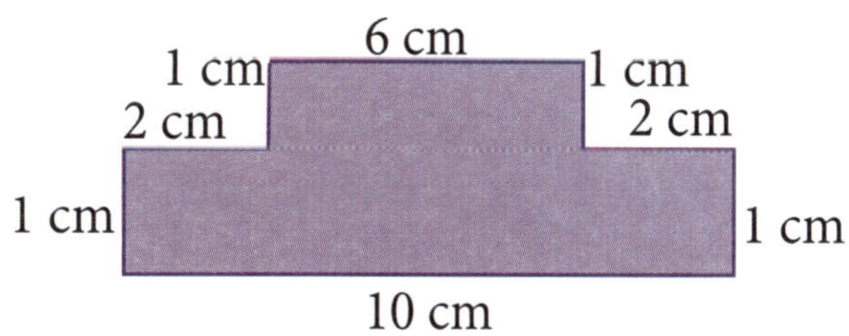

3.

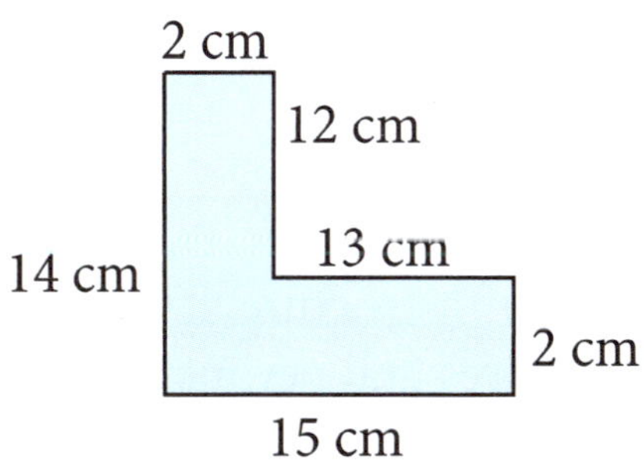

4.

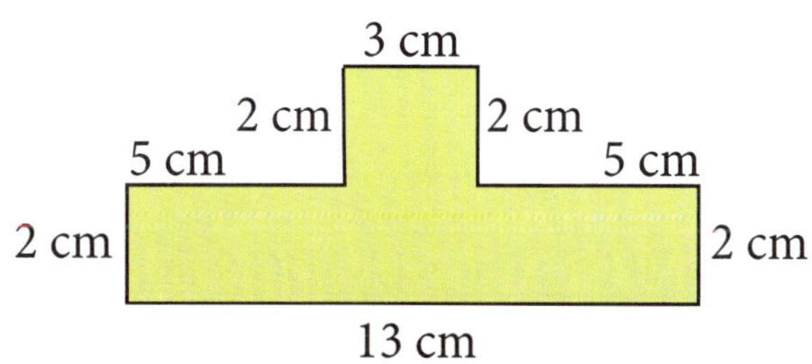

D. Solve the following.

1. Find the perimeter of a square with side 12 cm.
2. Find the perimeter of a rectangle with length 13 cm and breadth 9 cm.
3. Find the perimeter of a hexagon with each side equals to 8 cm.
4. Find the area of a rectangle whose length is 25 cm and breadth is 4 cm.
5. Find the area of a square whose side is 25 cm.
6. Find the length of the side of a square if the perimeter is 128 cm.
7. Find the length of a rectangle whose perimeter is 54 cm and breadth is 12 cm.

SKILL UP!

A. 21 CS Critical Thinking, Information Literacy — EL

Find the perimeter and area by tracing different types of objects in your school bag. Make a table as shown below. Estimate the perimeter and area of the traces. Then measure the actual perimeter and area. How accurate were you in your estimate?

Objects	Estimate	Actual
Pencil box	Perimeter: Area:	Perimeter: Area:
Maths book	Perimeter: Area:	Perimeter: Area:

B. 21 CS Creativity and Innovation, Life Skills — EL — STEAM CHALLENGE

9 INDUSTRY, INNOVATION AND INFRASTRUCTURE

Professional builders, gardeners and architects apply the concept of perimeter and area in their everyday work. Even at home, the concept of perimeter and area is applied almost every day. Suppose you need to design a backyard garden, what things would you need? Draw and design your garden detailing the perimeter and area.

C. 21 CS Information Literacy

Find out the different units of measurement such as inches, feet and yard. Where are these units usually used?

SUSTAINABLE DEVELOPMENT GOALS

Question B is in line with SDG 9 Industry, Innovation and Infrastructure. If you want to fence your garden, which entity would you choose between area and perimeter? A piece of land can be measured in sq. ft. Is it referring to the area?

Worksheet 12

21 CS Critical Thinking AI

Close your eyes and point your pencil inside this number wheel. Do this two times to get two numbers. Draw a polygon using these two numbers. Find the perimeter and area of your polygon. Repeat this activity till the whole grid is filled up with polygons. How many polygons did you get?

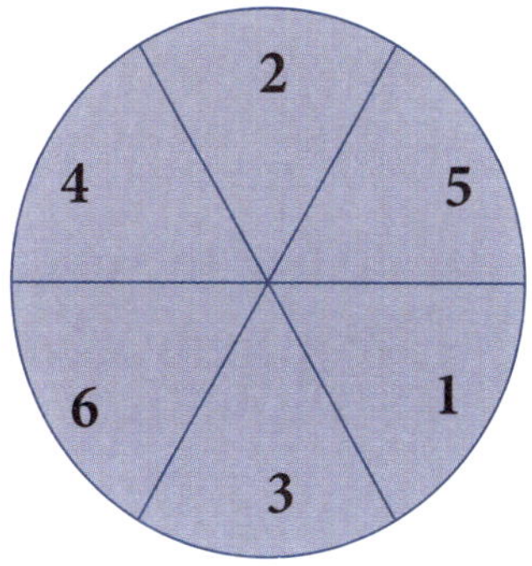

P = 3 + 5 + 3 + 5 = 16 cm

A = 15 sq. cm

13 Volume and Nets

Learning Objectives

- To understand the difference between volume and capacity
- To find the volume of 3D shapes by counting the number of unit cubes
- To identify the nets and views of different 3D shapes

Let's Get Started

21 CS Critical Thinking

Do you know how to measure capacity? Which of the following objects have capacity? Tick (✔) the objects that have capacity and cross (✘) that do not have capacity.

1. 

2. 

3. 

4. 

5. 

6. 

Is capacity the same as volume? How is capacity different from volume? Let us learn about the difference between capacity and volume.

VOLUME

Volume is the amount of space occupied by a container or an object.
Capacity is the amount of substance a container can hold.

Look at the jug of juice given here. The amount of juice this jug can hold (in mℓ or ℓ) is its capacity. Whereas volume is the space occupied by both the jug and juice.

The most common unit of volume is cubic centimetres (cu. cm).

One cubic centimetre will hold one millilitre of liquid. 1000 cubic cm will hold 1000 millilitres of liquid.

$$1000 \text{ m}\ell = 1000 \text{ cu. cm}$$

NOTE

1000 mℓ = 1 ℓ
So, 1 ℓ = 1000 cu. cm
The value of capacity and volume stays the same, but the units change.

Volume of Solids

The volume of solids or containers can be found by using unit cubes. To find the volume of an object, fill the object completely with unit cubes, that is, cubes of size 1 × 1 × 1 cubic units. Depending on the size of the objects whose volume is measured, any one of the following three units can be used. (The figures are just for representation, not to scale.)

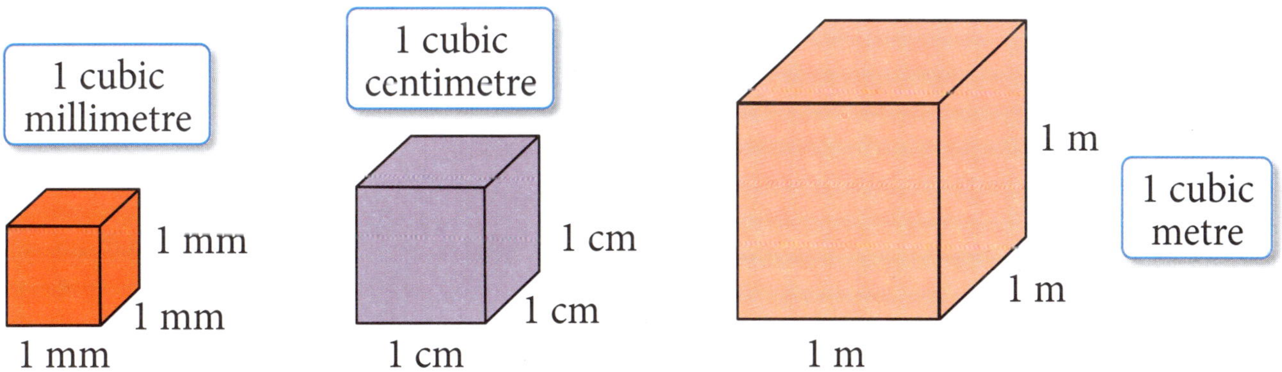

Now, let us measure the volume of this cubical box.

Let us use 1 cubic centimetre cubes to fill the container. Suppose it takes 3 cubes in three rows and three layers to fill the box; then the volume of the box would be $3 \times 3 \times 3 = 27$ cu. cm.

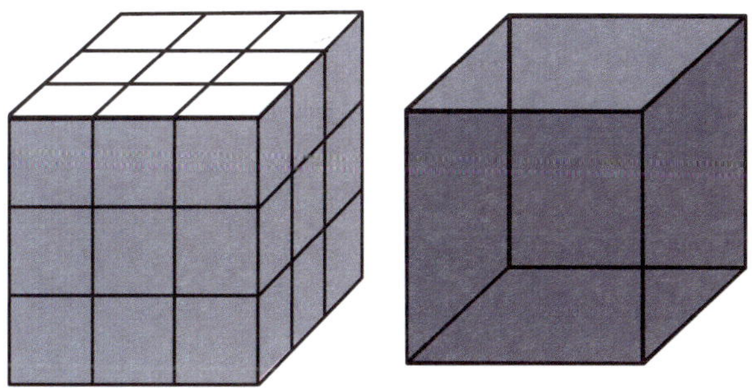

Exercise 13A

Find the volume of the objects given below. ▢ **= 1 cu. cm**

1. 

2. 

3. 

4. 

5. 

6. 

7. 

8. 

9. 

10. 

11. 

12. 

NETS

Remember the different shapes and figures you learnt in your earlier classes. Two-dimensional (2D) shapes such as lines, circles and triangles are flat shapes and can be drawn on paper. Three-dimensional (3D) objects such as cubes, cones, cylinders and pyramids have height, length and width.

A 2D shape can be folded to form a 3D shape. A 3D shape can be unfolded into its 2D components. A pattern or a 2D shape that can be folded to form a 3D shape is called a **net**. A solid can have one or more nets.

> **DO YOU KNOW?**
> There are altogether 11 possible nets for a cube.

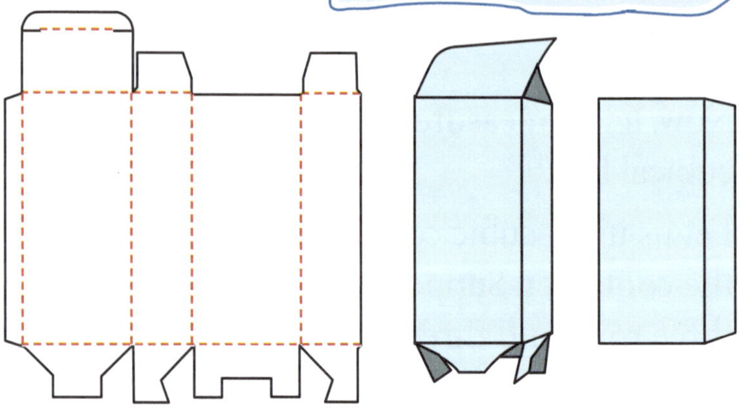

Net of a cuboid

The nets of some solid shapes are given below.

Shapes	Nets		2D drawings
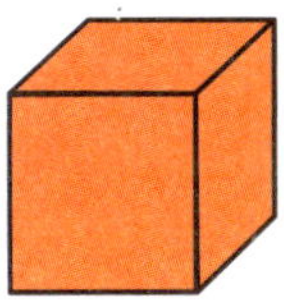 Cube	It has 6 squares.	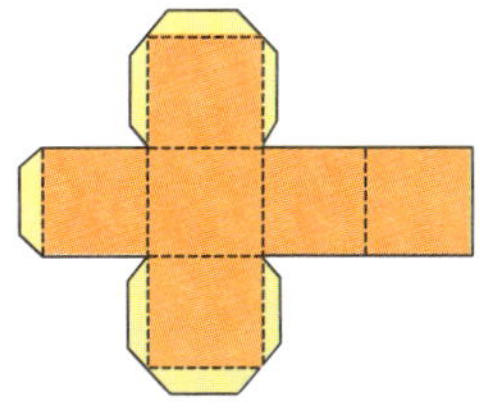	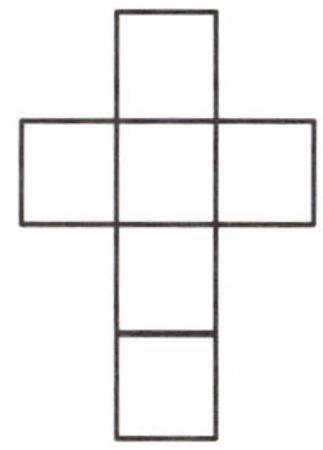
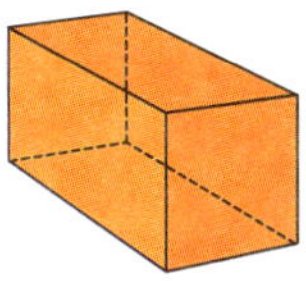 Cuboid	It has 4 rectangles (opposite faces of same size) and 2 rectangles of another size.	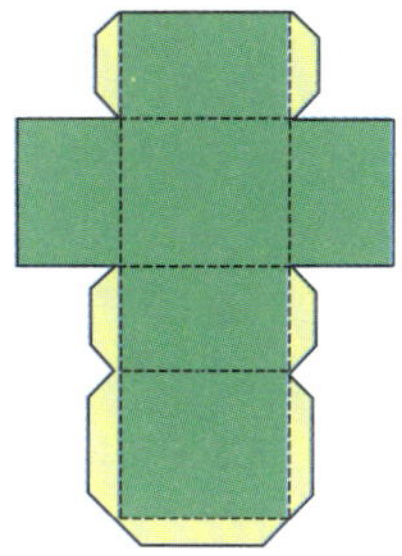	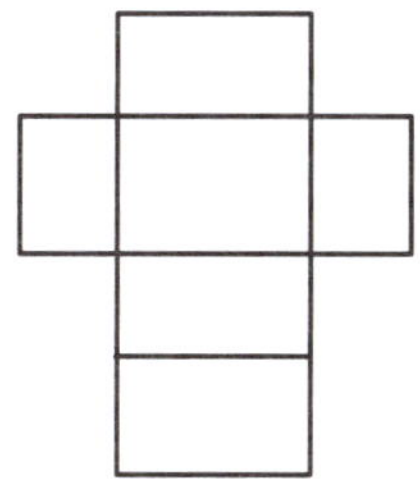
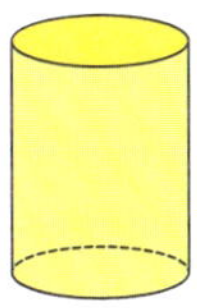 Cylinder	It has 1 rectangle and 2 circles.	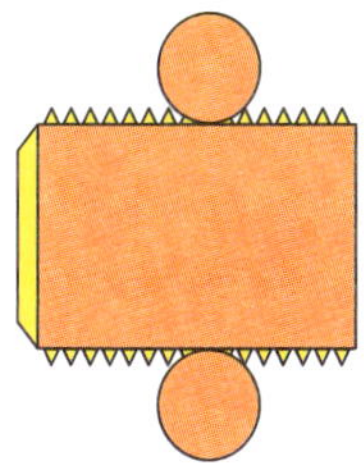	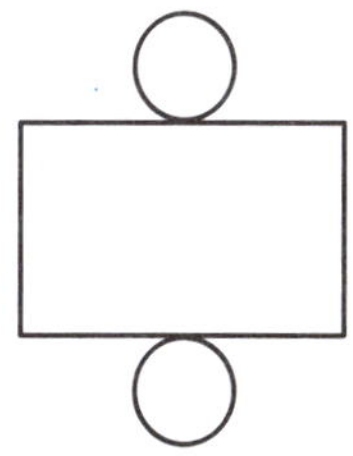
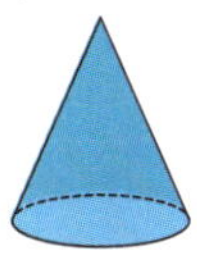 Cone	It has 1 complete circle and 1 sector of another circle.	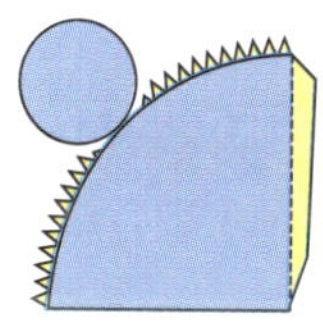	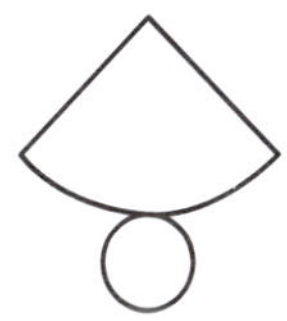

View of Solid Shapes

Most solid shapes appear different when viewed from different sides. For example, for a solid shape such as a hut or a tumbler, the view from the top, side or the front would look different as shown below.

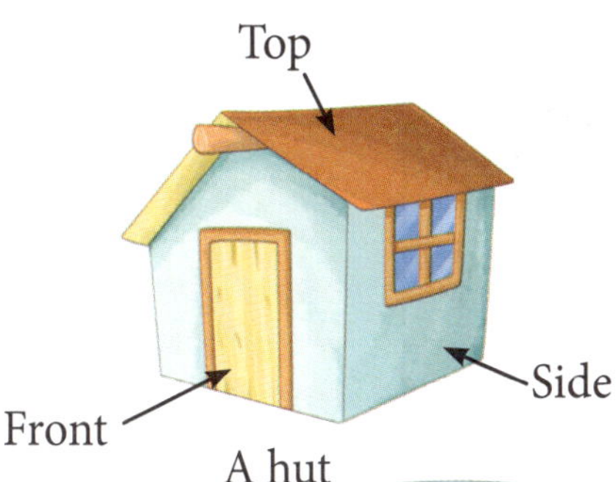

A hut

Front view

Side view

Top view

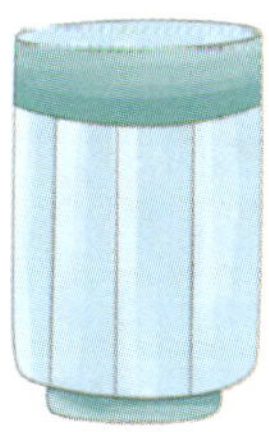
A tumbler

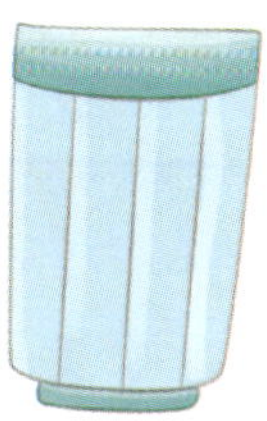
Side view

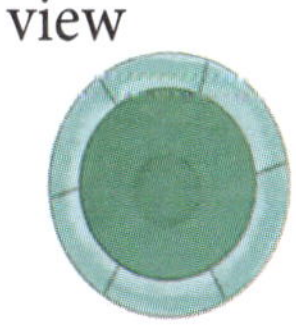
Top view

Exercise 13B

1. Colour the net of a cube in green, the net of a cuboid in blue, the net of a cone in red and the net of a cylinder in yellow.

a. 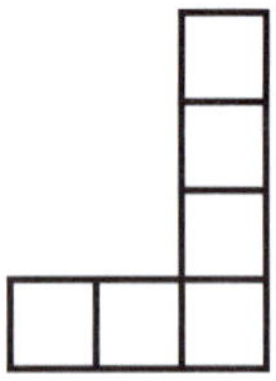

b. 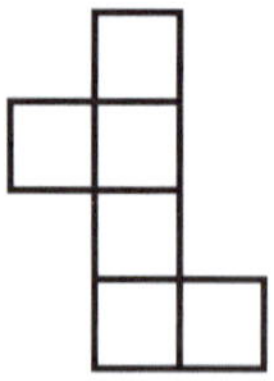

c. 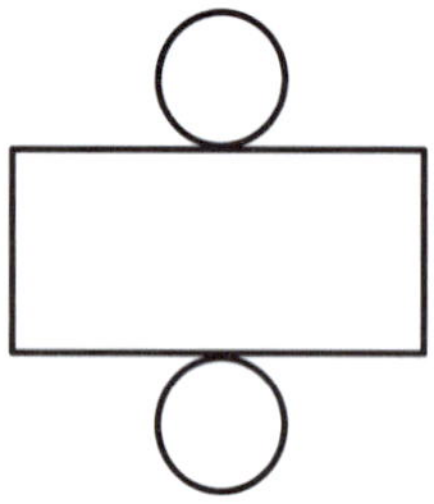

d. 

e. 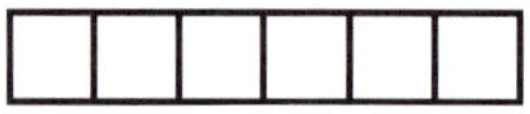

f. 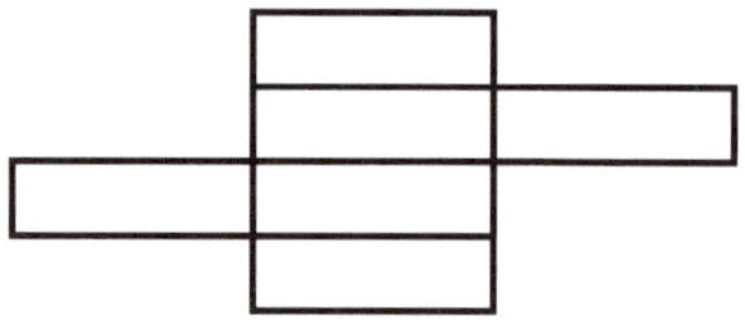

g. 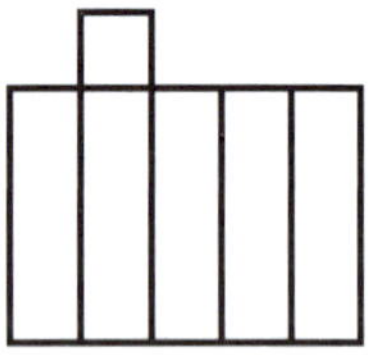

h. 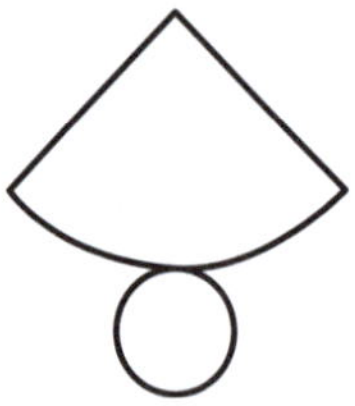

i. 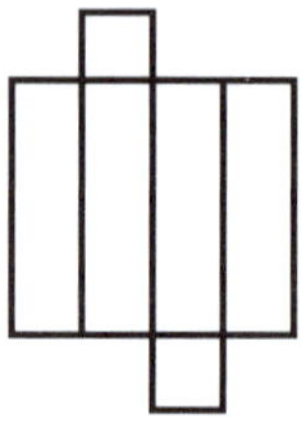

j. 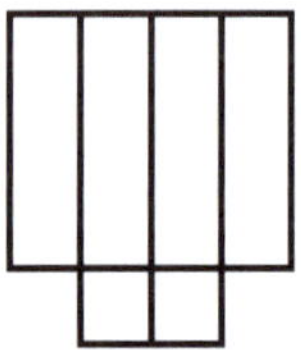

2. Which flat shape would be the top view of these solids?

a. 

Sphere

b. 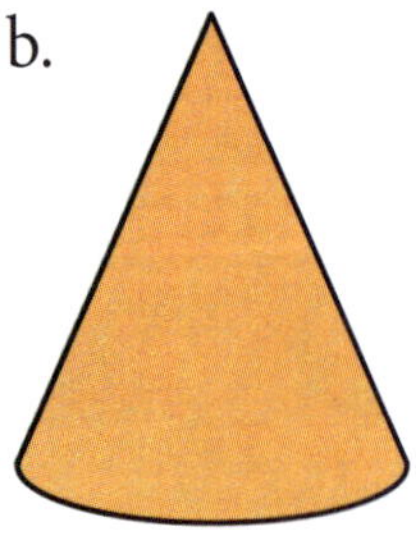

Cone

c. 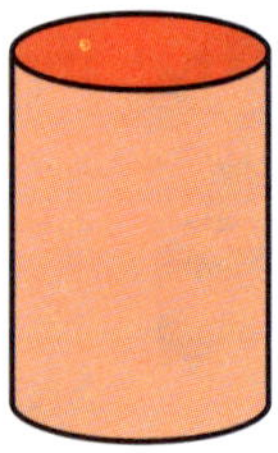

Cylinder

Maths Lab Activity

21 CS Creativity and Innovation | AI | STEAM Challenge

Aim: To make 4-faced, 5-faced and 6-faced solids from the given nets

Materials required: Five chart papers, scissors, ruler, pencil, glue or adhesive tape

Procedure:

1. On each chart paper, draw each of the given nets by using a ruler and a pencil.
2. Using scissors, cut along the dotted line to obtain nets for five different solids.
3. Fold the nets along the solid lines.
4. Use glue or adhesive tape to make the solids.
5. Name the solids you just created.

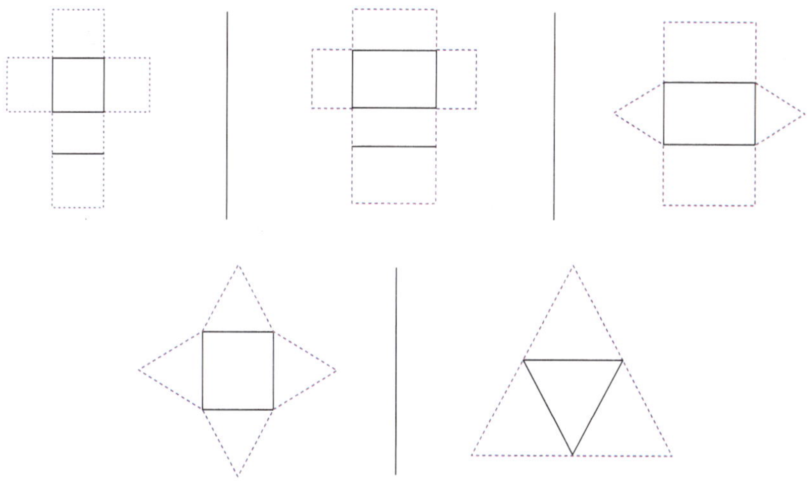

Concept Map

Measured in cubic units ← **Volume** → 3D Shapes → Nets

Key Concepts

- **Volume:** The amount of space occupied by a container or an object
- **Capacity:** The amount of substance a container can hold
- **Net:** The pattern or a 2D shape that can be folded to form a 3D shape

CHAPTER REVISION

A. Find the volume of the objects given below.  **= 1 cu. cm**

1. 

2. 

3. 

4. 

5. 

6. 

B. Draw three different nets for a cube and a cuboid in your notebook.

C. Identify the views of the objects. Write front view, side view or top view for each object given below.

1. A Car

a. 

b. 

c. 

2. A table

a. 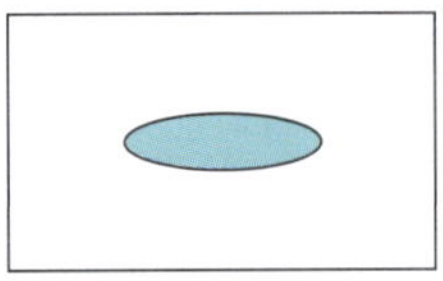

b. 

c. 

3. A cupboard

a. 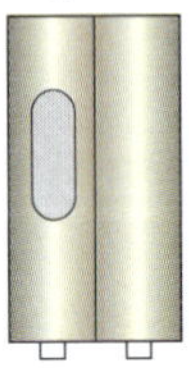

b. 

c. 

SKILL UP!

A. 21 CS Creativity and Innovation, Life Skills | EL

Collect any five cartons or boxes lying around your house. Unfold each box and observe the net of the boxes. Make a chart based on the nets of the boxes you have collected.

B. 21 CS Critical Thinking, Information Literacy

Collect a variety of small boxes such as matchboxes, mobile phone boxes, etc. Estimate the volume of each box. Also, find out the actual volume. Note down your readings in a tabular format and compare your results. How accurate were you in your estimation?

C. 21 CS Critical Thinking, Life Skills | EL | AI | STEAM CHALLENGE

1 NO POVERTY

Suppose you have to attend a donation camp in your school. For this camp, you need to bring boxes that would hold 50 english books, 50 maths books, 50 science books, 50 social studies books. Design and build a box that could fit all these books. You can also think of creating more than one type of box.

D. 21 CS Critical Thinking

There are 11 possible nets for a cube. Which of these nets will not make a cube?

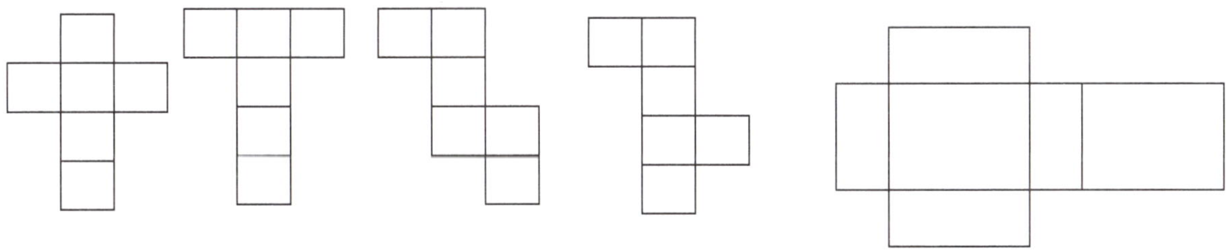

SUSTAINABLE DEVELOPMENT GOALS

Question C is in line with SDG 1 No Poverty. Have you ever donated something such as clothes, money, etc.? How does it feel? Donation has some positive effects like it gives you more pleasure and at the same time we can meet the needs of poor people.

Worksheet 13

21 CS Creativity and innovation AI

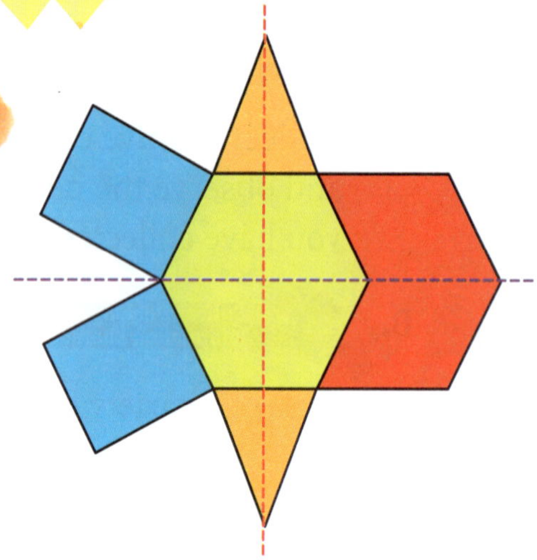

The figure given here has different 2D shapes in it. How many can you see? Make accurate drawing of the 2D shapes using a ruler on the dot grid given below. Colour them.

14 Data Handling

Learning Objectives

- To draw and interpret bar graphs
- To interpret circle charts

Let's Get Started

21 CS Critical Thinking, Information Literacy

Label the different parts of a bar graph using the keywords given below.

Labels Title Bars Equal intervals

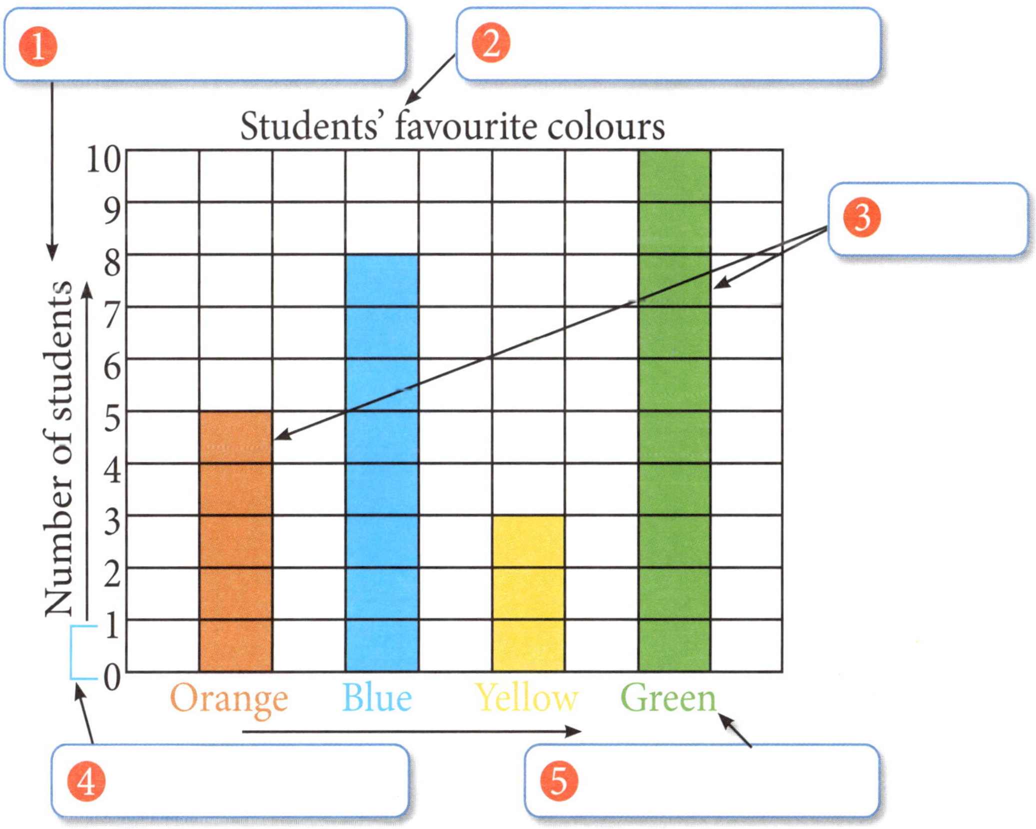

Data is a collection of information. We collect data to find answers to certain questions. These answers help us to understand situations and take decisions accordingly. Bar graphs and circle charts are some ways of representing data.

BAR GRAPH

A bar graph has bars of different heights and same width to display information. It helps in easy visualisation, comparison and interpretation of data.

The bars can be represented horizontally or vertically. The shorter the height of the bar, the lesser the value. The longer the height of the bar, the greater the value.

The marks obtained by Anuradha in different subjects in her final test is given here. This data can be represented in the form of a vertical bar graph or a horizontal bar graph.

Before making the graph, identify the following:

Title: Final test score of Anuradha

Categories: Subjects

Data: Marks obtained

Scale of the graph: 1 box = 10 marks

Subjects	Marks obtained
English	60
Maths	65
Science	60
Social Studies	55
Hindi	45

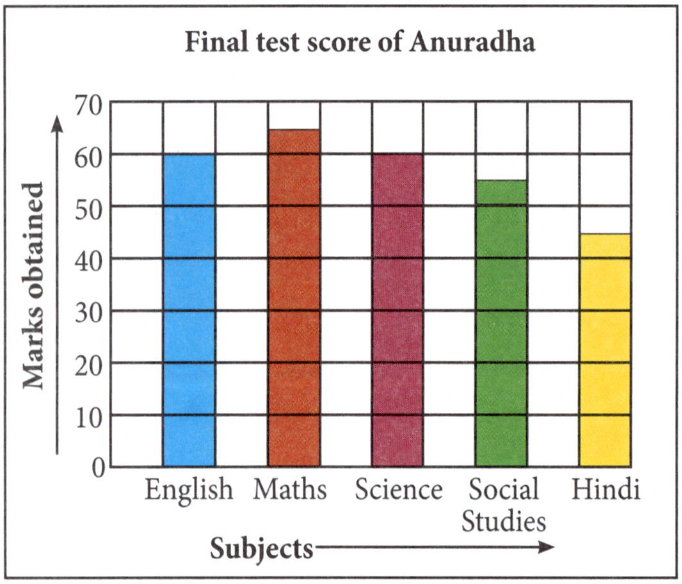

Bar graph with vertical bars

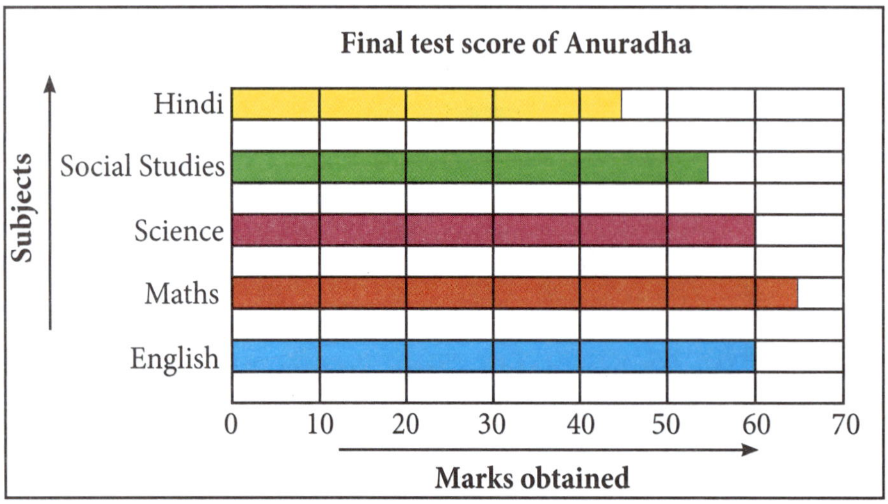

Bar graph with horizontal bars

SOLVED EXAMPLES

Example 1: The bar graph shows the number of ice creams a vendor sold from Monday to Friday. Study the graph and answer the questions.

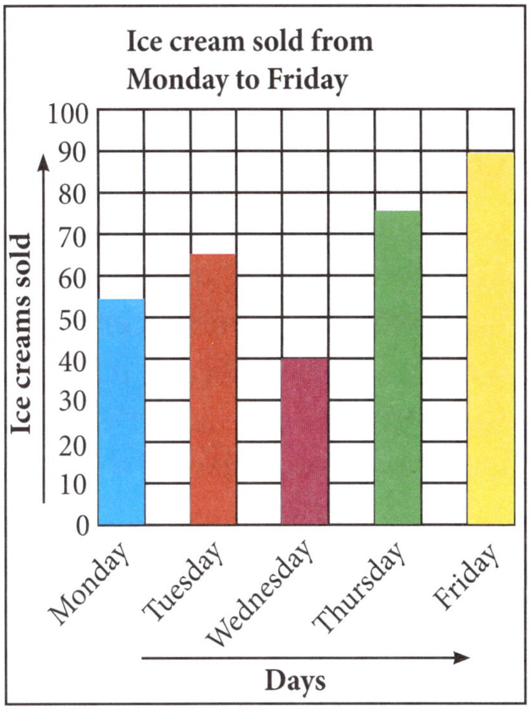

1. How many ice creams were sold on the following days?
   a. Monday b. Tuesday
   c. Wednesday d. Thursday e. Friday
2. On which day were the most ice creams sold?
3. On which day were the least ice creams sold?
4. On which day the vendor sold 65 ice creams?
5. How many more ice creams were sold on Thursday than on Monday?

Solution:

1. a. 55 b. 65 c. 40 d. 75 e. 90
2. Friday (see the longest bar)
3. Wednesday (see the shortest bar)
4. Tuesday (identify the bar that ends at 65)
5. 75 – 55 = 20; twenty more ice creams were sold on Thursday than on Monday.

EXERCISE 14A

The graph given here shows the number of students from Class I to Class V in a school. Study the graph and answer the questions.

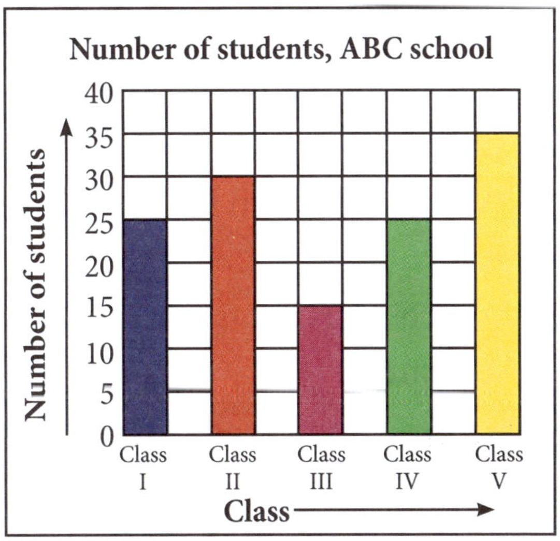

1. How many students are there in the following classes?
   a. Class I b. Class II
   c. Class III d. Class IV
   e. Class V

2. Which class has the maximum number of students?
3. Which class has the least number of students?
4. How many more students are there in class II than in class IV?
5. How many more students are there in class I than in class III?

CIRCLE CHARTS

Circle charts represent data in the form of a circle. A circle is divided into many parts. Each part represents a certain part of the whole. The size of each part is related to its value in the data. Larger-sized part means larger portion or larger share.

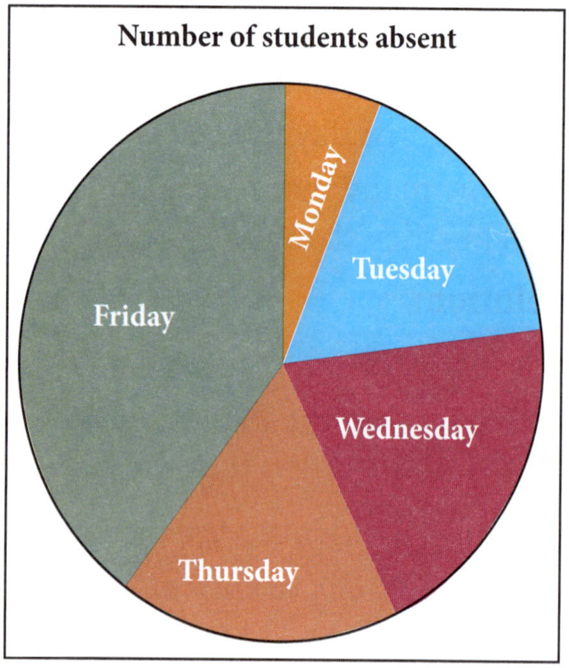

The circle chart given here shows the number of students that were absent from school from Monday to Friday.

The part for Friday is the biggest. So, the maximum number of students were absent on Friday.

Look for the smallest part in the chart. It is Monday. That means the least number of students were absent on Monday.

SOLVED EXAMPLES

Example 2: The circle chart shows the data of food items bought by students from their school canteen.

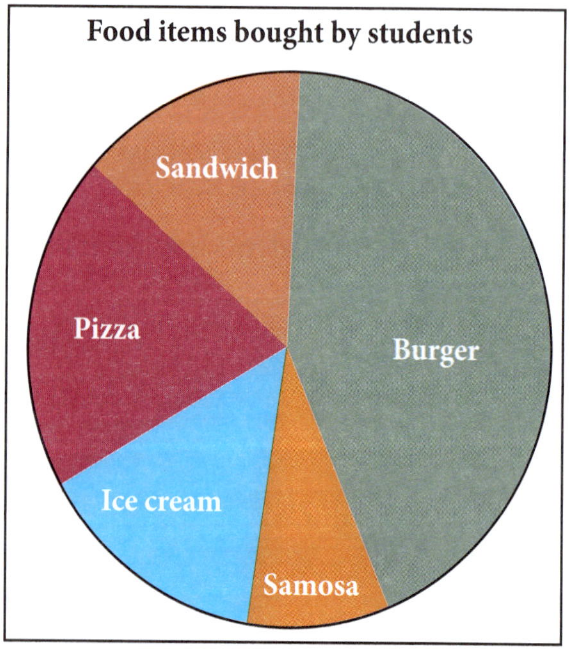

1. Which food item is liked by most students?
2. Which food item is liked by least students?
3. Which food items were equally liked by students?

Solution:

1. Burger   2. Samosa
3. Sandwich and ice cream

Exercise 14B

Given here is a circle chart which shows the favourite colour of Class IV students. Study the circle chart and answer the questions.

1. Which is the favourite colour of most of the students?
2. Do more students like pink or blue?

Favourite colour of Class IV students

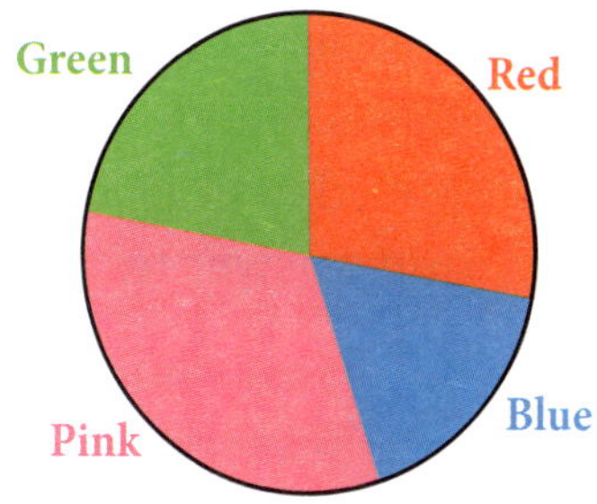

Maths Lab Activity

21 CS Collaboration, Communication | AI

Aim: To collect data, create a bar graph and analyse the bar graph

Materials required: A square grid graph paper, sketch pens, rough paper to collect data

Procedure:

1. Divide the class into five groups.
2. Group I asks the question "What do you want to become in the future?" from each of their classmates in other groups.
3. Group II sorts the information by counting the number of students having the same future goal. Use tally marks to sort the data.
4. Group III writes the labels and title of the bar graph on the graph paper.
5. Group IV draws the bar graph. Consider 1 square grid as one count. Refer to the data sorted by Group II and fill the square grids with colour for each future goal.
6. Group V analyses and interprets the data and presents a conclusion to the whole class.
7. Repeat the activity till each group understands how to draw the bar graph.

Concept Map

Data handling

- Bar graphs: data displayed using bars of equal width
- Circle charts: data displayed using parts of a whole circle

Key Concepts

- Bar graph helps in easy visualisation, comparison and interpretation of data.
- Circle charts represent data in the form of a circle.

Answer the following questions.

1. The bar graph shows the number of pages of a storybook read by Meher from Monday to Friday. Study the bar graph and answer the questions.

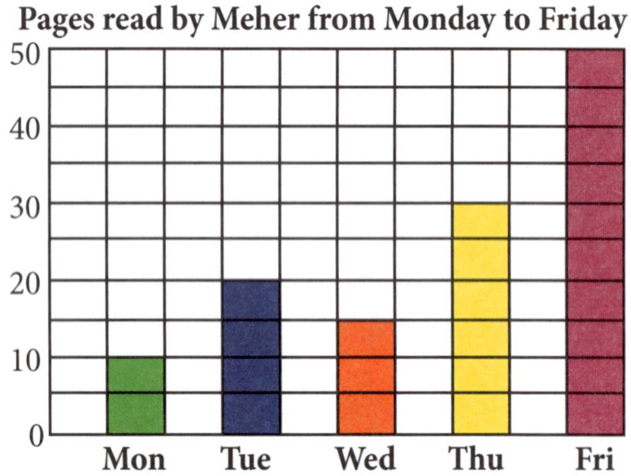

   a. How many pages did Meher read on Thursday?
   b. On which day did Meher read 15 pages?
   c. How many more pages did Meher read on Tuesday than on Monday?
   d. How many pages did Meher read on Monday and Tuesday?
   e. On which day did Meher read the maximum number of pages?

2. Given here is a circle chart showing different games that some children play in a sports club. Study the circle chart and answer the questions.

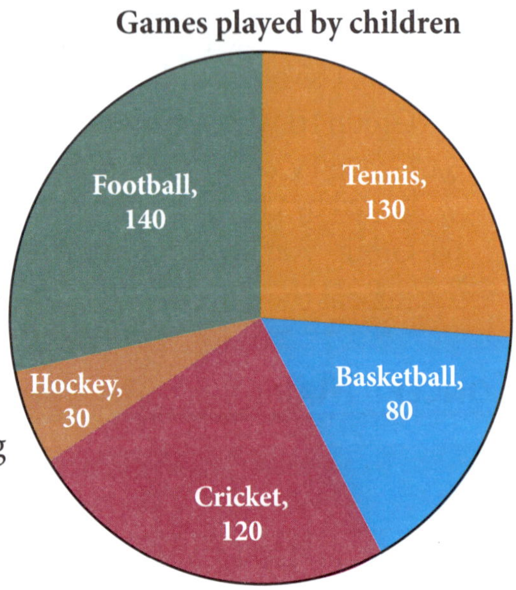

   a. How many children play basketball?
   b. Which game is played by the maximum number of children?
   c. Which game is played by the least number of children?
   d. How many more children play cricket than basketball?
   e. Which game is played by 80 children?

3. On this page, find the number of words starting with M, N, O, P, S and T.

   Make a bar graph depicting the above data and answer the following.

   a. How many words are there starting with M?
   b. How many words are there starting with N?
   c. Which letter has the maximum number of words starting with it?
   d. Which letter has the least number of words starting with it?

Skill up!

A. 21 CS Communication, Information Literacy | EL

Visit a grocery shop near your house and record the price of any five items. Create a bar graph to show comparison of prices of these items. Then ask your classmate a few questions based on the data collected such as

a. Which item costs the most? b. Which item costs the least?

B. 21 CS Information Literacy, Technology Literacy | EL | CC Integration with Computer Science

Find out how your classmates come to school. Recreate a table as shown below to collect your data.

Modes of transport	Tally marks	Number of students
Car	𝍸 ||	7
Bus		
Cycle		

Now create a circle chart based on your findings. You can use your computer to create the circle chart.

C. 21 CS Information Literacy, Life Skills

4 QUALITY EDUCATION

The given bar graph shows the marks scored in a mathematics test by students A, B, C, D and E. What would you do if you obtained the highest score and your best friend the lowest score in a test? Is it important to always get the highest score?

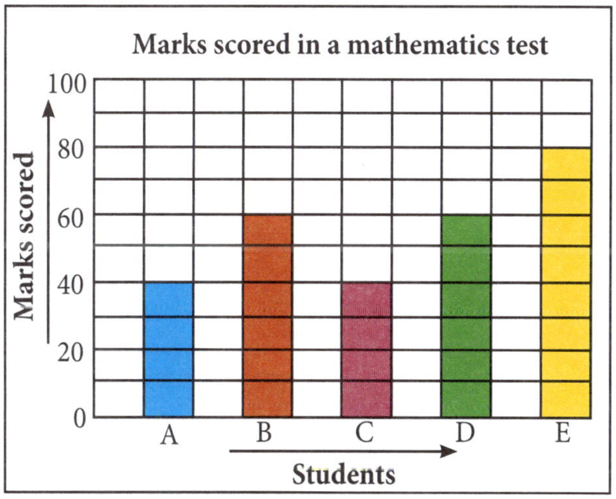

D. 21 CS Information Literacy, Media Literacy | EL

Read and check the newspaper or a magazine for a week. How many bar graphs or circle charts can you find? Do these graphs look the same as the types of graphs you have studied so far? Write a report on your findings.

SUSTAINABLE DEVELOPMENT GOALS

Question C is in line with SDG 4 Quality Education. Which is more important, good marks or knowledge? Are both terms inter-related to each other? Mention an example to prove the above statement true.

WORKSHEET 14

21 CS Critical Thinking AI

Have you tried graphing in reverse? Draw pictures and colour them for the data from which the graph given below has been created. (*Hint*: 1 small rectangle shows 1 shape.)

SHAPES AROUND US

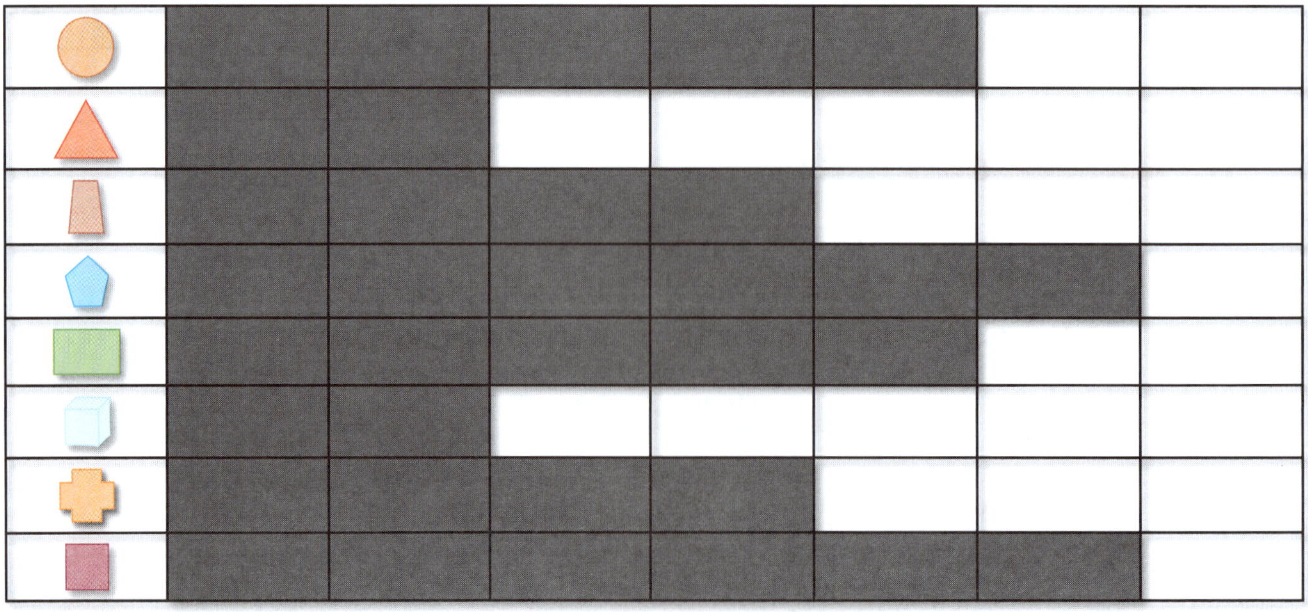

Reasoning Worksheet 3

1. Which of the given figures has the least perimeter?

a. Fig. I b. Fig. II c. Fig. III d. Fig. IV

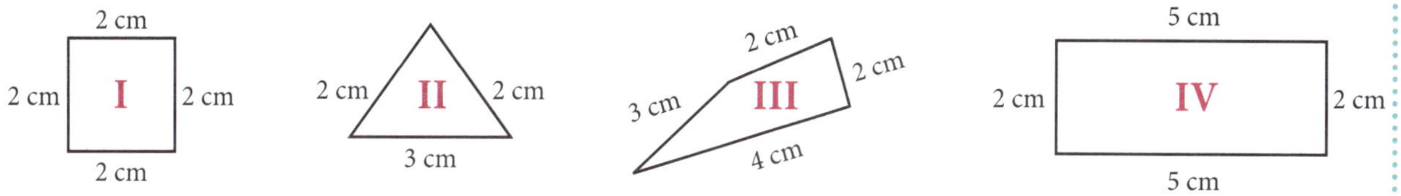

2. Identify the solids in the given figure?

	A	B	C	D
a.	Cone	Cube	Sphere	Cylinder
b.	Cone	Sphere	Cylinder	Cube
c.	Cone	Sphere	Cube	Cylinder
d.	Cone	Sphere	Cuboid	Cylinder

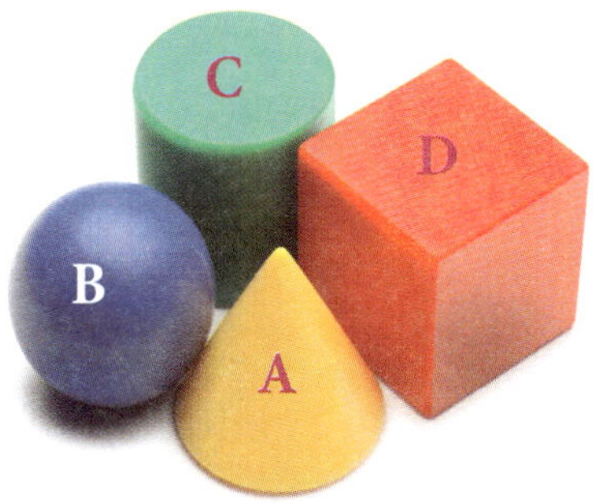

3. Identify the missing symbols in the pattern.

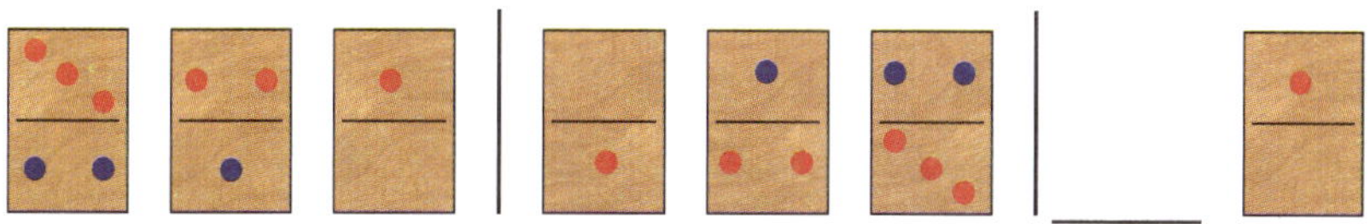

a. 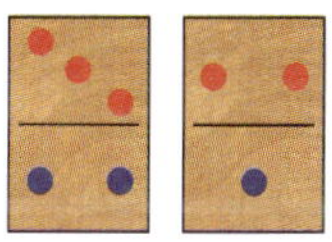 b. 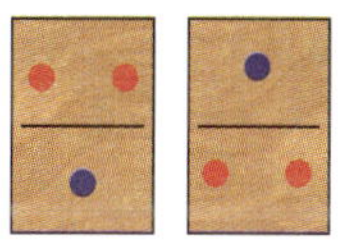 c. 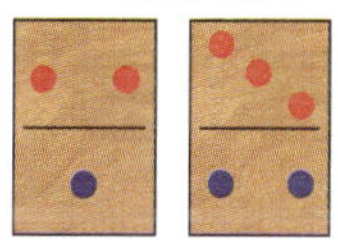 d. 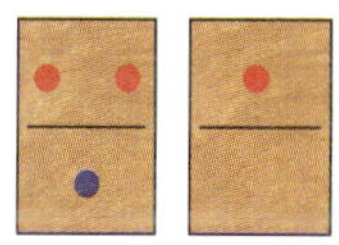

4. Select the image that would complete the sequence given below.

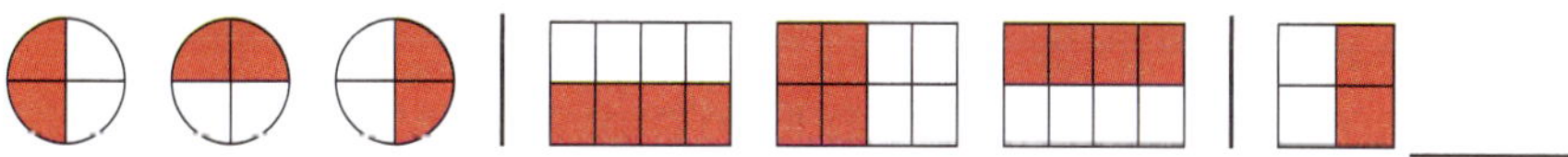

a. 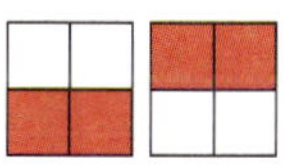 b. 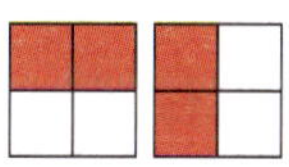 c. 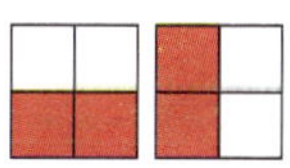 d. 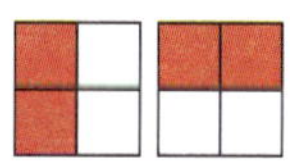

5. The given bar graph shows the savings of five people. Which of the following option is correct based on the data given in the bar graph?

a. Least savings: Mansi, ₹10,000

b. Least savings: Lekha, ₹20,000

c. Highest savings: John, ₹13,500

d. Highest savings: John, ₹15,000

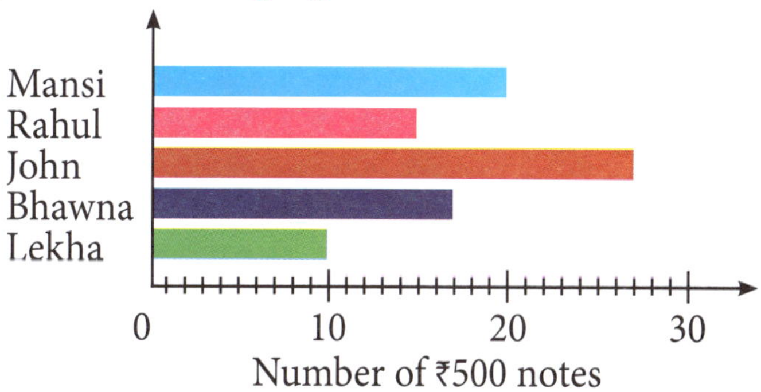

Review Corner

Review 1 — **Chapters 1–3**

Maximum Marks = 40

A. Choose the correct option. [3 × 1]

1. The numeral for five lakh seventy-two thousand one hundred ninety-six is

   a. 5,70,296 b. 5,72,196 c. 5,72,096 d. 5,79,600

2. 500000 – 200000 =

   a. 500000 b. 300000 c. 200000 d. 100000

3. In 245 × 3 = 735; 735 is the

   a. multiplicand b. multiplier c. subtrahend d. product

B. Solve the following. [3 × 2]

1. Write the expanded form of 3,15,624.
2. 23 × 10000 3. 200 + 300 + 100

C. Answer the following questions. [5 × 3]

1. Arrange in ascending and descending order.
   56,984; 72,130; 3,72,140; 3,72,104; 9,10,000; 8,99,999
2. Write the Roman numerals for the following.

   a. 9 b. 26 c. 40

3. Round off the following numbers to the nearest 100 and 1000.

   a. 5621 b. 5,71,832 c. 20,845

4. Add the following.

   a. 32,051 + 20,927 b. 48,653 + 25,741 c. 3,58,076 + 25,741

5. Subtract the following.

   a. 31,740 – 1665 b. 8,53,142 – 3,58,076 c. 9,78,657 – 2,12,301

D. Solve the following word problems. [4 × 4]

1. Javed spent ₹5,82,000 to buy a car and ₹73,000 to buy a scooter. How much money did Javed spend altogether?
2. Out of 9,57,600 people in a town, 8900 people left to live in another city. How many people were left in the town?
3. If one toy car costs ₹495, what will be the cost of 72 such toy cars?
4. Estimate the product of 82 and 37.

Rough Work

Review 2

Chapters 4–7

Maximum Marks = 40

A. Match the following. **[3 × 1]**

1. $5 \div 1$ a. Mixed fraction
2. 2, 3, 5, 7   b. 5
3. $6\frac{4}{9}$ c. Prime numbers

B. Write Yes or No. **[3 × 2]**

1. Are 2 and 4 factors of 8?
2. Is $\frac{14}{9}$ a proper fraction?
3. Is 5.8 = 5.80000?

C. Solve the following. **[5 × 3]**

1. $5782 \div 4$
2. Find all the factors of 18.
3. Arrange these fractions in ascending order: $\frac{5}{6}, \frac{1}{12}, \frac{3}{4}$
4. Convert $\frac{79}{10}$ into a decimal.
5. Arrange the decimals in descending order: 2.59; 8.3; 5.47; 9.1; 5.48

D. Solve the following word problems. **[4 × 4]**

1. Tripti purchased 6 boxes of pencils. There were 60 pencils in each box. She repacked the pencils into 9 boxes equally. How many pencils did she put in each box?
2. Frame a word problem for $(12 + 6) \div 3$.
3. Raj ate $\frac{1}{4}$ part of the cake in the morning and $\frac{2}{5}$ part of the cake in the evening. What fraction of the cake is left?
4. Vijay weighs 48.9 kg. His sister weighs 34.2 kg. Who weighs more and by how much?

Rough Work

Comprehensive Review 1

Chapters 1–7

Maximum Marks = 80

A. Write T for true and F for false. **[6 × 1]**

1. The smallest number formed by using the digits 6, 5, 0, 9 and 8 is 05689.
2. The Hindu–Arabic numeral for XXXIV is 36.
3. $5 \times 7 = 7 \times 5$
4. 2, 4, 6 and 8 are prime numbers.
5. $\frac{5}{8} + \frac{2}{8} = \frac{7}{8}$
6. $15.03 > 12.99$

B Solve the following. **[6 × 2]**

1. Write the number name of 598,603.
2. 7,85,000 – 1,42,000
3. 43×200
4. $4682 \div 2$
5. A number divisible by both ______ and ______ is divisible by 6.
6. Convert $5\frac{1}{12}$ into an improper fraction.

C. Answer the following questions. **[10 × 3]**

1. Write Roman numerals for the following numbers.
   a. 15 b. 27 c. 36
2. Add the following.
   a. 1,92,835 + 5,49,017 b. 6,35,874 + 2,87,316 c. 1,46,240 + 20,004
3. Subtract the following.
   a. 9,35,874 – 2,87,316 b. 7,34,694 – 2,87,316 c. 6,64,204 – 10,004
4. Multiply the following.
   a. 146×24 b. 3529×471 c. 450×60
5. Divide the following.
   a. $5829 \div 17$ b. $9810 \div 10$ c. $1765 \div 15$
6. Find the common multiples of 2 and 4, less than 25.
7. Solve $2\frac{1}{5} + 7\frac{2}{4}$.
8. Add 259.35, 16.072, 481 and 5.7.
9. Solve $6\frac{5}{7} - 2\frac{1}{3}$.
10. Arrange these fractions in ascending order: $6\frac{1}{5}, 7\frac{2}{4}, 6\frac{5}{7}, 7\frac{1}{3}$

D. Solve the following word problems. **[8 × 4]**

1. Trisha earned ₹1,24,000 in 2019, ₹3,45,900 in 2020 and ₹98,000 in 2021. How much money did she earn in these three years?
2. If 5200 people go to see the Taj Mahal every month, how many people would go in 21 months?
3. Pinky bought 10 kg of fruit for ₹1280. She bought 6 kg of mangoes at ₹150 per kg and 4 kg of oranges. At what price per kg did she buy the oranges?
4. Find the lowest common multiple of 5 and 7.
5. Find the highest common factor of 6 and 15.
6. Out of $\frac{5}{8}$ of the book, Shalu read $\frac{3}{16}$ of it. What fraction of the book is left to be read?
7. Salma walks 1.7 km to the bus stop, travels 5.395 km by bus and then takes a taxi for 12.86 km. What is the total distance that Salma travels every day?
8. Describe the different types of fractions with one example each.

Rough Work

Review 3

Chapters 8–10

Maximum Marks = 40

A. Write T for true and F for false. [3 × 1]

1. 1 km = 1000 m 2. ₹2 = 20 paise 3. 9:11 p.m. = 2111 hours

B. Fill in the blanks. [3 × 2]

1. 5 m 80 cm = ________ cm
2. 2 hours 45 min = ________ min
3. 19 rupees 50 paise = ________ paise

C. Solve the following. [5 × 3]

1. Convert into metres.
   a. $\frac{1}{2}$ of 8 m b. 210 km c. 9 km 100 m
2. Convert into litres.
   a. 67 kℓ b. 7260 mℓ c. 400 dℓ
3. Convert into kilograms.
   a. 1583 g b. 6675 mg c. 6300 g
4. Convert into seconds.
   a. 2 hours 37 min b. 9 min 14 s c. 3 hours
5. Convert into paise.
   a. ₹29.50 b. 64 rupees 600 paise c. 58 rupees 7 paise

D. Solve the following word problems. [4 × 4]

1. Zehra cycled 1 km 750 m to her friend's house and then 2 km 625 m to the park. What is the total distance that Zehra covered?
2. I left the house at 2:30 pm and came back at 5:45 pm. For how long was I away?
3. How many days are there from 7th of February to 25th of February?
4. On my holidays, I spent 5 days in Lucknow, 4 days in Kochi and 6 days in Shillong. How many weeks and days did I spend in all these 3 places?

Rough Work

Review 4

Chapters 11–14

Maximum Marks = 40

A. Write T for true and F for false. **[3 × 1]**

1. The line dividing B is a line of symmetry.
2. Perimeter of a polygon is the distance covered along its boundary.
3. Capacity is the amount of substance a container can hold.

B. Solve the following. **[3 × 2]**

1. Define vertex and arms of an angle.
2. Find the perimeter of square with side = 3 cm.
3. Find the volume of 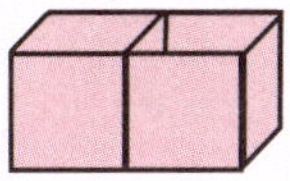 if 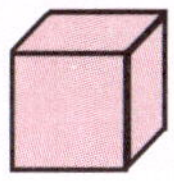 = 1 cu. cm.

C. Answer the following questions. **[5 × 3]**

1. Describe the parts of a circle.
2. How many sides do the following polygons have?
   a. Triangle b. Quadrilateral c. Pentagon
3. Write the formulae for the following.
   a. Perimeter of a square b. Perimeter of a rectangle c. Area of a rectangle
4. What do you understand by tiling and tessellation?
5. Draw the top view, front view and side view of a cuboid.

D. Solve the following. **[4 × 4]**

1. Find the perimeter of a rectangle with length 14 cm and breadth 8 cm.
2. Find the area of a square with side equals to 9 cm.
3. Study the bar graph and answer the questions.
   a. How many students are there in each class?
   b. Which class has the least number of students?
   c. Which two classes have 25 students each?
   d. How many more students are there in Class IV than in Class I?
4. What is a circle chart? Explain with the help of a diagram.

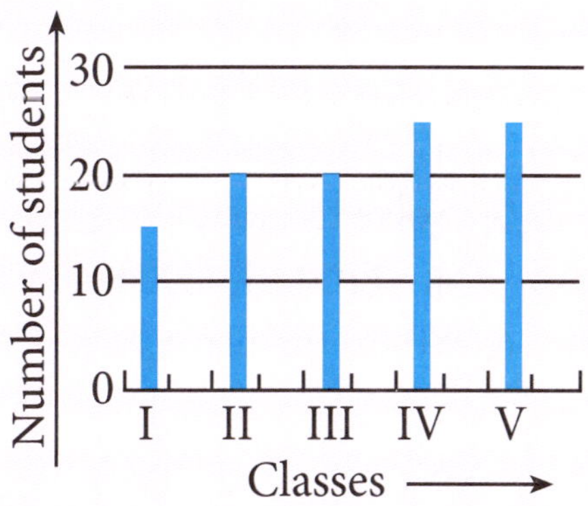

Rough Work

Comprehensive Review 2

Chapters 8–14
Maximum Marks = 80

A. Fill in the blanks. **[6 × 1]**

1. 1 dam = ________ m
2. 3 hours = ________ min
3. 2315 hours in the 12-hour clock = ________
4. 15 rupees 3 paise = ________ paise
5. The side of a square whose perimeter is 12 cm is ________ cm.
6. The area of a square with side equals to 5 cm is ________.

B. Convert the following. **[6 × 2]**

1. 7 kg 4 hg 3 dag 9 g = ____ g
2. $\frac{3}{4}$ of 5000 hℓ = ____ ℓ
3. 100 min = ____ hour ____ min
4. The time duration from 2 pm to 9 pm = ____ hours
5. 8 days = ____ week ____ day
6. 5 p.m. = ____ hours

C. Solve the following. **[10 × 3]**

1. Convert into metres.
   a. 2398 km b. 5476 cm c. 6018 dm
2. Convert into hours.
   a. 4 hours 17 min b. 12 min 56 s c. 328 s
3. Convert into 24-hour clock.
   a. 7 a.m. b. 2:37 in the afternoon c. 6 p.m.
4. Convert into days.
   a. 2 weeks 5 days b. 18 weeks c. 64 hours
5. Solve the following.
   a. ₹1000 + ₹600 + ₹7 b. ₹23.75 + ₹58 c. ₹18 – ₹3.45
6. Fill in the blanks.
   a. A rectangle has ______ sides.
   b. A triangle has ______ sides.
   c. A quadrilateral has ______ sides
7. Label Fig. A with its different parts.
8. Name the angle in Fig. A in three different ways.
9. Find the perimeter of the given triangle B.
10. Draw the nets of a cone and a cylinder.

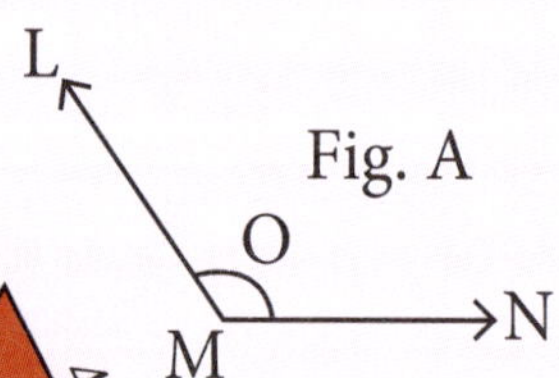

Fig. A

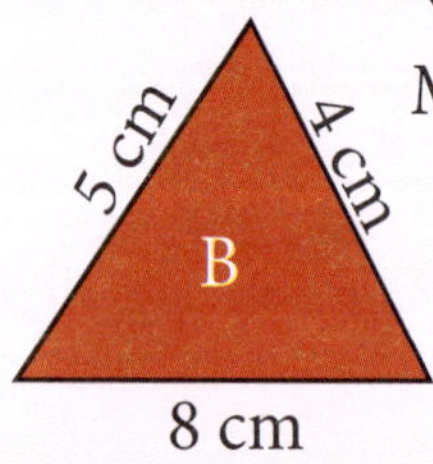

D. Answer the following questions. **[8 × 4]**

1. Kinana's bag weighs 1.003 kg and her books weigh 2.700 kg. What is the total mass of the bags and the books?
2. One bottle has 750 mℓ of water and another bottle has 900 mℓ of water. How much water is there in both the bottles?
3. A bus leaves Meerut at 2:45 p.m. and reaches Delhi at 5:30 pm. How long was the journey?
4. Convert 28 months into years and months.
5. Thoibi learned kathak for 25 days during the summer vacation and for 18 days during the winter vacation. For how many weeks and days did Thoibi learn kathak?
6. How many days are there between July 15 and August 9?
7. Jaspreet bought a book for ₹275. He gave the shopkeeper a ₹500 note. How much money will the shopkeeper return to him?
8. The bar graph shows the monthly savings done by Benu. Study the graph and answer the questions.
    a. How much money did Benu save in January and May?
    b. What was the total amount she saved in these 5 months?
    c. In which month did she save the most?
    d. How much more did she save in January than February?

Monthly savings done by Benu

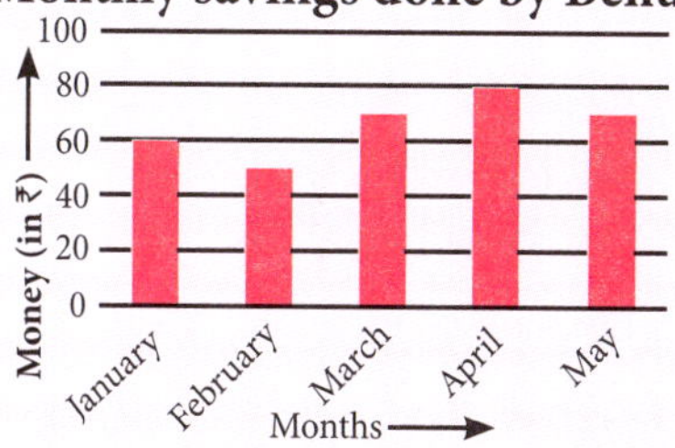

Rough Work

CLASS 4

QUESTION PAPER SET A

IMO

SOF INTERNATIONAL MATHEMATICS OLYMPIAD 2020-21

DO NOT OPEN THIS BOOKLET UNTIL ASKED TO DO SO

Total Questions: 35 | Time: 1 hr.

Guidelines for the Candidate

1. You will get additional ten minutes to fill up information about yourself on the OMR Sheet, before the start of the exam.
2. Write your **Name, School Code, Class, Section, Roll No.** and **Mobile Number** clearly on the **OMR Sheet** and do not forget to sign it. We will share your marks / result and other information related to SOF exams on your mobile number.
3. The Question Paper comprises four sections:

   Logical Reasoning (10 Questions), **Mathematical Reasoning** (10 Questions), **Everyday Mathematics** (10 Questions) and **Achievers Section** (5 Questions)

   Each question in Achievers Section carries 2 marks, whereas all other questions carry one mark each.
4. All questions are compulsory. There is no negative marking. Use of calculator is not permitted.
5. There is only ONE correct answer. Choose only ONE option for an answer.
6. To mark your choice of answers by darkening the circles on the OMR Sheet, use **HB Pencil** or **Blue / Black ball point pen** only. E.g.

   Q.16: Sonia had 80 sweets. She gave 15 sweets to Danish and 15 sweets to Megha. How many sweets are left with her?

   A. 50 B. 30 C. 60 D. 40

   As the correct answer is option A, you must darken the circle corresponding to option A on the OMR Sheet. 16. ● Ⓑ Ⓒ Ⓓ
7. Rough work should be done in the blank space provided in the booklet.
8. Return the OMR Sheet to the invigilator at the end of the exam.
9. Please fill in your personal details in the space provided on this page before attempting the paper.

SOF
SCIENCE OLYMPIAD FOUNDATION
Inspiring Young Minds Through Knowledge Olympiads

Name:..

Section:............ SOF Olympiad Roll No.:.. Contact No.:..

1. Some numbers are given which are numbered 1, 2, 3, 4, 5 and 6. Find the combination of numbers so that the letters are arranged accordingly to form a meaningful English word.

E G W H I T

1 2 3 4 5 6

A. 3, 1, 5, 2, 4, 6 B. 3, 1, 5, 2, 6, 4 C. 2, 4, 6, 1, 3, 5 D. 3, 2, 1, 5, 4, 6

---

2. Which of the following is the unfolded form of the given figure along the dotted line?

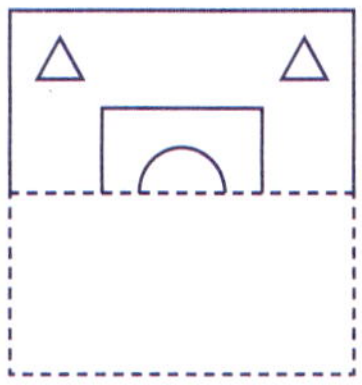

A. 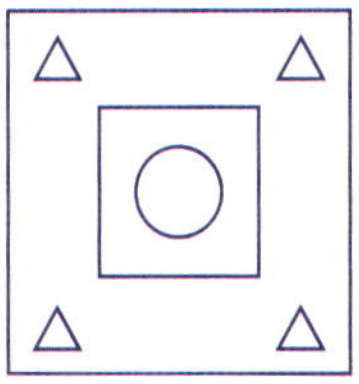

B. 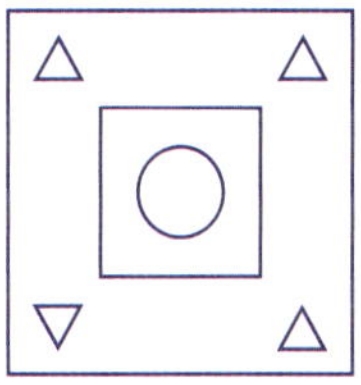

C. 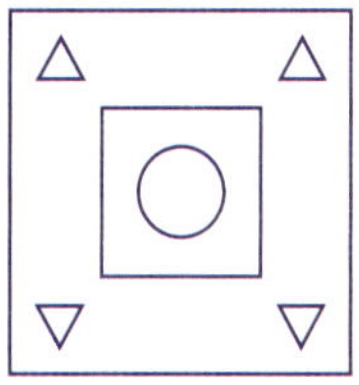

D. 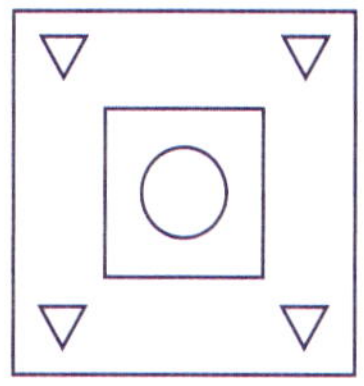

---

3. How many of the following letters have at least one line of symmetry?

IGNORED

A. 2 B. 3 C. 4 D. 5

---

4. How many possible combinations of 1 boy and 1 girl can be formed from the given boys and girls?

Boys	Girls
Sachin	Kanika
Amit	Gunjan
Ankit	Kajal
Ashish	Sonia
	Mitu

A. 10

B. 15

C. 16

D. 20

---

5. Find the missing number, if a certain rule is followed either row-wise or column-wise.

3	9	81
8	6	144
6	9	?

A. 196

B. 185

C. 162

D. 84

SPACE FOR ROUGH WORK

6. Which of the following figures will continue the given figure pattern?

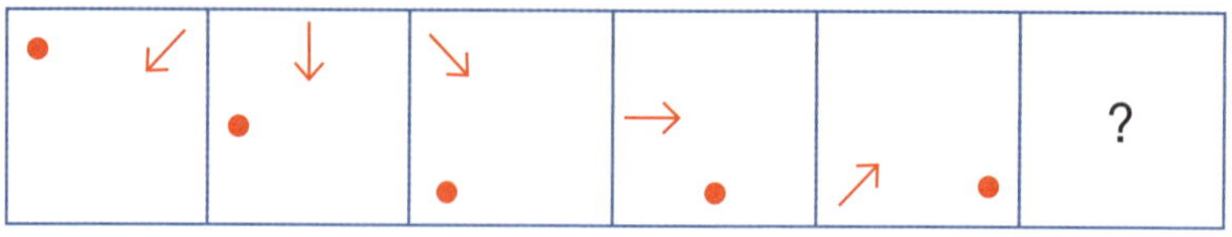

A. 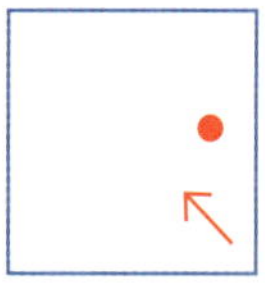 B. 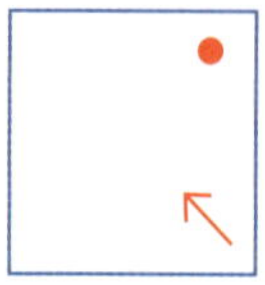 C. 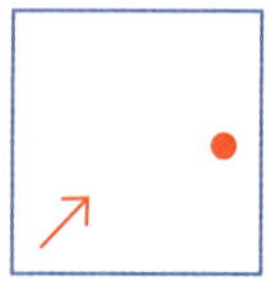 D. 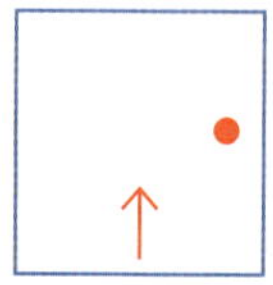

7. Who is in South-West of Prachi?

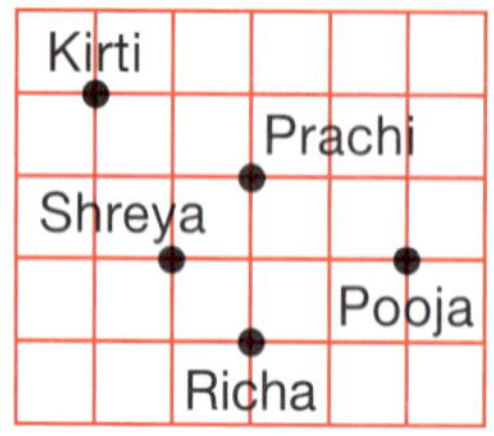

A. Pooja
B. Shreya
C. Richa
D. Kirti

8. Which of the following figures is exactly embedded in the given figure as one of its parts?

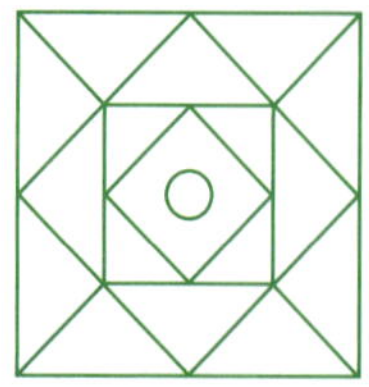

A.  B. 

C.  D. 

9. If  means 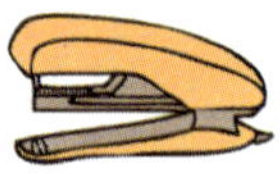, 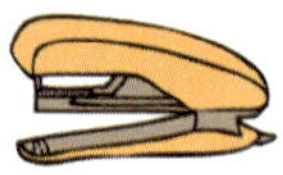 means 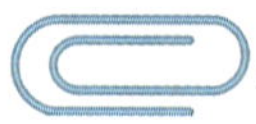, 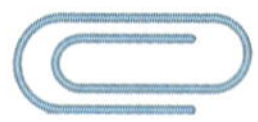 means 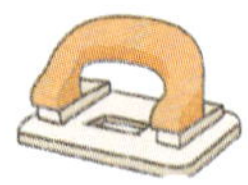 and 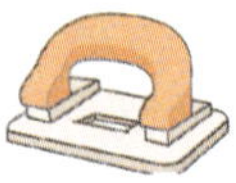 means , then _________ is used for punching the paper.

A. 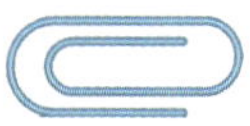 B. 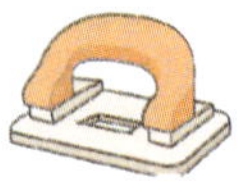 C.  D. 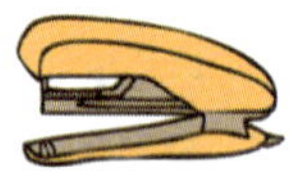

10. Select the correct mirror image of the given figure.

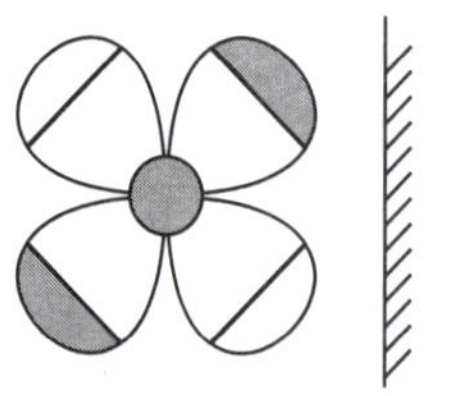

Mirror

A.  B. 

C. 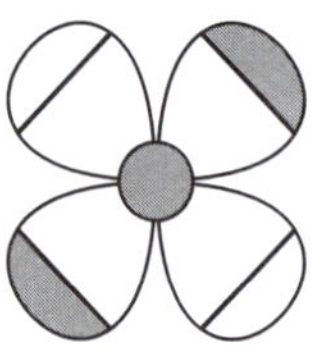 D. 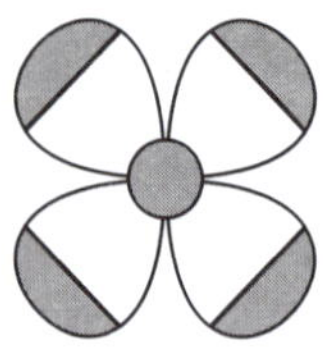

SPACE FOR ROUGH WORK

11. Identify it.
    - I am a 4-digit number.
    - All my digits are different.
    - They add up to 20.
    - The hundred's digit is double the one's digit.

    A. 6734 B. 9236 C. 2864 D. 2963

---

12. Which of the following shows $\frac{9}{8}-\frac{5}{8}$ shaded part?

    A. 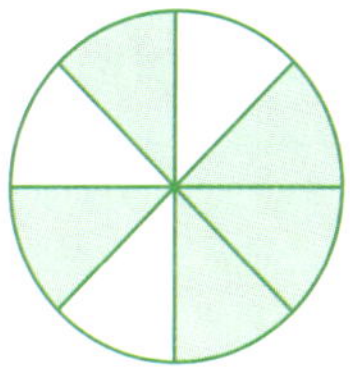
    B. 
    C. 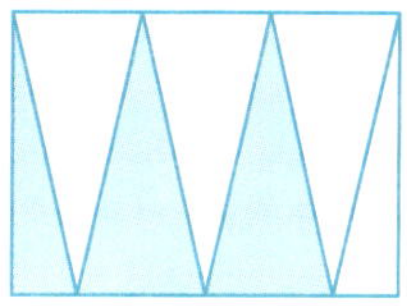
    D. 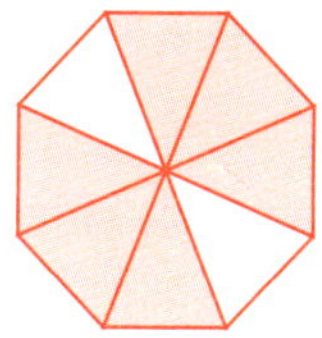

---

13. Which of the following has the greatest number of factors?

    A. 12 B. 24 C. 48 D. 32

---

14. Which of the following figures is not symmetric?

    A. 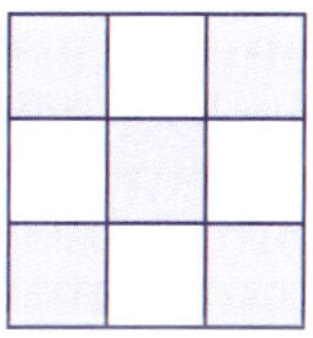
    B. 
    C. 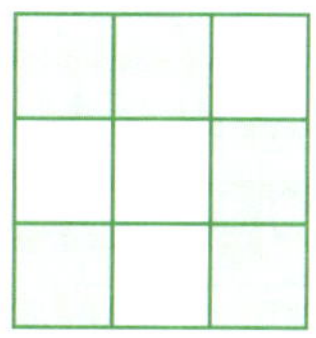
    D. 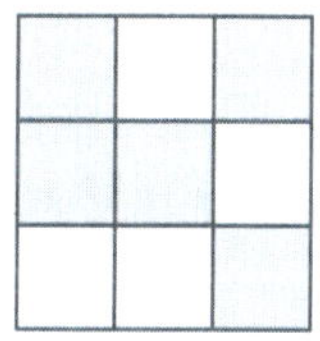

---

15. The given pictograph shows the different types of vehicles in a locality.

    There are ______ fewer scooters than cars in the locality.

    A. 0

    B. 20

    C. 40

    D. 60

Vehicles	Number of vehicles
Car	
Bus	
Motorcycle	
Scooter	
Bicycle	
Each  represents 20 vehicles.	

SPACE FOR ROUGH WORK

16. 500 poles were erected along one side of a straight road. Two poles were 5 m apart. What is the distance between the first pole and the last pole?

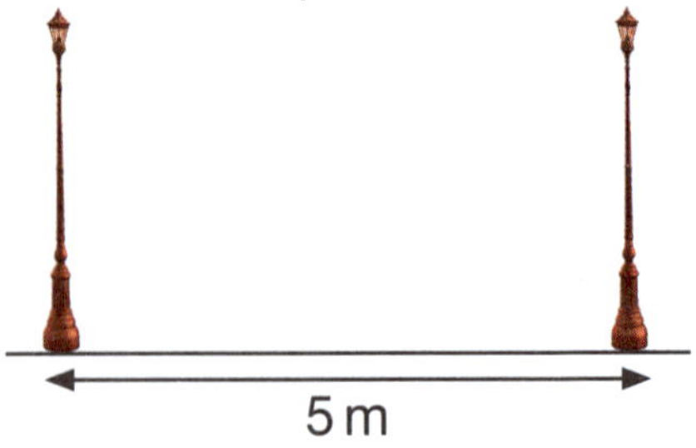

A. 2 km 90 m B. 3 km 495 m C. 2 km 500 m D. 2 km 495 m

17. Subtract 49876 (when rounded off to nearest thousands) from 95846 (when rounded off to nearest hundreds).

A. 45800 B. 35700 C. 85000 D. 46000

18. Find the perimeter of the shaded figure (not drawn to scale).

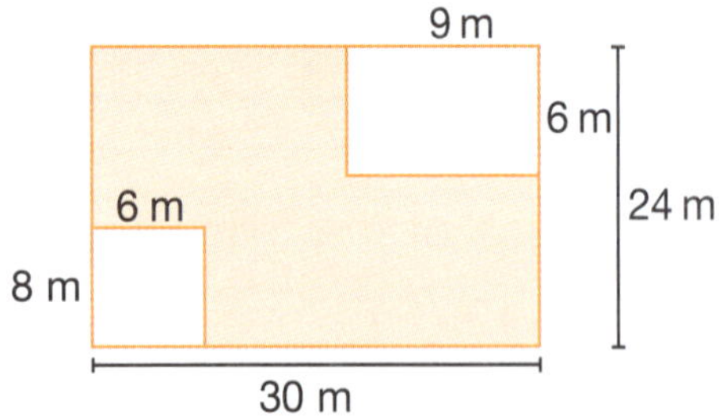

A. 96 m
B. 108 m
C. 120 m
D. 110 m

19. Which of the following are arranged in the ascending order?

A. CXLVI, CLXXXIX, DLXVIII, CMLXXVII
B. CXLVI, CMLXXVII, CLXXXIX, DLXVIII
C. CMLXXVII, DLXVIII, CLXXXIX, CXLVI
D. CMLXXVII, CLXXXIX, DLXVIII, CXLVI

20. Find the value of  + , if  +  +  +  +  = 2700 and  −  = 428.

A. 652 B. 540 C. 112 D. 684

EVERYDAY MATHEMATICS

21. A rectangular playground is 120 m long and 80 m wide. What distance did Avantika cover in going 4 times around this field?

A. 400 m B. 1600 m C. 800 m D. 3200 m

SPACE FOR ROUGH WORK

22. Anjana has to cover 20 km 560 m distance. She walked 1 km 200 m. She covered 10 km 150 m by an auto and rest of the distance by car. How much distance did she cover by car?

A. 9 km 21 m B. 9 km 210 m C. 7 km 350 m D. 7 km 300 m

23. Arjun's weight is 34 kg 375 g. Kapil's weight is two times of Arjun's weight. What is the total weight of both of them?

A. 103 kg 125 g B. 103 kg 375 g C. 68 kg 750 g D. 98 kg 250 g

24. Deepak filled 17 L 450 mL of water in a tank every day. How much quantity of water did he fill in 7 days?

A. 110 L 120 mL B. 102 L 150 mL

C. 150 L 122 L D. 122 L 150 mL

25. Manoj reads $\frac{8}{9}$ of a book. If there are total 1431 pages in the book, then how many pages are left to be read?

A. 140 B. 113 C. 159 D. 195

26. Aman is XXI years old. Raghav is XV years older than Aman. The sum of their ages (in years) is ________.

A. 57 B. 52 C. 29 D. 38

27. Vishal draws some figures as given below.

How many closed figures does he draw?

A. 2 B. 3 C. 4 D. 5

28. 20 chairs and 15 tables were purchased for a hotel. If each chair costs ₹ 110 and a table costs ₹ 235, then the total amount to be paid is ________.

A. ₹ 5725 B. ₹ 5000 C. ₹ 8250 D. ₹ 7359

29. The XYZ company estimated the cost to build a new baseball stadium which is Rupees ninety four thousand. What is this number in numeral form?

A. ₹ 90400 B. ₹ 94000 C. ₹ 90004 D. ₹ 90040

SPACE FOR ROUGH WORK

30. 950 nuts are manufactured in a factory every day. How many nuts can be manufactured in 60 days?

A. 57000 B. 58000 C. 60000 D. 62000

ACHIEVERS SECTION

31. Which of the following has the greatest perimeter?

A. 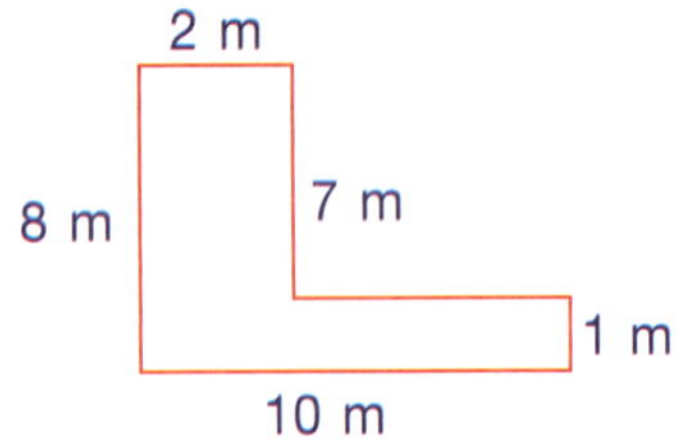

B. 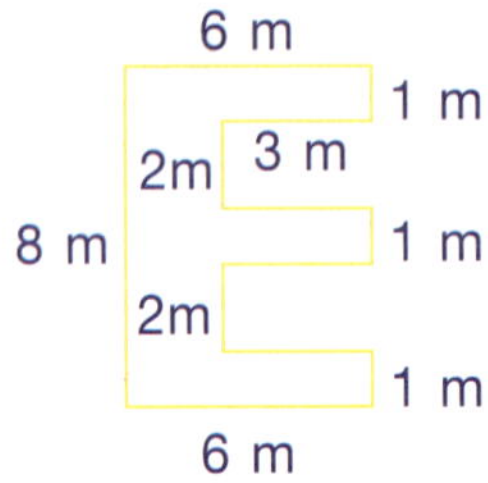

C. 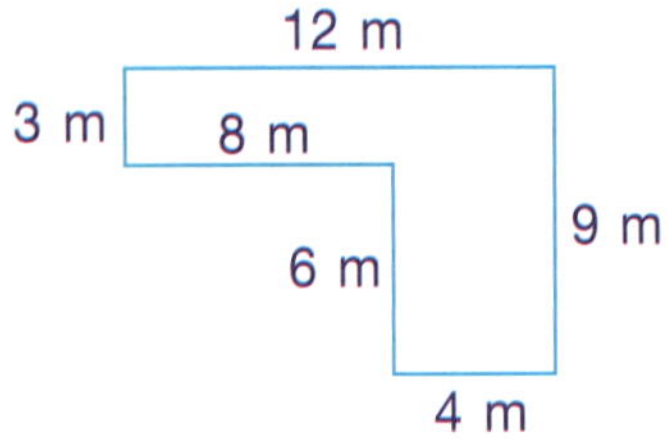

D. 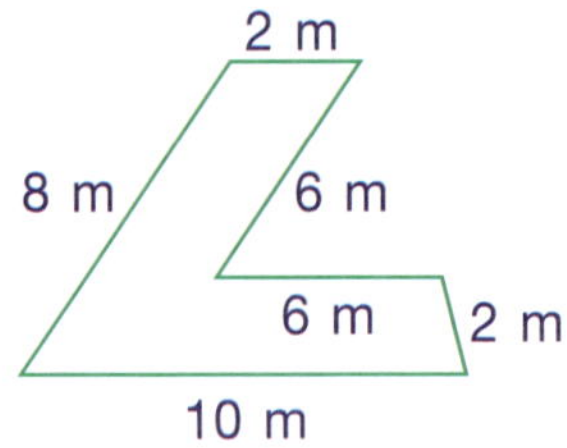

32. Match the following and select the CORRECT option.

	Column I	Column II
P.	The number of factors of 125 is ____.	(i) 5
Q.	Common prime factor of 15 and 50 is _____.	(ii) 272
R.	L.C.M. of (16, 34) is ____.	(iii) 14
S.	H.C.F. of (98, 14) is ____.	(iv) 4

	P	Q	R	S
A.	(iv)	(i)	(ii)	(iii)
B.	(i)	(ii)	(iv)	(iii)
C.	(iv)	(i)	(iii)	(ii)
D.	(i)	(ii)	(iii)	(iv)

33. Find the difference between the shaded fractions of the given figures.

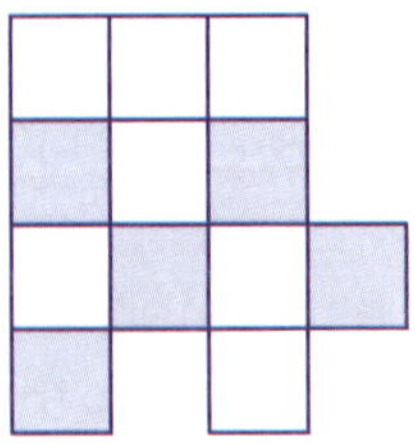

P

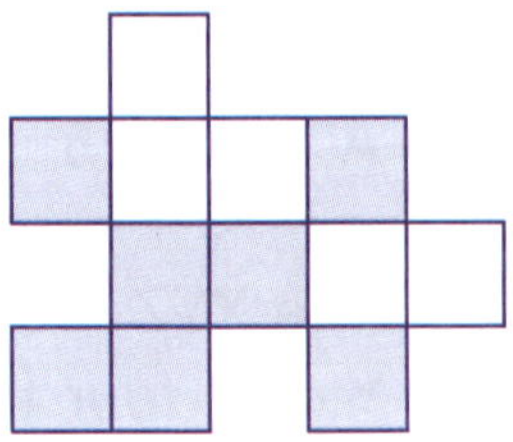

Q

A. $\frac{1}{6}$ B. $\frac{1}{12}$

C. $\frac{1}{4}$ D. $\frac{1}{3}$

SPACE FOR ROUGH WORK

34. Read the given statements carefully and state T for true and F for false.

(i) Roman numeral for largest 3-digit number is CMXCIX.

(ii) The sum of face value of 8 and 6 in the number 85642 is 100.

(iii) The largest 5-digit number formed from the digits 9, 6, 0, 5, 2 (without repetition) is 95062.

	(i)	(ii)	(iii)
A.	T	T	F
B.	T	F	T
C.	T	F	F
D.	F	T	T

35. Fill in the blanks and select the CORRECT option.

(i) The number 82564 when rounded off to nearest thousands becomes __(P)__.

(ii) __(Q)__ will be added to 56492, to make 98492.

(iii) Difference between largest 5-digit number and smallest 6-digit number is __(R)__.

	(P)	(Q)	(R)
A.	8000	4000	1
B.	80000	4200	1
C.	8000	42000	1
D.	83000	42000	1

SCIENCE OLYMPIAD FOUNDATION

National Office: Plot 99, First Floor, Sector 44 Institutional area, Gurugram -122 003 (HR) India

Email: info@sofworld.org | Website: www.sofworld.org

Regd. Office: 406, Taj Apt., Ring Road, New Delhi-110 029

Note: Please address all communication to the National Office only.

ANSWERS

CHAPTER 1

Exercise 1A

1. a. 6 thousands or 6000; b. 7 lakhs or 7,00,000; c. 3 ten thousands or 30,000; d. 0 hundreds or 0; e. 0 ones or 0;
2. a. Two lakh thirty-five thousand seven hundred thirty-four;
   b. One lakh twenty-six thousand five hundred seven;
   c. Eight lakh thirty-five thousand one hundred forty-nine;
   d. Three lakh seventy thousand eight hundred fifteen;
   e. Eight lakh forty-six thousand seven hundred twelve;
3. a. 50,000 + 6000 + 100 + 90 + 8
   b. 20,000 + 3000 + 700 + 0 + 6
   c. 200,000 + 10,000 + 7000 + 500 + 60 + 2
   d. 300,000 + 40,000 + 2000 + 900 + 80 + 4
   e. 5,00,000 + 20,000 + 9000 + 100 + 0 + 3
4. a. 23,462 b. 7,52,105 c. 5,81,428
5. a. 3,29,658 – Three lakh twenty-nine thousand six hundred fifty-eight; Indian place value system;
   b. 9,00,632 – Nine lakh six hundred thirty-two; Indian place value system
   c. 284,210 – Two hundred eighty-four thousand two hundred ten; International place value system;
   d. 791,004 – Seven hundred ninety-one thousand four; International place value system

Exercise 1B

1. a. <; b. >; c. <; d. <;
2. a. 5,81,049 < 5,81,723 < 5,81,856 < 5,81,900;
   b. 3,58,907 < 4,39,185 < 8,21,063 < 9,10,259;
   c. 6,81,999 < 7,00,000 < 9,98,998 < 9,99,999;
3. a. 9,00,724 > 8,14,295 > 5,63,102 > 4,39,180;
   b. 7,29,546 > 7,27,000 > 7,21,987 > 7,21,526;
   c. 9,99,999 > 9,99,909, 99,999 > 9999;
4. a. 7,28,564; b. 2,14,869; c. 5,72,007; d. 6,89,994; e. 9,50,008;
5. a. 8,53,763; b. 9,21,304; c. 4,68,714; d. 9,99,588; e. 5,99,060;
6.

	Smallest	Largest
a.	2,46,789	9,87,642
b.	3,04,578	8,75,430
c.	2,00,678	8,76,200
d.	1,02,567	7,65,210

Exercise 1C

1. a. VII; b. X; c. IX; d. XIII; e. XV
2. a. 10; b. 39; c. 28; d. 11; e. 24

Exercise 1D

1. a. 30; b. 180; c. 7350; d. 82,160; e. 9,18,260
2. a. 100; b. 500; c. 1600; d. 83,400; e. 6,43,300
3. a. 4000; b. 5000; c. 73,000; d. 8,43,000; e. 9,36,000
4. a. 50,000; b. 40,000; c. 2,60,000; d. 7,30,000; e. 5,70,000
5. a. 8900; b. 2600; c. 7,17,000; d. 57,870; 57,900; 58,000; 60,000

Chapter Revision

A. 1. c; 2. c; 3. b; 4. a; 5. c; 6. c; 7. b; 8. d; 9. c; 10. b

B. 1. 5300; 2. 5; 3. 32,549; 4. 0

C. 1. F; 2. F; 3. T; 4. F

D. 1. c; 2. a; 3. e; 4. b; 5. d

E. 1. 10; 99; 2. 100; 999; 3. 1000; 9999; 4. 10,000; 99,999; 5. 1,00,000; 9,99,999

F. 1. 268,149 Two hundred sixty-eight thousand one hundred forty-nine;
   2. Both the numbers are the same. Only their name is written using different number systems;
   3. 1,99,999; 4. 3,00,489;
   5. 2,00,000 + 40,000 + 3000 + 500 + 60 + 7;
   6. 7,30,029; 7. 5,49,700;
   8. 7,77,777 > 7,70,777 > 7,00,777 > 7,00,077 > 7,00,007;
   9. 120000

CHAPTER 2

Exercise 2A

1. a. 83,305; b. 8,77,699; c. 9,75,846; d. 5,65,375; e. 4,92,867; f. 9,52,405

Exercise 2B

1. a. 9,29,690; b. ₹8,07,400; c. 1,65,670; d. 4,22,000; e. 1,17,490
2. a. Raj had 32,941 books in his store. He ordered 18,596 more books. What is the total number of books he has in his store now?
   b. 46,723 people visited the zoo on Monday and 18,095 people visited the zoo on Tuesday. How many people visited the zoo on Monday and Tuesday together?
   c. Population of city A is 7,35,298 and population of city B is 1,67,403. What is the total population of city A and B?
   d. 6,10,527 people went to see the movie on Saturday and 2,78,149 people went to see the movie on Sunday. How many people went to see the movie on Saturday and Sunday?

Exercise 2C

1. 8,32,910; 2. 7,85,878; 3. 7,42,133; 4. 5,66,784; 5. 42,737; 6. 6,00,001

Exercise 2D

1. a. 43,449; b. ₹2,65,790; c. 4,65,160; d. 87,320; e. 2,61,220

2. a. A book store had 25,694 books. Out of which 13,827 were sold. How many books were left in the store?
   b. Out of 69,250 toys produced today 48,794 were defective. How many toys were not defective?
   c. A company manufactured 2,78,658 cars in a day and sold 1,56,984 cars. How many cars were left with them?
   d. By how much is 9,50,000 more than 8,00,000?

Chapter Revision

A. 1. d; 2. d; 3. b; 4. a; 5. d; 6. a

B. 1. 2594; 2. 15,398; 3. 57,809; 4. 1,00,008; 5. 3,45,079

C. 1. F; 2. T; 3. F; 4. T; 5. T

D. 1. 6,34,941; 2. ₹4,56,700; 3. ₹2,80,200; 4. ₹1,65,400; 5. 1,27,000

Chapter 3

Exercise 3A

1. a. 0; b. 0; c. 72; d. 0; e. 0; f. 289; g. 3; h. 5; i. 11
2. a. factors; b. product; c. 1; d. 0; e. Commutative

Exercise 3B

1. a. 50; 500; 5000; 50,000;
   b. 230; 2300; 23,000; 2,30,000;
   c. 370; 3700; 37,000; 3,70,000;
   d. 410; 4100; 41,000; 4,10,000;
   e. 750; 7500; 75,000; 7,50,000;
   f. 840; 8400; 84,000; 8,40,000;
2. a. 460; b. 53,00,000; c. 15,36,900; d. 2860; e. 1,06,700

Exercise 3C

1. a. 426; b. 69,784; c. 37,563; d. 1075; e. 74,613
2. a. 642; b. 3,41,754; c. 27,984; d. 4,76,766; e. 5,00,966

Exercise 3D

1. a. 35 days; b. 420 seconds; c. 14,400 seconds; d. ₹56,700; e. ₹11,900
2. a. 1200; b. 3200 c. 1,00,000; d. 2,40,000

Exercise 3E

1. a. 16; b. 162; c. 256; d. 625; e. 512; f. 1250
2. b. 90; 900; c. 16; 160; 1600;
3. a. 1380; b. 325; c. ₹1,56,100; d. 6204

Chapter Revision

A. 1. c; 2. b; 3. c; 4. b; 5. c

B. 1. 0; 2. 0; 3. 2584; 4. 450; 5. 13; 6. 2,70,000; 7. 1,01,480 ; 8. 41,160; 9. 5,02,146; 10. 80,017

C. 1. 4284 people; 2. a. ₹13,950; b. ₹13,500; 3. ₹5,86,500 people

4. ₹1,35,200; 5. 4,62,500 passengers; 6. ₹6,81,850 7. ₹1,02,120; 8. ₹8,64,000; 9. ₹2,54,400

Chapter 4

Exercise 4A

1. a. 2858; b. 787; c. 194; d. 325
2. a. 14; R = 1; b. 1; R = 2; c. 7; R = 1; d. 4; R = 0
3. a. 16,973; R = 1; b. 18,515; R = 3; c. 11,541; R = 1; d. 10,459; R = 1; e. 21,097; R = 1; f. 16,705; R = 4; g. 4209; R = 1; h. 2607; R = 2

Exercise 4B

1. a. 7; b. 8; c. 400; d. 27; R = 26; e. 102; R = 9; f. 32; g. 18; h. 65

Exercise 4C

1. a. 14; b. 8; c. 23; d. 99; e. 4; f. 29; g. 240
2. a. 25 students; b. 13 teams; c. 18 notebooks; ₹9; d. 150 marbles
3. a. Aarav bought 10 kg of mangoes and 15 kg of apples. He wants to distribute the fruit equally into 20 boxes. How much weight does each box carry?
   b. During the Covid19 outbreak, many people donated whatever they can for the needy. Three people donated 15 kg, 18 kg and 17 kg of pulses. These donations need to be shared among 25 families. How many kg of pulses will each family get?
   c. A school has Classes 1 to 10 with 2 sections in each class. There are 25 students in each section.
   How many students would be in each group if all the students are to be arranged in 50 groups?

Chapter Revision

A. 1. a; 2. c; 3. a; 4. c; 5. c

B. 1. ÷; 2. Dividend; 3. 0; 4. 354; 5. 15; 12; 6. Divide; 7. Divide

C. 1. 42 rows; 2. 12 books; 3. 25 boxes; 10 apples; 4. 21 bags

D. 1. If a box has 25 apples. How many apples will be there in 20 such boxes?
   2. A group of students are standing in 20 rows and 25 columns. How many groups of 50 students can be made from the given number of students?
   3. Raj has 20 apples. His mother gave him 25 more apples. How many apples does he have now?
   4. Rita has 20 sweets, she bought 25 more sweets. She must divide them equally between her 3 children. How many sweets will each child get?

Chapter 5

Exercise 5A

1. a. 392; 5,34,176; 1,73,590; b. 1,25,682; 6,14,250;

c. 5,18,612; 2,13,736; 7,38,104; 9,16,532;

d. 2,35,490; 7,38,165; 29,170;

e. 57,432; 29,796; 4,36,716; f. 5,93,824; 49,296; 4,62,408;

g. 47,916; 69,831; 2,13,579; h. 73,490; 43,120

2. Even numbers: 2, 14, 280, 5718, 9354; Odd numbers: 5, 7, 69, 1697, 6791

Exercise 5B

1. a. yes; b. yes; c. no; d. no
2. a. 1, 2, 5, 10; b. 1, 2, 3, 4, 6, 12; c. 1, 2, 3, 4, 6, 8, 12, 24; d. 1, 5, 7, 35; e. 1, 2, 4, 5, 8, 10, 20, 40; f. 1, 3, 9; g. 1, 5; h. 1,11;
   i. 1, 2, 3, 4, 5, 6, 8, 9, 10, 12, 15, 18, 20, 24, 30, 36, 40, 45, 60, 72, 90, 120, 180, 360;
   j. 1, 2, 3, 4, 5, 6, 7, 9, 10, 12, 14, 15, 18, 20, 21, 25, 28, 30, 35, 36, 42, 45, 50, 60, 63, 70, 75, 84, 90, 100, 105, 126, 140, 150, 175, 180, 210, 225, 252, 300, 315, 350, 420, 450, 525, 630, 700, 900, 1050, 1260, 1575, 2100, 3150, 6300.
3. a. 1, 2; HCF = 2; b. 1, 5; HCF = 5; c. 1, 2, 3, 6; HCF = 6; d. 1, 2, 3, 6; HCF = 6; e. 1, 5; HCF = 5;

Exercise 5C

1. 3, 6, 9, 12, 15, 18 2. 6, 12, 18
3. a. 6, 12, 18, 24; b. 10, 15, 20; c. 14, 21, 28, 35;
   d. 4, 8, 12, 16, 20 (Plot these numbers on number line);
   e. 20; f. 10; g. 12;
   h. Multiples of 3 are 3, 6, 9, 12, 15, 18, 21, 24, 27, 30; Multiples of 5 are 5, 10, 15, 20, 25, 30; First common multiple of 3 and 5 is 15
4. a. 9, 18; b. 30, 60; c. 24, 48
   d. 18, 36; e. 12, 24
5. a. 24; b. 30; c. 99; d. 65; e. 27

Exercise 5D

1. Prime numbers: 2, 3, 5, 7, 11, 13, 17, 19, 23, 29;
   Composite numbers: 4, 6, 8, 9, 10, 12, 14, 15, 16, 18, 20, 21, 22, 24, 25, 26, 27, 28
2. 31, 37, 41, 43, 47
3. 30, 32, 33, 34, 35, 36, 38, 39, 40, 42, 44, 45, 46, 48, 49, 50
4. a. 2, 3; 2 × 3; b. 2; 2 × 2 × 2; c. 2, 5; 2 × 5;
   d. 2, 5; 2 × 2 × 5; e. 3; 3 × 3 × 3;
   f. 2, 3, 5; 2 × 3 × 5; g. 2, 3, 7; 2 × 3 × 7;
   h. 2, 3; 2 × 2 × 2 × 2 × 3; i. 2, 3, 5; 2 × 2 × 3 × 5

Chapter Revision

A. 1. c; 2. b; 3. a; 4. c; 5. c

B. 1. F; 2. T; 3. T; 4. F; 5. T

C. 1. Yes, as sum of digits is divisible by 3;

2. Yes as the number formed by last 3 digits is divisible by 8;

3. 537, 4391, 5723;

4. Prime numbers: 2, 3, 5, 11, 41, 43;
Composite numbers: 8, 16, 20, 32, 39, 58, 63, 72;

5. 3, 4; 6. 6, 12, 18, 24, 30, 36, 42, 48; 7. 3, 9;

8. 24: 2, 3; 2 × 2 × 2 × 3; 27: 3; 3 × 3 × 3; 36: 2, 3; 2 × 2 × 3 × 3;

9. 4 – 8, 12, 16; 6 – 12, 18, 24; LCM 12;

10. 1, 3; 3

CHAPTER 6

Exercise 6A

1. a. shade 1 of the 4 parts; b. shade 1 of the 4 parts; c. shade 3 parts out of 4;
2. a. $\frac{3}{5}$; b. $\frac{3}{5}$; c. $\frac{3}{7}$; d. $\frac{12}{13}$;
3. a. $\frac{2}{4}, \frac{3}{6}, \frac{4}{8}, \frac{5}{10}, \frac{6}{12}$; b. $\frac{4}{6}, \frac{6}{9}, \frac{8}{12}, \frac{10}{15}, \frac{12}{18}$;
   c. $\frac{8}{10}, \frac{12}{15}, \frac{16}{20}, \frac{20}{25}, \frac{24}{30}$;
   d. $\frac{6}{14}, \frac{9}{21}, \frac{12}{28}, \frac{15}{35}, \frac{18}{42}$;
4. a. $\frac{4}{12}$; b. $\frac{8}{20}$
5. a. $\frac{2}{5}$; b. $\frac{5}{11}$; c. $\frac{6}{13}$

Exercise 6B

1. unit fraction $\frac{1}{7}$; proper fraction $\frac{2}{3}, \frac{5}{9}$; improper fraction $\frac{23}{20}, \frac{15}{11}$; mixed fraction $8\frac{5}{9}, 19\frac{3}{9}$;
2. a. $1\frac{2}{3}$; b. $9\frac{1}{2}$; c. $23\frac{1}{2}$; d. $24\frac{5}{7}$;
3. a. $\frac{28}{3}$; b. $\frac{78}{7}$; c. $\frac{67}{5}$; d. $\frac{155}{8}$

Exercise 6C

1. a. > b. > c. < d. < e. <;
2. a. $\frac{3}{10} < \frac{1}{2} < \frac{3}{5}$; b. $\frac{1}{4} < \frac{7}{12} < \frac{5}{6}$;
   c. $\frac{1}{12} < \frac{5}{24} < \frac{7}{8}$;
3. a. $\frac{4}{5} > \frac{6}{20} > \frac{1}{10}$; b. $\frac{3}{5} > \frac{7}{20} > \frac{1}{4}$;
   c. $\frac{5}{6} > \frac{7}{18} > \frac{2}{9}$

Exercise 6D

1. $\frac{3}{5}$; 2. $\frac{5}{7}$; 3. $\frac{3}{4}$; 4. $\frac{2}{3}$; 5. $\frac{2}{3}$;

6. $\frac{13}{20}$; 7. $8\frac{1}{2}$; 8. $11\frac{3}{7}$; 9. $7\frac{3}{5}$; 10. $7\frac{7}{18}$;

11. $14\frac{11}{12}$; 12. $13\frac{1}{4}$

Exercise 6E

1. a. $\frac{3}{8}$; b. $\frac{5}{9}$; c. $\frac{3}{2}$; d. $3\frac{8}{9}$;

e. $2\frac{15}{28}$; 2. $\frac{3}{5}$; 3. $5\frac{3}{10}$ m

Chapter Revision

A. 1. b; 2. d; 3. c; 4. d; 5. b;

B. 1. 1; 2. numerator, denominator;
3. numerator; denominator; 4. 1;

C. 1. a. U; b. M; c. I; d. P;
2. a. $\frac{3}{4}$; b. $\frac{3}{8}$; c. $\frac{3}{5}$; d. $\frac{4}{5}$;
3. a. $4\frac{4}{7}$; b. $\frac{119}{9}$;
4. a. $\frac{5}{18} < \frac{1}{3} < \frac{8}{9}$; b. $\frac{2}{5} < \frac{9}{20} < \frac{7}{10}$;
5. a. $\frac{13}{15} > \frac{7}{30} > \frac{1}{5}$; b. $\frac{19}{20} > \frac{3}{4} > \frac{7}{10} > \frac{1}{5}$;

D. 1. $\frac{7}{25}$; $\frac{18}{25}$; 2. $\frac{1}{4}$ kg; 3. $42\frac{3}{4}$ kg;
4. $\frac{3}{5}$; 5. $6\frac{1}{4}$ kg

Chapter 7

Exercise 7A

1. 7 thousands, 3 hundreds, 4 tens, 5 ones, 2 tenths, 1 hundredth, 6 thousandths;
2. a. 9; b. 900; c. $\frac{9}{10}$; d. 90;
e. $\frac{9}{1000}$
3. a. $8 \times 100 + 1 \times 10 + 5 \times 1$;
b. $9 \times 100 + 3 \times 10 + 7 \times 1 + 2 \times \frac{1}{10}$;
c. $2 \times 100 + 1 \times 10 + 6 \times 1 + 5 \times \frac{1}{10} + 7 \times \frac{1}{100}$;
d. $9 \times 100 + 5 \times 10 + 3 \times 1 + 4 \times \frac{1}{10} + 8 \times \frac{1}{100} + 1 \times \frac{1}{1000}$
4. a. 518.3; b. 471.59; c. 682.349
5. a. Three point five; b. Two point four seven;
c. Six point two one three; d. Twenty-nine point five;
e. Fifty-one point eight three;
f. Eighty-two point nine one six;
g. One hundred seventy-six point nine;
h. Three hundred fifty-eight point zero four

Exercise 7B

1. a. 0.02; b. 0.7; c. 0.019; d. 562.1; e. 3.47;
2. a. 1.2; b. 5.37; c. 8.59; d. 2.53; e. 12.003;
f. 19.024; g. 3.147; h. 12.3;
3. a. 0.4; b. 0.5; c. 0.75; d. 0.14; e. 0.25;
f. 0.6; g. 0.6; h. 0.45; i. 0.4; j. 0.76;
k. 0.26; l. 1.75

Exercise 7C

1. a. $\frac{1}{5}$; b. $\frac{7}{10}$; c. $\frac{29}{100}$; d. $\frac{31}{100}$; e. $\frac{13}{25}$;
f. $\frac{447}{500}$; g. $\frac{5}{8}$; h. $\frac{1}{1000}$;
2. a. $\frac{12}{5}$; b. $\frac{29}{5}$; c. $\frac{87}{5}$; d. $\frac{31}{10}$;
e. $\frac{158}{25}$; f. $\frac{239}{25}$; g. $\frac{302}{25}$; h. $\frac{391}{25}$;
i. $\frac{2353}{250}$; j. $\frac{11503}{1000}$; k. $\frac{1074}{125}$; l. $\frac{301}{250}$

Exercise 7D

1. Like decimals – a and c
2. a. 5.780, 25.193, 14.600; b. 29.300, 4.780, 63.152
3. a. <; b. >; c. =
4. a. 82.003 < 82.17 < 82.478 < 82.560 < 82.9
b. 569.1432 < 569.299 < 569.6849 < 569.814
5. a. 9182.1 > 468.3 > 25.7 > 7.9999;
b. 273.8 > 273.4007 > 273.25 > 273.006

Exercise 7E

1. a. 120.9; b. 779.41; c. 4459.9;
d. 8209.08; e. 3545.99; f. 312.531
2. a. 446.3; b. 2667.7; c. 480.3;
d. 1835.4; e. 4565.085; f. 7740.264
3. a. 65.5 kg; b. 7.7; 9.9; second bag weighs 2.2 kg more;
c. ₹6736

Chapter Revision

A. 1. b; 2. c; 3. b; 4. b; 5. d; 6. c;

B. 1. 9.7; 2. 0.2; 3. 15.13; 4. 36.478; 5. 79.027

C. 1. $\frac{2}{5}$; 2. $\frac{31}{50}$; 3. $\frac{31}{100}$; 4. $\frac{13}{5}$;

D. 1. a. 295.7; b. 528.394;
2. a. 7 tenths; b. 7 hundredths; c. 7 thousandths;
3. 8.003 > 7.9 > 5.8 > 4.382 > 1.9999;
4. 934.68;
5. Sunita has ₹268.84 more than Ashok;
6. ₹2.75; 7. 130.5 m, 261 m

Chapter 8

Exercise 8A

1. a. cm; b. m;
2. a. 4000 m; b. 300 cm; c. 1200; d. 5023;
e. 725; f. 304; g. 7032; h. 5 km 629 m

Exercise 8B

1. a. kg; b. 7000; c. 3275; d. 1333.33; e. 1800;
f. 5213; g. 8903; h. 2 kg 350 g i. 2 kg 359 g

Exercise 8C

1. a. 1 ℓ; b. 200; c. 9000; d. 6 kℓ 700 ℓ; e. 800;
f. 6 kℓ 701 ℓ; g. 125000; h. 9203

Exercise 8D

1. a. 257.26 hg, 2572.6 dag, 25726 g;

b. 93.1 hg, 931 dag, 9310 g;
c. 4823.05 hg, 48230.5 dag, 482305 g;

2. a. 357.63 hm, 3576.3 dam, 35763 m;
b. 2961.4 hm, 29614 dam, 296140 m;
c. 50.09 hm, 500.9 dam, 5009 m;

3. a. 196.8 hℓ, 1968 daℓ, 19680ℓ;
b. 52.47 hℓ; 524.7 daℓ; 5247 ℓ;
c. 6258.03 hℓ, 62580.3 daℓ, 625803 ℓ;

4. a. 26.571; b. 35.821; c. 82.732; d. 6.941;
e. 249 ℓ 3 dℓ 6 cℓ 1 mℓ

Exercise 8E

1. a. Vijay; b. Ajay; c. 146 kg 407 g;
2. 15 kg 350 g; 3. 28 ℓ 550 mℓ;
4. 37 km 310 m; 5. 23 m 81 cm;
6. Meher weighs 17 kg 230 g more;
7. 5 ℓ 80 mℓ; 8. 151 km 705 m;
9. 9 kg 509 g; 10. 12 ℓ 823 mℓ

Chapter Revision

A. 1. c; 2. a; 3. d; 4. a; 5. d;
6. c; 7. a; 8. a; 9. c; 10. b;

B. 1. 10,000; 2. divide; 3. 100; 4. 100; 5. mℓ;
6. m; 7. kg; 8. km;

C. 1. 10,000 dg < 2 kg < 5000 g < 250 hg
2. Raj weighs more by 34.9 kg; 3. 5 kg;
4. 29.658 kg; 5. 397.525 km;
6. 258.76 hℓ; 2587.6 daℓ; 25876 ℓ

Chapter 9

Exercise 9A

1. 6:51; 2. 12:51; 3. 8:51

Exercise 9B

1. 205; 2. 100 min, 6000 s; 3. 2533;
4. 11,520; 5. 6 min 12 s; 6. 10 h 21 min;
7. 1 h 13 min 12 seconds; 8. 1 h 26 min 23 seconds

Exercise 9C

1. a. a.m.; b. a.m.; c. a.m.; d. a.m.; e. noon;
f. p.m.; g. p.m.; h. p.m.;
2. 0435 hours, 0620 hours, 1050 hours, 1200 hours, 1235 hours, 1257 hours;
3. 3:20 a.m.; 2:10 p.m.; 11:50 a.m.; 12:45 p.m.

Exercise 9D

1. 1 h; 2. 5h 5 min; 3. 6 h 55 min; 4. 1:30 p.m.

Exercise 9E

1. a, c, d; 2. 12 months; 52 weeks 1 day; 365 days;
3. a. July 11; b. July 18; 4. 2 years 11 months;
5. 4 weeks 3 days; 6. 3 weeks 5 days;
7. a. 17 days; b. 14 days;
8. a. 18 days; b. 23 days

Chapter Revision

A. 1. b; 2. a; 3. d; 4. c; 5. b; 6. c; 7. a

B. 1. 12; 2. 31; 3. 29; 4. 14 October; 5. 366;
6. 10 days

C. 1. F; 2. T; 3. F; 4. T

D. 1. 1 h 40 min; 2. 10:50 a.m.;
3. a. 12 April; b. 19 April; c. 26 April;
4. 10 years; 5. 20 days

Chapter 10

Exercise 10A

1. a. 300 p; b. 700 p; c. 1100 p; d. 2300 p; e. 8100 p;
f. 50000 p; g. 140000 p; h. 500300 p; i. 250 p; j. 1325 p;
k. 4530 p; l. 1350 p; m. 2475 p;
2. a. ₹1; b. ₹7; c. ₹9.50; d. ₹8.25; e. ₹4.30; f. ₹14.50;
g. ₹82.09; h. ₹11.50; i. ₹2.30

Exercise 10B

1. a. ₹114.43; b. ₹476.63; c. ₹658.31; d. ₹350.53;
2. a. ₹45.51; b. ₹97.45; c. ₹191.95; d. ₹31.86

Exercise 10C

1. ₹175; 2. ₹407; 3. ₹544; 4. ₹280; 5. ₹75; 6. ₹1075;
7. 1, 2; 8. 2; 9. 1

Chapter Revision

A. 1. a; 2. b; 3. c; 4. b; 5. b

B. 1. 300 p; 2. 1700 p; 3. 25000 p; 4. 670 p; 5. 1989 p

C. 1. ₹2; 2. ₹19; 3. ₹3.47; 4. ₹18.35

D. 1. ₹120; 2. ₹350; 3. ₹3088.87; 4. ₹2967.23;
5. ₹730; 6. ₹750; 7. ₹78.14; 8. ₹676.91

E. 1. ₹85; 2. ₹70; 3. ₹133; 4. ₹402;
5. ₹52.85; 6. ₹79.95; 7. ₹188.11

F. 1. ₹145; 2. ₹118; 3. ₹223.25; 4. ₹200

Chapter 11

Exercise 11A

1. Draw line segment as per the given length using a ruler;
2. a. 2.1 cm; b. 2.5 cm; c. 3.3 cm;
3. a. B; b. BC, BA; c. CBA, ABC, B, D;
d. acute angle

Exercise 11B

1. a. centre of the circle; b. radii; c. radius
2. Circumference is the length of the outer boundary, O is the centre, OA is the radius, BC is the diameter

Exercise 11C

1. a. closed; b. 3; c. 3; d. 4; e. equal;
2. a, b; 3. a. Triangle; b. Quadrilateral

Exercise 11D

2. 2; 3. infinite

Exercise 11E

Follow the pattern and colour accordingly.

Chapter Revision

A. 1. b; 2. c; 3. b; 4. b; 5. a; 6. d; 7.d

B. 1. Draw line segments as per the given length using a ruler;
2. Refer p. 179 to draw a circle;

C. 1. Yes; 2. No; 3. Yes; 4. Yes; 5. No; 6. Yes

D. 1. 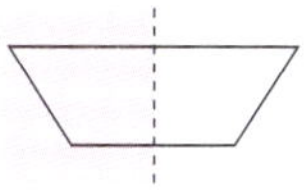 2. 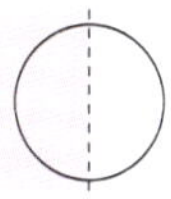

3. 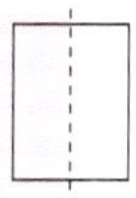 4. 

E. 1. No line of symmetry; 2. Infinite lines of symmetry;

3. 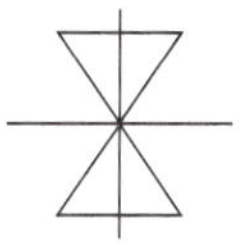
2 lines of symmetry

4. 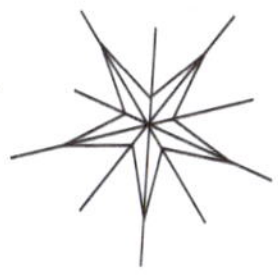
5 lines of symmetry

5. 
1 line of symmetry

6. 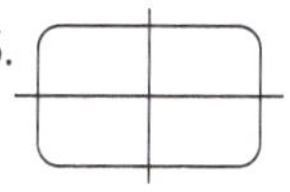
2 lines of symmetry

F. 2, 3, 4, 5

Chapter 12

Exercise 12A

1. a. 8 cm; b. 16 cm; c. 19 cm;
d. 22 cm; e. 12 cm; f. 34 cm

Exercise 12B

1. a. 16 cm; b. 24 cm; c. 56 cm; d. 72 cm;
2. a. 14 cm; b. 20 cm; c. 28 cm; d. 38 cm;
3. a. 12 cm; b. 29 cm; c. 33 cm; d. 45 cm;
4. a. 3 cm; b. 5 cm; c. 7 cm; d. 13 cm;
5. a. 5 cm; b. 6 cm

Exercise 12C

1. a. 15 sq. cm; b. 40 sq. cm; c. 91 sq. cm;
d. 152 sq. cm; e. 200 sq. cm; f. 144 sq. cm;
2. a. 25 sq. cm; b. 64 sq. cm; c. 225 sq. cm;
d. 576 sq. cm; e. 1024 sq. cm;
3. a. 6 sq. cm; b. 11 sq. cm; c. 20 sq. cm;
d. 6.5 sq. cm

Chapter Revision

A. 1. b; 2. c; 3. a; 4. b; 5. d; 6. a

B. 1. 4; 2. breadth; 3. $2(l + b)$; 4. Side; 5. Add

C. 1. 18 cm; 2. 24 cm; 3. 58 cm; 4. 34 cm

D. 1. 48 cm; 2. 44 cm; 3. 48 cm; 4. 100 sq. cm;
5. 625 sq. cm; 6. 32 cm; 7. 15 cm

Chapter 13

Exercise 13A

1. 2 cu. cm; 2. 4 cu. cm; 3. 5 cu. cm; 4. 8 cu. cm;
5. 3 cu. cm; 6. 5 cu. cm; 7. 5 cu. cm; 8. 7 cu. cm;
9. 5 cu. cm; 10. 7 cu. cm; 11. 6 cu. cm;
12. 12 cu. cm

Exercise 13B

1. b. Net of cube, colour it green;
i. Net of a cuboid, colour it blue;
h. Net of a cone, colour it red;
c. Net of a cylinder, colour it yellow
2. a. circle; b. circle; c. circle

Chapter Revision

A. 1. 9 cu. cm; 2. 11 cu. cm; 3. 14 cu. cm;
4. 14 cu. cm; 5. 10 cu. cm; 6. 11 cu. cm

B. Three different nets of a cube:

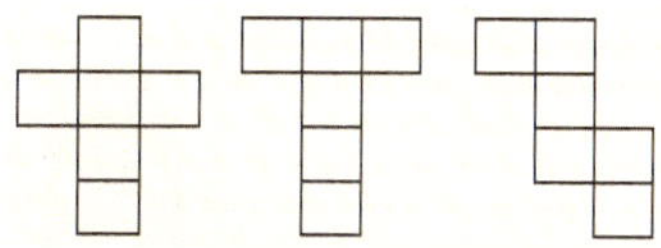

Three different nets of a cuboid:

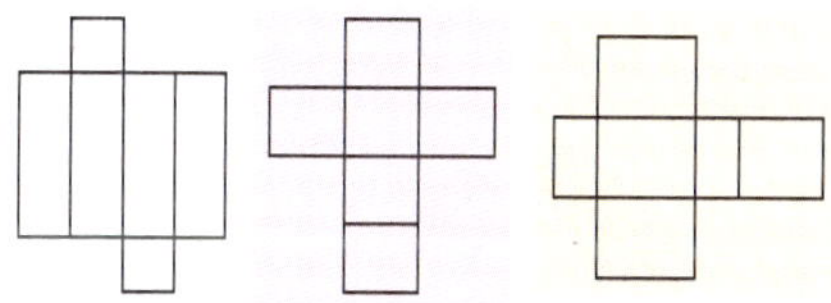

C. 1. a. front view; b. side view; c. top view;
2. a. top view; b. side view; c. front view;
3. a. front view; b. side view; c. top view

Chapter 14

Exercise 14A

1. a. 25; b. 30; c. 15; d. 25; e. 35; 2. Class V;
3. Class III; 4. 5; 5. 10

Exercise 14B

1. Pink; 2. Pink

Chapter Revision

1. a. 30; b. Wednesday; c. 10; d. 30; e. Friday;
2. a. 80; b. Football; c. Hockey; d. 40;
e. Basketball;
3. a. 24; b. 7; c. T; d. N

SEE Social Emotional Ethical Learning

Every Penny Is A Life Saver

21 CS Collaboration

HQ Harmony In The Self

13 CLIMATE ACTION

My SEE (Social Emotional Ethical) Space

A. Answer the following questions.

1. At what time is the cyclone supposed to make landfall? Convert it into 12-hour clock.

____

2. How many hours left for the storm to strike while the children were watching the news?

____

3. Write the time 15 minutes to 4 in the evening using a.m./p.m.

____

B. Apart from contributing money, what else can you do to support those affected by natural disasters?

____

____

C. Find out the names of the government agencies in our country that are involved in disaster management. Write their names in the box.

21 CS Creativity and Innovation AI EL

Maths Mela

Let us demonstrate fractions.

All you need is... 2 circular bowls (1 big and 1 small), 2 different coloured pastel sheets, toothpicks, glue, scissors, sketch pens and a paper cutter

Note:
Do not use scissors or cutter yourself. Take help of an elder while cutting.

Let's Start!

1. Place a big bowl on a pink pastel sheet and trace its outline. Cut-out the circle.

2. Mark its centre and divide the circle into 8 equal parts.

3. Make a cut on one of the lines that runs from the centre to the circle's boundary. The cut should end 1 cm before the circle's boundary.

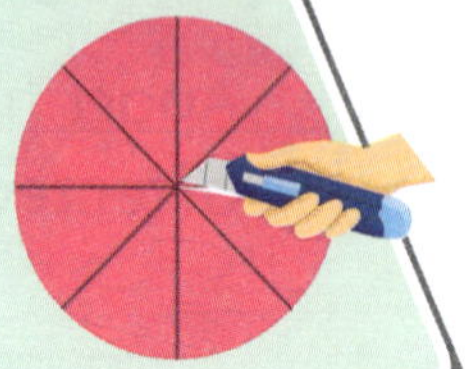

4. Now, place a small bowl on green pastel sheet. Trace and cut-out the circle.

5. Now, make a cut in small circle from the centre to the circle's boundary. This time the cut should be through the boundary.

6. Now, start inserting the small circle from its cut into the cut you have made on the big circle.

7. Turn over and paste a toothpick on either side of the small circle.

8. Write $\frac{1}{8}$ in the first part, $\frac{2}{8}$ in the second and so on till you reach the last part on the big circle.

9. Similarly, divide the opposite side of pink circle into 4 equal parts. Write $\frac{1}{4}$ for the first, $\frac{2}{4}$ for the second and so on.

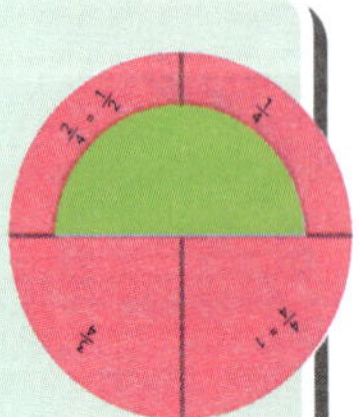

10. Your fractions model is ready. Now, rotate the green circle and see on which fraction it lands.

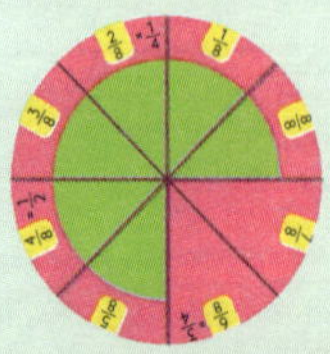

Do It Yourself!

Can you demonstrate fractions using any other model? Give a brief idea about the model in the space given below.

Create the model you chose. Write the materials required and the steps of its construction. Draw a picture of your model in the space given below.

All I Need Is:

Let's Start:

Eminent Mathematicians

D.R. Kaprekar
(17 January 1905–1986)

Dattathreya Ramchandra Kaprekar was an Indian Mathematician born in Dahanu, Maharashtra.
He is also known as Ganitanand and wrote extensively on various topics such as magic squares, recurring decimals, integers with special properties and much more. He even has a constant named after him! The number 6174 is known as Kaprekar's constant.

Euclid
(Around 300 BC)

Euclid was a Greek mathematician often referred to as the 'Father of Geometry'.
His ideas are considered revolutionary. He wrote the book 'Elements' around 300 BC, which can be referred for teaching history of mathematics.

Terence Chi-Shen Tao
(born 17 July 1975)

Terry Tao is an Australian of Chinese heritage. Together with Ben Green (a British mathematician), he proved an amazing result about prime numbers.
Together they found that you can find sequences of primes of any length in which every number in the sequence is a fixed distance apart. For example, the sequence 3, 7, 11 has three primes spaced 4 apart. The sequence 11, 17, 23, 29 has four primes that are 6 apart.

John Napier
(1550–4 April 1617)

John Napier was a Scottish mathematician, physicist and astronomer.
He popularised the use of the decimal point in arithmetic and mathematics. He created a calculating device called the "Napier's bones" that helped in multiplication and division.

Marjorie Lee Browne
(9 September 1914–9 October 1979)

Marjorie Lee Browne was a mathematics educator. She was one of the first African-American women to receive a PhD in mathematics. She worked with secondary school mathematics teachers, instructing them in "modern math." She focused especially on encouraging math education for minorities and women.